Across America on Foot

27 Stories of Adventure, Endurance, and Inspiration

by

Nick Ashill, Newton Baker, Noah & Robert Barnes, Patrick Binienda, Jay Birmingham, Thomas Curran, LouisMichael Figueroa, Rosalynn Frederick, Frank Giannino, Jeff Grabosky, Pete Kostelnick, lazarus lake, Benjamin Lee, Doug Masiuk, Lindsay Monroe, Jim McCord, Milton Miller, Helene Neville, Chris Finill & Steve Pope, Amanda Standley, Brian Stark, Jim Starkovich, Henrik Aarup Svendsen, Alan Tardy, Sandra Villines, Jan Walker, John Wallace III

Copyright © 2023 Across America Author Group

All rights reserved. No part of this publication may be reproduced, distributed, or transmitted in any form or by any means, including photocopying, recording, or other electronic or mechanical methods, without the prior written permission of the publisher, except in the case of brief quotations embodied in critical reviews and certain other noncommercial uses permitted by copyright law.

ISBN: 979-8-61441330-9 (Paperback)

Cover image by Johannes Plenio.
Cover design by John Wallace III.

Printed by The Bean Counting Crosser LLC,
DBA Across America Author Group, in the United States of America.

First printing edition March 2020.

http://acrossamericaonfoot.us

This book is a collection of stories by different people; as such, each author's words, experiences, and contributions are theirs alone.

Dedicated to our friends and family, to those who helped us along the way, and to everyone who has ever wondered what it would be like to go there on foot.

Contents

1. Alan Tardy (1978) 1
2. Frank Giannino (1979, 1980) 13
3. Jay Birmingham (1980) 24
4. LouisMichael Figueroa (1982, 1996, 2005) 34
5. Jim Starkovich (1994) 45
6. Brian Stark (1998) 50
7. Jim McCord (2002) 58
8. John Wallace III (2004-2005) 68
9. Helene Neville (2010, 2013, 2014, 2015, 2017) 81
10. Jeff Grabosky (2011) 86
11. Milton Miller (2011, 2014) 97
12. Chris Finill and Steve Pope (2011) 111
13. Doug Masiuk (2012) 121
14. Rosalynn Frederick (2013) 132
15. Benjamin Lee (2013) 143
16. Newton Baker (2015) 154
17. Henrik Aarup Svendsen (2016) 166
18. Pete Kostelnick (2016, 2018) 180
19. Jan Walker (2016) 189
20. Lindsay Monroe (2017) 196
21. Noah & Robert Barnes (2017) 204
22. Nick Ashill (2017) 214
23. Amanda Standley (2017) 229
24. Sandra Villines (2017) 250
25. lazarus lake (2018) 252
26. Thomas Curran (2019) 257
27. Patrick Binienda (2019) 264
About the Authors 275

Life is either a daring adventure or nothing.
Helen Keller

Foreword
by
Dean Karnazes, Harvey Lewis, and James E. Shapiro

Dean Karnazes

"The women and men profiled in this book are true pioneers and trailblazers. Each story is fascinating, at times harrowing, not infrequently hilarious, and always awe-inspiring. As I flipped through the pages I found myself cheering for my fellow crossers, drawn in to their meanderings, misadventures and milestones. And flipping through the pages I could not stop! *Across America on Foot* is a must read for anyone with an adventurous spirit, regardless of whether you run great distances, modest distances, or not at all."
~*Dean Karnazes, ultramarathoner*
& one of TIME *magazines 100 Most Influential People in the World*

* * *

Harvey Lewis

"There is a timeless allure to setting out on a great adventure, a spiritual quest, a pilgrimage discovering oneself and America. This book sheds light on uncommon stories of individuals who set out on lesser known paths. The collection of perspectives is as riveting as it is insightful, with colorful characters, across numerous decades, you'll be left inspired by their audacious feats!"
~*Harvey Lewis*
5-time 24-Hour National Team
Badwater 135 Champion and 9-time finisher
Featured in film, "Like Harvey, Like Son"

* * *

James E. Shapiro

"Running across America reminds us that we and the world inhabit the exact same space. We don't conquer mountains and deserts; we travel with them. When we glimpse that truth we abandon watch, calendar and map. Perhaps then we can truly say we are wayfarers."
~*James E. Shapiro*
Author, Meditations from the Breakdown Lane and Ultramarathon
Coast-to-coast runner

Introduction
by
Jay Birmingham and Brian Stark

The history of crossing America on foot dates to 1909, a walk from New York City to San Francisco by 70-year-old Edward Payson Weston.

For 12 decades since, men and women have run or walked across the United States. Some have pushed the pace and covered more than 60 miles per day. Others have taken more than a year to complete the challenge.

There is no standard starting line or finish location, but by far, a Los Angeles--New York City route has been used most often, due largely to two transcontinental foot races in 1928 and 1929 where runners completed the route in stages.

John H. Wallace III, who is also a crosser and an author in this book, created and maintained an Internet website, *usacrossers.com* that is complete through 2012. The 279 crossings by 248 individuals include 228 men and 20 women up to that date. Seven of our writers have crossed since.

Contributors to this book are a random lot. Our backgrounds cover every sector: a teacher and a real estate agent, a bartender, a recovering alcoholic and an alcohol counselor, a data analyst and a baseball player, an opera singer and a house painter, a 10-year-old, and everything in between.

However, one most unusual common trait binds us: at one time, we have all stood at the edge of land, our toes to the water, and traversed the entire breadth of North America on foot. We are Transcontinental Crossers, an accomplishment almost as long as the name itself and far rarer than summiting Mount Everest.

What causes one to want to attempt this incredibly difficult task? Each answer is as unique as our various professions.

An editorial from the Lincoln Star in 1964, commenting on Don Shepherd as he ran through Nebraska is appropriate:

"...there are the most of us who, if the thought of a cross-country run did enter our mind, would be unable to execute the plan.

"Mr. Shepherd, however, has maintained and developed his physical ability and has, somehow, made himself the opportunity. For his efforts, he has the satisfaction of fulfilling a great desire and many of us live a lifetime and never quite get the job done."

"Secondly, the South African runner has become acquainted in detail with the beauty and grandeur of the woods and waters, deserts and mountains and plains and valleys of this nation. Whether he now has or ever will have wealth of a monetary nature, he has a great wealth of experience that will reward him for the rest of his days."

During those after years of rosy-tinted memories, any alum of this endeavor is likely to pick up on news of a fellow repeating the journey. And that is how each of the authors in this book have come together, thanks in large part to Facebook. Through the access of that site, we formed a group and became friends. Eventually, one of our members, Jim McCord, suggested we compile our stories into one book, a chapter from each person. It took several years to assemble words from our group of diverse, rogue, norm-bending pedestrians, but we are pleased to present this first ever compilation of transcontinental crossers.

We hope that each of you enjoys reading these brief accounts of this life-changing experience.

---Jay Birmingham,
Coast-to-coast runner, coach, and teacher

---Brian R. Stark,
Coast-to-coast runner, teacher, and editor of Across America on Foot

Chapter 1

Alan Tardy
May 23 to Aug 5, 1978
San Francisco, CA to Northampton, MA

It was May 23, 1978. I was 23 years old, I was born and raised in the Northampton, MA area. I had never been away from the east coast in my life. And there I stood, on one side of the Golden Gate Bridge (the first and last time I've ever seen it) about to start a run across the United States.

Picture of me training in 1977

Suddenly a year and a half of training and organizing had led to that day, that time and that place, with me standing there that morning ready to start my journey. There was a very small group of well-wishers in the parking lot as well as two men from a local television station who were there to film the start of my run.

In my preparation to do this run, and during my two months of running, I learned many things about attempting an undertaking such as this. Running across the United States was not an "in vogue" thing to do in 1978. I had no one who had already accomplished this feat to draw knowledge from. I also did not have a 24-hour support crew with me during the journey. So, some of the things I say may, or may not fit into your preparations to join the USA crossers.

I am going to title these points "Tid Bits." These items I feel can prove helpful to you if you have a support team or if you're carrying your supplies with you on a solo journey. Some of them I will give you right away and some I will weave into my story. I hope I can put into words ideas that might help and inspire you.

And here is the first of 11 and the most important Tid Bit.....

Tid bit #1. "YOU" MAKE YOUR DECISION TO DO THIS. It is your life, your journey. Your dream and your accomplishment. Not someone else's (although others will voice their opinions). This is something you can look back on for the rest of your life. An accomplishment nobody can ever take away from you. If it's in your head to do this GO FOR IT. Stop thinking about it and move towards getting it done.

Once you've made the decision to GO FOR IT the rest of my Tid Bits will help you to accomplish YOUR mission.

Tid Bit #2. STUDY YOUR ROUTE. Look over every step of your journey so you can be as best prepared as possible for things that may occur. Things such as long distances between towns and possible places to which you can send supplies ahead of your arrival. This might seem like common sense, but you still need to study your route.

Tid Bit #3. USE MORE THAN ONE BRAND OF SHOES. There is a basic starting shoe structure in almost all models of running shoes that a brand produces. By using two or more brands of shoes, you actually give some of your muscles a rest as you switch back and forth.

On May 23, 1978 early in the morning, I strapped my knapsack on, said my goodbyes and off I went. Inside my Jansport backpack I had a second pair of shoes, vitamins, powdered protein, a diary, a second set of running clothes, multiple small containers for water and a small amount of cash with some credit cards. At the bottom of the knapsack was strapped my Jansport tent. My run was being sponsored by The National Council of Corvette Clubs (NCCC).

I was working with Roger Clancy, their national fundraising organizer, to whom I had spoken only two months prior to the start of my run. I had another charity and sponsor that bailed out on me at the 11th hour (that story in itself would fill a chapter).

But Roger learned I had a 22-person organizing committee who had helped put this together, and he stepped out on faith and said "yes, let's do this!" He helped set up people to put me up wherever possible. That turned out to be 25 nights during the run. The NCCC would then reimburse me for the money spent on food and nights that I would spend in motels along the way.

Tid Bit #4. FIND A CAUSE. If you are going to do this, find a charity that can benefit from your efforts. It should be one that will become embedded in your heart. Also, a charity that will not, for any reason, disappear while you are running. A short term need that may no longer exist by the time you finish, for instance. This will be most important when you mentally and physically hit "a wall." Others relying on you will pull you through it all.

The NCCC had a nationwide effort going to raise funds for Spina Bifida research and was working with the Spina Bifida Association. This cause, and these people, would become the largest piece of the run when I at times felt like quitting, and was eventually told by a doctor to stop my run.

I mentioned in Tid Bit #2 to study your route. I had studied my route over and over. However I had studied my route on a map of the entire country. But, I hadn't studied individual cities. Within 20 minutes of having crossed the Golden Gate Bridge, I was lost. Remember this was 1978. No cell phones, no GPS, no tablets. And I had to stop at phone booths to place collect calls to people's homes.

I spent a large part of my beginning miles stopping to ask directions, running until I was unsure of where to go next and once again stopping to ask directions. Believe it or not I eventually made it by late that day to where I was scheduled to meet another couple who would put me up for the night.

Most of my route had been mapped out for me by a national travel agency. I realized then, that many of the roads were interstate highways and I was not allowed on them. That night the couple mapped out new roads that I could legally be running on.

The next morning, with new maps tucked under one of the straps to my knapsack, I continued my journey.

Over the next couple of days I ascended into the Sierra Mountains. The highest "mountain range" back in my home area might have reached around 1700 feet above sea level. I soon would be at 3 to 4 times that height. In western Ma. a "big" pine tree might be about 75 feet tall with pinecones 4 to 6 inches long. But here, I marveled at the trees that seemed to reach to the sky. I found pinecones that were a foot or more in length and actually picked one up and sent it home.

Tid Bit #5. VISUALLY AND MENTALLY take the time to take in all that you will see during your run, because there may be things you might never experience again. Having to slow my pace due to both running up mountains and to compensate for thinner air, I had more time to look at the world around me. There were times that I would come around a bend in the

'Me, 40 years later holding THE pinecone

road and the scenery, with its trees and streams, would take my breath away almost as much as the altitude change. It was awe inspiring. These were the beginnings of my cherished memories associated with crossing the country, one stride at a time. Seeing so many things on foot that I would never have experienced in a car. Eventually I reached a point in the road high above Tahoe where I just had to stop, stand, and look at the enormous beauty that was laid out in front of me.

Upon arriving in Tahoe (now Tahoe City), I stopped into a sporting goods store. The shoulder straps on my knapsack were causing soreness and chafing on my shoulders. And I could see that it could become a problem. I purchased a strap that I was able to put between the shoulder straps and tighten just enough to distribute the weight differently. I couldn't explain any scientific data associated with this, all I knew was that it allowed the pain to go away and stopped the irritation.

After having another wonderful night's stay with a couple associated with the NCCC, I was on my way eastward. After Tahoe, I began the descent down towards the "flats" of Nevada. I had made it over my first real mountains and was headed for the first time in my life into a desert.

I was to stay with NCCC member Barry Bjorkman in Carson City. Upon arriving in Carson City I called Barry and he met me on the east side of the city. He took my knapsack and left me with one of my bottles of water. He then said he would come back and pick me up when he got out of work.

I was suddenly running without the 25-30 pounds on my back and on flat terrain. WOW. I set my sights on a rise in the road a ways away and set a goal to reach it before Barry returned. And sure enough, I did. Upon returning and picking me up, Barry seemed quite astonished. He informed me that it had been 1 hour and 50 minutes since he had left me. And in that time I had covered 16 miles! The next many days were lessons to be learned.

Tid Bit #6. LEARN TO BE ALONE IN YOUR RUNNING. Many of my days were 12-16 hours long and covered 60 to 80 miles. The aloneness can be all right if you are ready for it.

Tib Bit #7. ELIMINATE YOUR THOUGHTS ABOUT SPEED AND PACE. Unless you are trying to break a record, there is no clock on you during this run. Learn to expand your distance in your training and don't worry about time.

Tid Bit #8. DO NOT RUN ON JUST ONE SIDE OF THE ROAD. Alternate between the sides or you will develop knee, leg and/or hip pain and possibly injuries. I have personally helped four people do their run and this was vital to them.

Tid Bit #9. PLEASE, PLEASE BRING AND WRITE IN A DAIRY. Pictured is my diary from 1978, which I still have. Don't just type

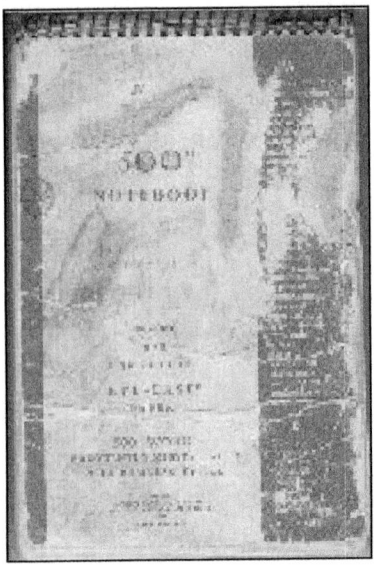

your thoughts. Most people can express what they are feeling better by writing rather than typing and it will be something you can look back at and hand down.

Amongst the things in my knapsack were a set of sweats I used while running in the desert. "SWEATS!! Were you crazy!?" you are asking. These sweats my mother had made for me out of bed sheets. They were lightweight, reflective because they were white, and kept the sun from sucking all the liquids out of my body.

"Take it all in...." I saw "sand mountain," my first prairie dogs, cacti and a lot of dead rattlesnakes on the road. One evening, between Ely, Nevada and Delta, Utah, I noticed that it had been awhile since I'd seen a dead rattlesnake, so I put up my 5 pound 8 ounce Jansport tent about 20-30 feet off the road and went to sleep. The next morning I woke up and upon exiting the tent, found a dead rattler in the road. Killed by a passing car during the night.

During those two days I averaged almost 70 miles/day and pushed my body to its limits. And remember back then we didn't have iPods, cell phones, iPads, solar powered radios or any of the devices we have today to keep our minds occupied while we ran. Instead I focused on what was around me. I made a note in my diary that I found myself running to the cadence of the clicking of the fiberglass rods of my tent. They were strapped to the bottom of my knapsack and with each stride they would make a clicking sound. THAT SOUND, my friends, was my music.

The following picture, and another further along, are pictures of actual entries I made in my diary. By reading them you will get a sense of two of the times when my body, mind and spirit were pushed to their limits.

I have to pause here and tell you that very rarely did a day pass that someone, sometimes many people, didn't stop and check to see if I needed help. Awesome.

A brief stay around the Delta, Utah area and I was on towards my next challenge, the Rocky Mountains. Along with the mountains came my first "Why the hell am I doing this?" moment. I got to a point about 20 miles west of Dinosaur, Colorado and had to camp another night. It had been raining up ahead of me most of the day, but never actually on me.

So the area where I had set up my tent was damp and that evening it felt like the temperature had dropped into the 30s and 40s. I didn't have a sleeping bag because during training I felt that it would add too much weight to my load.

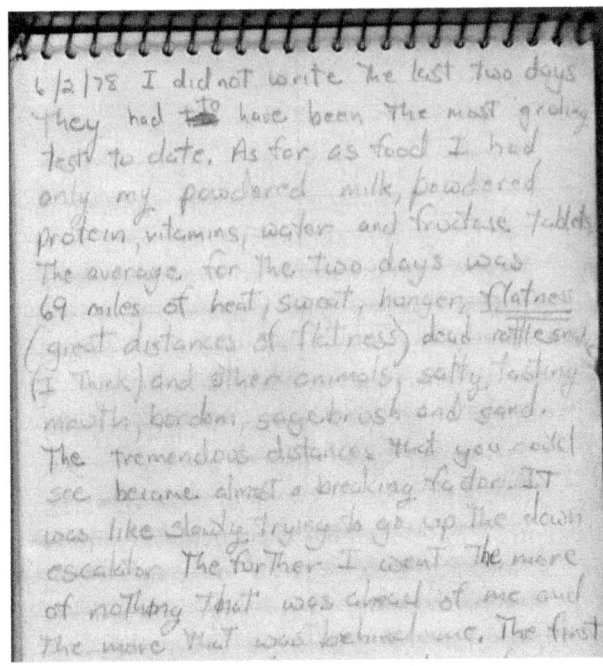

An excerpt from my diary on 6/2/78

In the middle of the night I woke up freezing cold. I put on all the clothes I had and then put my extra socks on my hands and began rocking back and forth. I carried a Bic lighter and would light it for short periods of time to warm the inside of the tent. But finally, long before dawn, I couldn't take it. I packed everything up and started my day's journey hoping that should a car pass by, it would not run me over in the pitch black of the Colorado night.

    Climbing the Rocky Mountains was both very challenging and very beautiful. Remember, I had never been away from the east coast, so I think the beautiful new surroundings helped me ignore the long, slow painful days.

    In Colorado I had an unexpected route change. I was headed toward Boulder when I was told that my NCCC connections changed and I was to head towards Denver. Well that change added 50-100 miles and a couple days of running. I was rerouted to Steamboat Springs. I saved this point in my trip to tell you about  another Tid Bit that I had been following and enjoying during the entire Journey. And I know you will like this one.

Tid Bit #10. Trainers, as you know them today, didn't really exist everywhere back then. My "trainers" were a biomechanics professor and a nutrition professor from UMass Amherst. The advice given to me by both of them was that at the end of every day. "YOU NEED TO DRINK BEER." We joke about the carbs in beer, but there is also nutritional value in the ingredients that are used to make beer. I put their advice into action and at the end of every day I drank a beer or two. My most unique experience with the "beer at the end of the day" came in Steamboat Springs. I would alternate my end of the day food experience. I would eat at a restaurant one night and go to a grocery store the next. Only when these venues were available, of course.

In Steamboat it was grocery store day. As I was wandering through the store I saw a young woman handing out samples of yogurt. After telling her about my journey, she gave her two containers of yogurt to me saying, "You need them more than anyone else I will see today." So, I took my yogurt and my beer, exited the store, wandered down the street a little ways and sat on a rock beside a stream to devour my feast. I was enjoying the food while sitting in the sun when I looked to one side and about 20 feet or so from me was a snake sunning itself on a rock. I turned back to my beer and yogurt and continued eating. The snake continued to bask in the sun. We seemed to have bonded in the middle of the beauty of Mother Nature. In the end, the snake and I went in our own directions for the night.

Getting over Berthoud Pass was a very trying day. That day's running (which included much walking) took me from about 7,000 feet above sea level to 11,400 and back down to 7500. I am not a skier, but at the top of the pass there was about 6 feet of snow. It was 60 degrees and people were skiing in cut-off jeans and tee shirts. Pretty cool. From Berthoud Pass I would eventually make my way to Denver.

Wow, Denver. Finally. After running over the Sierra Mountains, across the deserts of Nevada and climbing the Rocky Mountains, the worst parts of my run were behind me. Or so I thought.

During my stay in Denver I was finally amongst people that I could stay with and talk to. From Carson City to Denver, except for one night, it was long, long days of running and being alone. Motel stays and tenting is what it had been. Many times the only people I even talked with during my 12-16 hour running days were the people that would stop while driving by to make sure I was okay or the motel clerks behind the desks. But now, people and conversations, interviews with local television stations and newspapers, beer I didn't have to pay for...WOW!

But during a publicity run through some of the streets of Denver, with local politicians, Corvette Club people and people associated with Spina Bifida, I started feeling pains in my shin areas.

These were determined to be shin splints. A call homeward to my doctor started with him saying "Well, I know I can't convince you to stop." He advised me to shorten my stride, run in the dirt or grass on the side of the road and ice my shins at the end of every day. And that's what I did. The shin splints stayed with me for hundreds of miles every minute of every day before the pain went away.

The most important and vital part of my stay in Denver (and then more so along the way) was that I got to meet people with Spina Bifida. Babies are born with an open (or hollow) spine. This usually leaves a person as a paraplegic or quadriplegic. Also, the average life expectancy of a child born with Spina Bifida at that time was 16 years of age. I met them and got to really understand what and who I was running for. And trust me, there were times to come after Denver that the cause and the people were the ONLY things that kept me from quitting.

In Denver I was able to lighten my load as I sent home my tent and sweatsuit. These alone took about 7-10 pounds off my back. Also, from Denver on, there would be more people to stay with, which was a blessing.

I headed eastward from Denver, lighter knapsack, shin splints, knowledge of who I was running for and all. Plains of the midwest here I come.

I had run through Nevada in early June to avoid the heat that is expected in the desert. But I found the heat, BIG TIME, and all the humidity the midwest could muster in Nebraska. And it took until almost Lincoln before the shin splints went away.

Temperatures were in the 90's and the humidity was as high as it could get without actually raining. The cows in the fields seemed to be watching me as I slowly jogged past. They were probably thinking "What is that crazy human doing?"

Coming into Lincoln I hit my first rain of the entire trip. And boy did it come down. As I approached Lincoln I was running (or plodding) through 2-4 inches of water on the sides of the road. This led to my orthotic pads in my shoes beginning to break down. That too became a major problem later.

The people I was to stay with came and picked me up out of the deluge. The rain stopped, I had a hot shower, food and once again beers that other people were buying. Yeehaw! It all felt like heaven to me. A bunch of awesome people from the local Corvette Club took me out and we ate and drank and laughed. What a great pick me up this was. Then once again, off I went eastward. But the many miles of running through the water leading into Lincoln spelled the end of any support my orthotic pads were giving me.

Iowa, Illinois, Indiana were great, in that the towns were closer together, so I stayed with more people associated with the NCCC and Spina Bifida. I was realizing that I had passed the halfway point and somehow, despite the long distance still in front of me, I finally felt I was headed for home.

The heat continued as I traveled the midwest in July. I spent July 4th running into Markle, Indiana. The "Welcome to Markle" sign also read "Population 902 Happy People and 4 Grouches." It was a small town and had one diner that was closed. My holiday celebratory food

July on the roads in Iowa. I lost 25 lbs at this point in my run.

extravaganza consisted of 3 pounds of tomatoes, bought at a veggie stand, and a quart of Miller beer bought at the package store. Yeah. "Happy July 4th to me."

But, worse than that, I was starting to feel the effects of the broken down orthotic pads all throughout my body. My hips and knees kept wanting to stop. Just stop and give it up. But my mind kept flashing back to the kids I had met with Spina Bifida and their parents. I could not let them down.

When I arrived in Findlay, Ohio it was the beginning of a 10 day break. Roger Clancy had coordinated plans with NCCC club members and I joined them traveling to North Carolina. We went to their annual national convention. I was introduced to hundreds of fantastic people and was also able to regain a few of the almost 25 pounds that I had lost. But I could also tell that, despite the rest, my body was not doing well. Then it was back to Findley and off I went eastward once again.

As I came into Akron, Ohio, Roger had organized a large gathering of media people, Spina Bifida Association and Corvette Club members at the civic center. But along with celebrating my arrival, Roger could also see that I was in a lot of pain. So, he scheduled an emergency doctor's appointment. The doctor told me point blank that I needed to stop running or risk bad (and possibly permanent) damage to my ankles, knees and hips. But there was no option in my mind at this point. I was about 600 or so miles from home and in my mind I felt that the kids I had met with Spina Bifida were watching and counting on me. Also, my parents, siblings and my hometown were starting to make plans for my arrival back home. "My RUNNING arrival."

> and off again" I ran all day until late and instead of a motel I put my rain parka down and rolled up in it in a field. I slept only a few hours and started again moving into New York and Ohio then eastward to Wellsville, where I am now. However both my legs, feet and knees are hurting. I think the pads have bit the dust and it's going to be interesting to see how far I go, without falling apart.

So, once again, I was homeward bound. Except now I think my completing the journey was in question by many people. But there were no questions in my mind. "I would finish...I had to finish." When I am hurting physically, I have a tendency to withdraw into myself. I tend to be less social and very quiet and deal with it from within. This is what I did and how I handled my "limp to the end." I communicated with Roger, my family, and the local newspaper back home and that was about it. There were some days I hurt so bad that instead of a hotel, I would find some field at the end of the day, wrap myself in my rain parka, and sleep. But as I dozed off each night, I would remember and picture the kids that needed me to finish. Read the last entry in my diary on 7/23/1978 about my concerns.

Running, limping, plodding eastward through the Berkshires, and then crossing the Massachusetts border I thought "holy crap! I truly am almost home!". It took me a few more days to make my way down to within 3 miles of the finish. But I had reached that point on a Tuesday and I was told in a very strong manner by our mayor, that I couldn't finish until Saturday. The reasoning was that there was a major "Welcome Home" celebration planned and people were both flying and driving into town from all over the country. So on that Saturday I stood on top of a hill ready to run to the finish in the center of Florence, Ma. And behind me were 65 Corvettes that were going to follow me as I ran to the end of a journey that had started at the Golden Gate Bridge. I started down the hill with the roaring motors of the Corvettes right behind me. Starting from the bottom of the hill I could see were thousands of people lining both sides of the street cheering me to the end. At the finish area there were people from the NCCC, Spina Bifida, General Motors, media and an enormous crowd.

65 Corvettes as we started down the final hill

In the final stretch, (pictured) approaching the finish along with me are Jeff Easley in the mini Corvette (Jeff was the poster child for Spina Bifida), his dad Larry on the left and my brother-in-law Rocky. The mini Corvette was built for Jeff by General Motors.

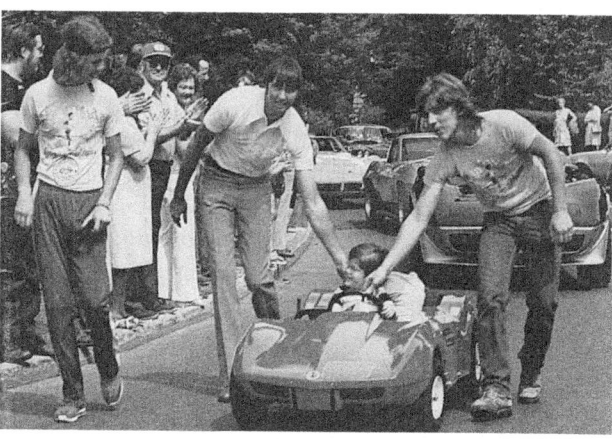

As I broke the "Welcome Home" banner, I hugged my mother, father, grandmother, and sisters. As they had also endured my journey (via phone calls and the media) and their journey's end was also being celebrated here.

There were parades and parties well into the evening. In the end it was determined that about $250,000 was raised for Spina Bifida research due to my run. And more importantly the world had started to become educated as to what Spina Bifida was. What a glorious venture. That brings me to my last Tid Bit.

Tid Bit #11. PLAN SOMETHING with your life after you are done with your cross-country journey. From the beginning of training until the end of my run took about two years. Those days were filled with training runs, meetings, planning and a million other things. And then, It was over. Then... NOTHING.

I have felt it myself and heard about it from other crossers. The empty or hollow feeling when you have finished. It can become a very depressing time if you don't plan on doing something beyond the finish. Plan ANYTHING, but don't plan NOTHING.

I hope these pages have helped you somehow. It has been 46 years since I started long distance running. And I still love it today. Follow your dreams. GO FOR IT.

Please read the next part and open your heart to how you can make a difference.

I ran in 1978 for Spina Bifida. In 2002 some friends of mine introduced me to a woman who had a special reason to meet me. She proceeded to tell me that she remembered my run for a special reason. She explained that in 1978 she had worked in a laboratory in one of the Springfield, Massachusetts hospitals. She told me that the staff in that hospital stayed close in tune with the progress of my run. The reason being that, at that time, there was little or no money being given to Spina Bifida research. It was the 2nd leading birth defect in the world. But very few people knew what it was. This woman said that my running gave the Spina Bifida Association a rolling podium from which to educate the world of their plight. The run had brought so much attention to Spina Bifida that laws were changed and money started flowing in for research from everywhere. With tears starting to form in her eyes, she said that because of those monies, it was in her laboratory that the first early pregnancy test for Spina Bifida was developed. And she was giving all the credit for that to me. I explained that in truth, it was a combined effort of many people. But she stopped me, grabbed my hands and looked me square in the eyes and said, "But it was your running that allowed everyone else to be as effective as their efforts were." Then with tears rolling down her cheeks she said, while staring into my eyes, "Alan, you changed medical history." Now with tears coming out of both our eyes she gave me a small hug and said, "Thank you for what you did." And she walked away.

What can one person do? Step to the plate. If you make the decision to run, or walk across the United States, do it for a cause that will motivate you and save you when you are down or questioning what you are doing. Don't just think about running or walking across the U.S.. Start to act on your thoughts and doors will open that will help you accomplish your mission. Do you really want later in life, to keep recalling how you had THOUGHT about it, or would you rather talk about all your experiences having DONE it?........ You choose.

To see more about my running past, present and future, log on to www.runningwithaltardy.com.

Chapter 2

**Frank Giannino
1979, 1980
My Two Runs Across the U.S. from California to New York**

I'm writing this chapter as a brief first-person account of my experiences running across America twice. A more detailed version of my story was chronicled a few years ago in the book: "46 Days" by Kevin Gleason.

My first "Run Across America" began on March 1, 1979 at 6:00 AM on the beach behind Gladstone's Restaurant near Los Angeles. My running partner, Billy Glatz, and I, scooped up a bottle of Pacific Ocean water, which we planned to pour into the Atlantic Ocean after our finish. The daunting task that lay ahead was christened with challenges right from the start. During the night before our start, our support motorhome was parked in the lot next to the restaurant. The motor home was like a large tin can as it was being pelted with rain. We managed very little sleep that night.

The rain poured on us through the entire first eight miles up Sunset Boulevard to Sepulveda. Billy and I missed the first turn onto Sepulveda, as the sign was covered with leaves from overhanging branches due to the rain. We were moving right along at about eight minutes per mile, before we realized we had missed our turn. In the downpour, we had also missed our support motorhome, which was parked (as planned) by the Holiday Inn. Drenched and in front of the UCLA campus, we stuck out our thumbs and hitchhiked back to Sepulveda. Our body heat thoroughly fogged up the front window of the VW van that picked us up. The driver all but threw us out of his vehicle when we arrived at the entrance to Sepulveda Boulevard. We were a little flustered after this rocky moment, as our motor home support vehicle was nowhere in sight!

We had charted our route through the Automobile Association of America. We were using TripTik's to guide us and we had no means of communicating with our support team (back in 1979 no internet, no cell phones). So onto Sepulveda we ran over the hill into Fountain Valley and beyond, sans support! A total of 42 more miles later we ended the day at a police station not far from Acton CA. While running we contacted the police. The police issued an APB to let our support team know we were on the planned route and to come meet up with us. Our support team also had an APB issued. End of the day comes, we rendezvous and the fireworks among the four of us, as all of us blamed one another for missing one another at Sepulveda. Soon after, the arguing stopped, together we all diffused the situation and planned for the next day.

Day Two's goal was to reach Victorville. Running through the

Mojave Desert was no easy task. Soft sandy shoulders presented a challenge for the motor home as it parked ahead waiting for us, and the hot desert was no picnic. Billy, already negative about being responsible "to so many masters" (referring to our sponsors), decided to run in a black t-shirt and black run shorts. With fair complexion and blonde hair, by the end of the day, he began to convulse from heat stroke. After sabotaging himself, the following morning, he announces he wants to drop out. I didn't see it coming!

Billy decided to continue the run, as a support person. On Day Eleven, after seeing I was comfortably managing the 50 miles per day routine, Billy stuck his thumb at an entry ramp to the interstate system in Phoenix and got a ride (amazingly) straight back to New Paltz, NY, with a tractor trailer driver. After the run Billy told me the drive only took 36 hours and he was back in the Paltz! Amazing!

A lifetime of running had prepared me for this run. Going into it, I did not know what would happen. My friendship with Billy, our marathon lifestyle and our combined passion for all things running, are what led to this moment. Billy had a lot of great ideas. Opening a running store in New Paltz, our training routes, our "running bum" lifestyles, the social scene in New Paltz, all these were happening at the height of a very adventurous period-of-time in our lives. The most powerful thing we shared back then, was a dream! When Billy departed in Phoenix, he stated to me: "You need this run more than I do, Frank!" I did not know it at the time, but he was right!

All I was focused on back then, was one day at a time. Thank God, I had Becky Wright as a handler. Becky drove and maintained the motor home, prepared meals, kept a diary. She was, as she put it, like a "little housewife on wheels." Becky had just finished college and was looking for her first teaching job. Her being available to be the support person for the Run was a stroke of luck.

Other lucky moments came before the start of the run as well. A key moment was when the United Way of Ulster County called to say they would support the Run. As it turned out, United Way had a new campaign chair that spring. His name was Tom Geyer. Geyer was recently hired as the new publisher of the Daily Freeman in Kingston NY. So, as campaign chair, he thought it would be a "splashy" move to support the run. What Geyer did was use the "power of the press" to market the event! He negotiated with Camper's Barn in Kingston to get us a brand-new Coachman MotorHome to use for the Run, in trade for advertising space in the newspaper. Camper's Barn planned to use the motor home as a rental following the Run's completion.

Prior to the beginning of the Run, the Freeman announced "above the front-page banner": *Pair Plans to Run Across America for United Way!* Geyer's splashy idea was off and running, literally. All of a sudden during the days leading up to the Run, Billy and I had become major celebrities in Ulster County. So the benefit to United Way was two-fold: promote the United Way Campaign and raise money through a mileage pledge campaign, which was unheard of prior to the run. I insisted that the monies go directly to the Cancer Society (in my mother's memory) which back then, was one of United Way's beneficiaries. The promise to the pledger was that for $10 of sponsorship (which UW said sponsored five miles of the Run), the runner would send you a thank you postcard from wherever I was on the Run. I did not keep this promise, but it did not stop the community from mailing $11,700 in small donations to United Way. The Freeman ran daily stories about the Run, as Becky called in each day to report, and on several occasions they placed a map of the USA Run route above the banner on the front page. Most of the donations poured in at the end, after the Freeman displayed that my mileage running was far ahead of the dollars coming in.

Looking back, I can tell you, I was literally running "on the seat of my pants!" I would be on the road no later than 6 am. There were moments of course, when Becky had to pick up supplies, gas up the RV, make phone calls, so I would be running sans support. So we planned all our moves around my ten to eleven minute per mile pace. I would do five mile runs throughout the day. Pretty much "grazing" food-wise throughout the day on those brief five-mile breaks. A lunch break at 25 miles was always my longest break. I would log the fifty miles per day, each day by around 6 pm.

There were many memorable moments on Run #1! The two most memorable had to do with the wind and the rain. The wind was brutal on two occasions: Mountainaire, New Mexico and on the way to and through the north Texas panhandle and Amarillo. Another unforgettable memory was in Tulsa. As I was being interviewed by Channel Five Alive, I inadvertently introduced Becky as my athletic supporter. She punched me on live television. I deserved that one. In Missouri on the way to St Louis the rain poured heavy and all day. As the rain pummeled down, I ran past a mobile home park. Some of the mobile homes began to float due to extreme flooding with occupants climbing on the rooftops. During the downfall, my left shin flexor extender began to act up. I sought help at an orthopedic clinic in town. The doctor there gave me my first pair of over-the-calf medical grade compression hose to wear under my Jobst OTC socks. He also gave me several heel lifts to experiment with.

While in Indiana, Daily Freeman staff writer, Edwina Henderson informed her parents that I would be running past their coffee shop. Her parents and the customers there were very welcoming.

In Ohio, I was running with traffic on a divided section of highway. On the right side of the grass median were two lanes of cement roadway. Same on the other side of the road. All of a sudden I hear a loud rumbling on the other side of the road. Turns out a runner is push rolling an empty keg of beer with a lawn mower handle. The keg has two pieces of rubber tread around the wide spots to help the barrel roll easily. A relay team of college fraternity brothers is taking turns pushing the keg from Boston to Los Angeles to raise money for charity. It is an annual event. The roadway is relatively quiet, as we enthusiastically share our stories with one another.

Pennsylvania was by far the toughest state to run through. Narrow road shoulders. Cars zipping along and lots of hills presented many challenges. Memories of running through eastern Pennsylvania were everlasting. Three Mile Island had just experienced a nuclear incident. Briefly I was asked to stop and speak to a meeting of Chamber of Commerce members in Chambersburg. Gettysburg was the most memorable. As I ran past a section of the battlefield an open top double decker tour bus guide was sharing the story on loudspeaker with the tourist on board. In Doylestown, I took a wrong turn, had to backtrack a bit. The Pennsylvania Dutch known known for their crafts, especially woodworking, did not fail to excite as I passed men and women clad in black and white outfits during a light rain in their horse drawn carriages trotting down the road as a I ran by the intersection of roads leading to Blue Ball and Intercourse. I was running by and there was a very large chair on the front lawn. I sat in it for fun, joking with Becky, and saying "See this is what happens to you when you run across the country". I looked like I had shrunk as I sat in the oversized ten foot high-chair.

The bridge authority closed down the upper level of the Verrazano Bridge for me as I was police escorted across and into Brooklyn. That Fall of 1979, I would return to run the NYC Marathon. The finish in the steps of NYC Hall came 60 days 6 hours after my start in California. I had covered 2,876 miles. A reporter asked if I planned to do another run. I "knee jerk" said yes! The reason: I knew I could log more miles per day. After finishing, friends and well-wishers walked with me to the Battery Park and I ceremoniously dumped Pacific Ocean water into the Atlantic Ocean, as a way of celebrating West Meets East. I was happy to be finished.

For the next three days I ran from the City to Kingston, NY. I was reunited with Billy Glatz and I ran through New Paltz and hundreds of people greeted me along the parade route and in Dietz Stadium. Many local runners joined me that day in Kingston. Becky and I were given the "Key to the City" in both New Paltz and in Kingston. Kingston made a big deal of my finish. For sixty straight days the residents of Kingston and Ulster County had been updated about my experiences running across America. It was truly one of the best moments of my life! I received a kiss on the cheek from Miss Ulster County. The Mayor spoke, as well as other officials from the community and the United Way. Three thousand dollars in proceeds were donated to the United Way. I asked the United Way to give the money to the American Cancer Society in my mother's memory. Many speeches to community groups would follow, some in front of large audiences. I never dreamed I would receive this much attention.

Shortly after my finish, I announced I was going to run across America again. This time from San Francisco to NYC. With the credibility of one run under my belt, I thought soliciting sponsors for the second run would be a little easier. Not so! One after the other, sponsors said no to my request for underwriting. United Way was excited to work with me. This time I was working with the United Way of Tri-State in NYC. They were very supportive and helped open doors. I had no problem receiving product donations for the second run. Cold hard cash was tough to come by.

Several things transpired during the sixteen months of planning for the second run. First, my running times really improved on the local running scene. I won several Hudson Valley road and trail races. The most notable was my win with a time of 1:12:05 in the Kingston to Saugerties Half Marathon. All of the mileage running across America had paid big dividends. I carried this level of fitness into the NYC Marathon. I would hit the half marathon split in 1:11:05, a personal record, only to blow up and drop out at mile 20, with Lasse Viren, no less! We both took the subway to Central Park where I was reunited with disappointed friends and family. "Just finishing" was not my goal. Running a good time was! In the end I was happy with my splits and my level of conditioning.

After NY, my family volunteered to be my support team for the second run. My stepmother Josephine nickname Ja would cook the meals in the motor home, provide a homey atmosphere and keep a diary. My dad Frank Sr, nicknamed Sonny, a recently retired male nurse, would drive the motor home, maintain it and look after my medical needs. My brother John would ride his bike while I ran, supporting my immediate needs for food and other supplies.

July 1980, the Times Herald Record in Middletown, NY wrote a Q&A piece about my upcoming run from SF to NY. Shortly after the article, I received a phone call from Bud Weiner, a local track and field official. Bud requested I go with him to NYC to meet with executives from the shoe company he was a sales rep for, The Intermark Shoe Company, a division of International Seaway Trading Corp in Cleveland. The meeting proved successful.

While at the NY Shoe Show at the Colosseum on Columbus Circle, to meet the guys from Intermark, I noticed the Keds booth. An ultramarathoner named Stan Cottrell had run across America from NY to SF in new running shoes from Keds. Keds! A large map of his run across the USA blazoned as a backdrop for Keds new uniquely designed running shoes. Around the corner at the Pro Specs booth, was fellow crosser, Dave McGillivray (Boston Marathon director). Stan, Dave and I went to lunch to share our stories running across America. There was no ego. It was one of the most memorable moments of my life. The topic of conversations mostly about our support teams. Not only did we all have support team challenges. Bottom line is the runner has to keep moving and get in the miles. The support team had to get along. Not an easy task when they are supporting some "nutty" runner, and they are there in most cases volunteering their time. Keeping the peace seemed as much a challenge for the three of us, as was all the running we had done.

Following the show, at a meeting in Cleveland with the owner of ISTC, Nate Gurdy, the company agreed to underwrite my second run. I had my cash sponsor. It was AAU Shoes, one of Intermark's labels. United Way would be on my running cap. AAU Shoes was emblazoned across the front of my t-shirt. The back of the shirt read "AAU Shoes Coast to Coast."

Things went into high gear after that meeting. A local sportswriter and runner, Bruce Goldberg, from the Daily Freeman volunteered to join the run as a media liaison. Few motor homes were available to use, so my parents drove to Canton Ohio, met with one of Intermark's executives, and they rented a motorhome. The vehicle was in bad shape. My parents drove it to San Francisco. It had problems, big time! My dad managed to fix all of them. Their "shakedown" drive across America would prove valuable to the run.

The week prior to the second run, I visited the SF office of the Automobile Association of America. While there I tweaked my planned route across the country based on the advice of one of the trip planners there. They gave me road maps, trip tiks, complete with arrows, highlights, and warnings about certain locations along the way. Remember back then we did not have cell phones. I also visited the California College of Podiatric Medicine (CCPM) at the suggestion of a student there, Jim Goff. I met with Biomechanics professor, Chris Smith DPM and Richard Bogdon DPM. They evaluated my gait and addressed my concerns. They made me two sets of functional in-shoe orthotics and donated a treasure trove of podiatric supplies, all of which were useful on the second run.

On September 1, 1980 at 8:17 AM, I began my second run across America from the steps of City Hall. Walt Stack and many runners and community members from the SF Bay area were there. All of my family members living in the Bay Area were there for the start, as well! CCPM parked their 40 foot "Podmobile" motorhome nearby. The same vehicle they use at Bay to Breakers to provide foot care and first aid to the participants. CCPM donated even more supplies to my run. Four student runners from CCPM were there to start the run with me as well as Dr Bogdon. It was a clear beautiful day in the City. Up the road we went headed to the Golden Gate Bridge and Sausalito.

Halfway across the bridge I saw a commotion. Without losing a step, the six of us leaped over the sidewalk rail, crossed several lanes of traffic, and finished running across the bridge to the other side. Two hours later, a cyclist caught up with me. He stated the commotion was a bridge jumper was threatening to jump off the bridge. The jumper waited for his wife to come, looked up at her and jumped to his death. A little further up the road I met a man on his way to SF to finish his Walk across America. Day One ended outside of Vallejo.

    The next three days were rough. My plan was to run seventy miles per day. We only managed fifty plus mile days to South Lake Tahoe. The support team wanted showers in a campground. Everyone's personal needs seem to outweigh the importance of my logging the miles toward a record. By the end of Day Five, everyone was focused on helping me get in the mileage. Day Five, for the first time began at 4:00 am and ended a little past Fallon, NV. Day Six things began to click with the support team. No more wasting time searching for or driving to campgrounds, just so everyone could shower and get a good night's sleep. John and I were awake at 3:00 am. We were on the road at 4:00 am sharp! At 25 miles, I would take a "One hour" break. Then another 25 miles, I would take another "One hour" break. Then I would try to get in as many miles in as I could until I'd had enough. Day Six ended with 63 miles completed, my first ever sixty-plus mile day!

    Day Seven miles I reached sixty miles on US 50. My confidence began to soar! Then a set back! I ended Day Eight at 46 miles, nine miles east of Austin, NV. My right anterior shin hurt. I needed a break to rest and figure things out. The following morning on Day Nine, I inserted a rear medial heel wedge under my right orthotic and added a tighter fitting gradient OTC compression sock on both legs. The modification worked, as I began shuffling down the road with no discomfort, and sixty miles of no major hardship, just ten miles shy of Eureka.

    The next day my Dad visited a doctor in Eureka. He had dysentery. By the time we were running through town, he had already gotten his medicine. I ran through Eureka to a rest area, where the motor home was parked. My brother had leaned his bike against the front of the motor home. As dad went to drive ahead, he ran over John's bike. Dad was pissed. The bike was crushed. Now I had no immediate support from my brother. The team decided to drive ahead to Ely and purchase a new bike for John. While in Ely Bruce decided to contact the radio station and let them know what had happened. A local businessman heard the story about the run for United Way and donated a bike for John to use. I ran the full sixty miles that day with almost no support.

    Day Eleven things really clicked as I rock and rolled through eastern Nevada 70.8 miles, only five miles from the Utah border. The day wrapped up at 8:20 pm. It was my longest day of movement yet and my first seventy plus mile day. On Day Twelve I covered 70.2 miles, as things wrapped up at 8 pm, twenty miles west of Delta. Day Thirteen got us to within 45 miles of Provo. Intermark had mailed another case of shoes to the United Way there, so we drove to a hotel to pick up the shoes. To our surprise the BYU cross country team was there to meet us. Its team captain was Ed Eyestone. The BYU guys thought we were nuts, but they were very supportive nonetheless, asking many questions. We spent the night at the hotel. Got up early to our last road marker and ran toward and through Provo.

Provo was most memorable because the motorhome stopped and wouldn't start. A good Samaritan stopped by. He used a tool to create a connection and the vehicle started. He demonstrated how to use the tool in case the vehicle stopped In the future. The man gave the tool to Dad. It came in handy the rest of the trip. Day Fourteen ended six miles up Provo Canyon.

The part of each day that I looked forward to the most was starting my run at 4:00 am. As I made my way east, I looked forward to the first signs of daylight on the horizon. This period of time, each morning, were some of the best running experiences of my life. Even today, I enjoy completing my run early in the day. I still look forward to sunrise in the morning.

Day Fifteen I finished the day five miles east of Fruitland with 64.8 miles and noticeable gain in elevation and the breathtaking beauty of Provo Canyon. Day Sixteen I covered 68 miles and got within nine miles of Vernal. A man, who ran like a duck in full waddle, ran quite a few miles with me. He and his wife later joined our team in the motorhome for dinner. They were very unique people, as if all of us in the motor home weren't!

Day Seventeen, Ja and dad drove ahead to Vernal to do laundry. I remember them saying I think we set some kind of record for all of the laundry we did in such a short period of time. The support team really had their work cut out. Planning meals, shopping when they could, preparing the meals on the fly every day, day in and day out, and for what? A 29 years old man obsessed with a goal! Crazy when you think about it. I finished the day with 63 miles just shy of Massadona, CO.

Day Eighteen I finished in the boomtown of Craig, CO. My forefoot was really hurting. Actually, they were numb all of the time from the daylong foot plants. My dad went into a Penny's in Craig and talked the store manager into giving him a shoe stretcher. From that moment on, my father would constantly be stretching my shoes. At the end of each day, my dad would massage my feet, using a technique he learned in medical school. He would push the lactic acid out of my arms and legs and massage my back and neck. The massage would follow a brief meal. I would go into a deep sleep on average of 4-6 hours. Only to wake up each morning to take on another day of all day running. It was all so amazing while it lasted.

Day Nineteen we ran to the edge of downtown Steamboat Springs, then another 22 miles. Most memorable were the switchbacks I ran up as we approached ten thousand feet in elevation. I finished the day with 62.4 miles. Day Twenty was most memorable as I had a brief encounter with a bear along the roadside before sunrise as I ran through Walden. Ironically, Walden is where my family is from (Walden NY, that is). I ran another 27 miles to finish the day at 62.5 miles. A brief snow squall greeted me at the end of day, with the poplars glistening as I ran by. Another great memory!

One of the most important milestones of my run came on Day 21. Early in the morning, I felt like I was running in a mountain church when crossing Cameron Pass. The nearby towering rock formation was absolutely breathtaking. The entire day was spent running downhill. It was a chore all day just dealing with descending over 5,000 feet. A TV crew was filming a documentary on how important Poudre Canyon was to the community. So many people use the area for recreation. So, my running just added fuel to their fire. The government wanted to build a dam in the Canyon. The locals were against it. I finished the day with 70.6 miles at the junction of CO14 and CO287. We spent the night at the home of United Way friends in nearby Fort Collins. I was most pleased at the end of this day, because I had surpassed my original goal, which was to reach Fort Collins averaging at least 60 miles per day.

The following morning, I was met by the owner of a running store called "Foot of the Rockies." We ran twenty miles together, moving right along the whole time. I finished day 22 at 70.6 miles in Raymer. We parked the motor home at the edge of the road next to the border fence of a man's ranch. The owner gave us a miniature windmill he made himself. He liked to make them and give them as souvenirs. Day 23 I ran 62 miles to four miles east of Crook.

Day 26 I covered 65.8 miles finishing five miles west of Elm Creek. Day 27, I covered 70 miles to Grand Island. All kinds of celebrations were happening there. It was also the harvest season. It was hard to breathe, the air and trucks were moving fast, dangerous to anyone trying to run on the roadside. A local man offered to let us park in his driveway, use his electric, and let me use the shower in his basement. It was a little weird, but it worked.

Day 28 I completed 70 miles to the junction of US 34 and Interstate 80. To avoid having to run through Lincoln, I began running at 4:00 am on the interstate for four miles. Only a half mile from the exit, a trooper stopped me. He stated that a man, only two hours earlier was killed by a tractor trailer while walking along the interstate, and that I had to get off the road immediately. I let him know what I was doing, and he let me go. I ran a little faster, got off at the exit, and began running north to Omaha. The local running club ran with me through the streets of Omaha, police escort all the way. Day 29 ended at the Missouri River. United Way put us up in a hotel. I gave a reporter an interview and then early on Day 30 I quickly ran across the "no pedestrian" bridge. As I began running in Iowa,

I was greeted by many passersby, who had read the newspaper that morning, and learned I was running across America for charity and to break Stan Cottrell's recent record of 48 days 1 hour 48 minutes from NY to SF. I was definitely "on pace" to achieve that goal. It was hammer time! Turns out these first 30 days were about getting into the rhythm of running 70 plus miles per day. The team and I were finally there. I kept pushing but never lost control. Staying healthy and constant movement were everything.

In Des Moines I received a large homemade key to the city. Bruce also departed in Des Moines, citing "it was time" to get back to work. From that day on my dad kept in touch with Intermark, United Way, and the media. My dad wasn't a professional like Bruce, but nonetheless he did get the job done! In Quad Cities I would ceremoniously carry a letter across the bridge from one mayor to another. From Omaha to the finish, I averaged 70 miles or more per day all the way to the finish at the Verrazano Toll Plaza in Staten Island, New York City, NY.

The two most exciting moments for me during the final sixteen days of 70-plus milers every day, were running with Stan Cottrell for seventy miles (55 miles on Day 36 and 15 miles on the morning of Day 37, south of Chicago), and meeting Pat Perry south of Youngstown.

Stan was basically checking on my progress and the legitimacy of my run and on the claims I was making. After all, I was chasing his "record", which was only two months old. Stan spent the night with us in the motorhome. He had a lot of questions for the support team, wanted to see our logbook, the witness signatures, Ja's diary, etc. A cool moment while running with Stan that morning was the local newspaper reporter who ran with us. She found the story to be interesting, because the wannabe record holder was running with "the" record holder! Stan followed my progress the entire way, as he would later tell me. I was doing the same with Marshall Ulrich and Pete Kostelnick many years later. I wish I had the internet and social media back then. I was one of many crossers over the years who were basically broke while doing it and had limited "ready" access to communication devices.

Running with Pat Perry was the beginning of a lifelong friendship. Pat had run a marathon, never farther. On his way to the gym in Boardman, he noticed me running and the support vehicle. He joined me as I ran past his gym. He would run over 50 miles with me on that Day 42 which ended in Pennsylvania at 73 miles. Pat was the manager at Athlete's Foot in the Boardman Mall. He was looking to advance in life both with his career and through his endurance exploits. For Pat, his running with me was life changing, as he would chase his dreams. He would want more! He would go on to become a marketing executive with Athlete's Foot in the national office and ultimately spend a great deal of time going back and forth to South Korea. For a while he was an executive with Asics America. He was in "on the ground floor" with the start of 361 USA. Endurance-wise, he excelled as an ultramarathon runner, an ultramarathon cyclist, and an Ironman triathlete. To this day, he claims that running with me, all those years ago, was a game changer for him.

Pennsylvania once again was the toughest state to run through. The mountains, the lay of the land, the roads, the drivers on the highway, were a challenge. I logged the highest mileage of both of my runs. The last two days in PA, I was just looking for the finish, to be done with this phase of my life.

I was so exhausted emotionally at the finish. I was elated and at the same time relieved that my obsession was over. I submitted my claim of crossing America on foot in 46 days 8 hours 46 minutes to the Guinness Book of Records. When the Guinness Board of Directors approved my claim as a new record, it would remain a record claim with them for 36 years. Pete Kostelnick eclipsed that mark in 2016.

In retrospect, I completed both crossings, literally, on the seat of my pants. Looking back, both runs were completed with very little experience on my part. I was not an ultramarathon competitor. I had run a 2:39 marathon in Maryland in 1975. I love to run and I cherish all of the memories, but that's about it. I most certainly cannot boast a running resume like Pete and so many great runners today. The end result of two runs across America was that I found my career path. For over forty years, I have been a shoe-fitter, fitting runners, walkers, everyone I meet professionally. I call the business Frank's Custom Shoe-Fitting. It's located in Middletown NY. My website is www.shoe-fitter.com

It was the dream of completing monumental goals that really motivated me in 1979 and 1980. The runs were the greatest accomplishments of my life and most cherished of all the things I've done. Again, the complete story of my journeys is documented in the book "46 Days" written by Kevin Gleason. Hope you enjoyed reading this and I hope you will take the time to read my book.

Chapter 3

Jay Birmingham
May 19 to July 30, 1980
Los Angeles to New York City

RUNNING LONG: The Transcontinental, 40 Years Later

1980 was a long time ago, but as the 40th anniversary of my 2,964-mile run from Los Angeles to New York City approaches, memories come flooding into the present. To call the completion of the journey life-changing would be an understatement. It defined my running persona as no other event has before or since.

I hope readers will forgive my nostalgic indulgence. I believe that the lessons I learned during those 72 days might be useful to my running friends. Our running is a profoundly selfish pursuit but I believe that our lessons from the road give us something that we can share, and perhaps, on occasion, make us better people.

The seed was planted in 1964. A Dayton Daily News article described a 48-year old miner from South Africa, Don Shepard, who was jogging across Northern Ohio, chasing the record for a coast-to-coast run. I was 18, a college student with a longest race of 10 miles, and weekly mileage of twenty. Covering 40 miles a day on foot had no appeal.

A decade later, the Ohio boy found himself in Florida, dreams of an Olympic marathon vanished with the realization that average leg speed can't be bullied into national class running performances. I could now run far, but I couldn't do it very fast.

Thoughts of a journey run germinated. By 1976, I'd managed some 140-mile training weeks and treks from Cleveland to Columbus, Ohio (161 miles) and Miami to Cocoa Beach, Florida (219 miles).

With a paid leave of absence from my desk job at a local construction firm, and a donated truck camper, I jogged down the steps of Los Angeles City Hall on April 19, 1977, supported by John Stanforth of Wilmington, Ohio, and his 10-year-old son. Adhering to 8:30 per mile pace in doses of 30 to 60 minutes for 45 miles, I dashed across the Mojave Desert toward the Atlantic. I lasted just one week.

238 miles into the adventure, my Achilles tendons went on strike, joined by two blistered soles and ten swollen toes. Ehrenburg, Arizona, was as far as we got. Ten days of recovery in the desert, icing and massaging, brought me back to the L.A. City Hall steps for a second start. I lasted two days. Listening to my body was not a skill I understood. I'd scheduled myself to cover 45 miles a day for two weeks, then 50, then 55. I was not a machine. I was not even a good runner.

Covered with a stress-induced rash, I drove my friends to Ohio, and then headed home to Jacksonville. I sheepishly resumed life as a normal runner until PRs at the marathon, 30 km, half-marathon, and 10 km in 1978 snapped me from my doldrums. As Sherlock Holmes might say, "the game is (once again) afoot."

Encouraged by ultramarathon legend Ted Corbitt to consider running with a backpack, unaccompanied, a la Don Shepherd, I logged 200-mile weeks through the winter of 1979 for two months. I was now teaching and coaching at Jacksonville Episcopal High School and managing a tiny running store in Arlington. But unlike 1977, there would be no income while on the road.

On May 19, 1980, I stood on the steps of the L.A. City Hall for a third time. I got the signature of a city official at 9:15 a.m. By late afternoon, I was 35 miles to the east, working my way around Riverside, California, searching for intact stretches of Old State Road 60 and Jackrabbit Trail to avoid the expressway. A week later, I trotted across the Colorado River to Ehrenburg, Arizona and on toward Phoenix.

I was healthy. My blisters were runnable. My leg soreness was bearable. I was finding cheap motels and enough food. I got President Gerald Ford's autograph on a newspaper photo of myself near Palm Springs. I stopped to chat with locals and to read historic markers. Without a timetable, I was absorbing the lessons of the road, and making progress toward my goal.

Arizona was the most beautiful state that I had ever run through. Its arid mountains and deep, moist canyons were a joy to cross on foot. Fearful family and friends received my reports: People are not trying to run me down or rob me. Most motorists yield a couple of feet to the thin-clad jogger along the roadway. Accommodating strangers often gave me complimentary meals and reduced room rates.

I gobbled down two pieces of pie in Pie Town, New Mexico, just short of the high point of my route, the Continental Divide, 9,000 feet above sea level. It was all downhill from there, I told myself. Over the green ribbon of the Rio Grande Valley, I approached the 1,000-mile point of my journey, the Texas border.

Before my departure, a Jacksonville sportscaster had asked, "When do you think you'll have it made? When will you be confident that you can make it all the way?"

"I think I'll be injury-proof by a thousand miles," I replied confidently.

Crisis in North Texas

I had told the three Jacksonville sportscasters that I'd call them every night, which in 1980 was a time-consuming ordeal. Find a pay phone, three quarters, and then spend at least 45 minutes on my feet after 40 miles of running. A few days into my 3,000-mile journey, a compromise was required: I'd phone each guy every three days and they would share the update among themselves.

Not content with how many miles I had run, the starting and finishing towns, or weather reports, they were keen to hear of blood, dirt, and pain. "Anything special happen today?"

Three days in eastern New Mexico served up plenty of news.

The Very Large Array (VLA) was on the south side of US 60, a few miles from Socorro. Jogging past the massive phalanx of radio telescopes, I wondered what might be signaling us across space. Years later, Jody Foster would star in the movie, "Contact." The first scene was at the VLA. That evening, Lloyd Pasco hosted me at his home, a veritable mansion surrounded by a junk yard.

Pasco and his sons were scavengers, buying up abandoned railroads and salvaging copper, steel rails, railroad ties, spikes, and glass insulators. He'd seen me trotting eastward around noon and offered me an apple and a place to stay that evening. I enjoyed their hospitality that night and the next morning, I was on my way again, with a hearty breakfast in my gut and two sandwiches in my backpack.

Thirty miles later, after running north along I-25 and beside the Rio Grande, I veered east to my day's goal, Blue Springs. "Si, I ain't been up that way for a few years, but there's a restaurant and a motel," said Juan Hernandez, a grizzled farmer who signed my witness card. So, I re-filled my water bottle, crossed the Rio Grande, and ran the 11 uphill miles to Blue Springs.

At length, I came upon a crumbling concrete statue of an elephant, its trunk broken and bullet marks all over it. Behind it was a dilapidated saloon. Nothing else was in sight, so I cautiously entered the dark building.

"How far to Blue Springs?" I asked, as I plopped my sweaty body on a bar stool and ordered a Pepsi.

"Thees ees Blue Springs," said the tiny Señora who tended the place.

"I was told there was a motel here," I said.

"I'm sorry, Señor, but it is closed."

After I explained that I was on foot, she said maybe she could find a room for me. Fishing through a cigar box full of keys, she found the right one, led me through a beaded curtain, and out the back door. There was the motel, more dilapidated than the saloon, adorned with a CONDEMNED sign from the State. She brushed aside a spider web, opened the padlocked door, and unfolded a rollaway bed. "Three dollars, Señor, if you want it."

Since Mountainair was 14 miles farther east, I gladly accepted the room. I washed up in a pan of water behind the saloon, put on a dry t-shirt, worked on my blistered feet, and then returned to the bar for dinner.

My dining options were few. I could eat hard boiled eggs from a 10-gallon jar (they were pink), potato chips, beer, Pepsi, or beef jerky. I explained that I had run forty-one miles that day, and the owner took pity on me.

"Mama is cooking chili tonight. Please eat with us." I spooned down a large bowl of the hottest New Mexico chili I had ever tasted, following each mouthful with a saltine cracker. My hostess could see the discomfort in my red face, teary eyes, and constant gulps of Pepsi. She ordered a refill for me. "Por favor, Mama," she told her mother, "no pimiento." They smiled, indulgently, at the gringo runner who couldn't stand the heat.

As I lay on my cot at midnight, several cars pulled up. I stuck my head inside the saloon to get another Pepsi. Eight teenage boys had arrived, to drink many beers and to play pool. They confirmed that Mountainair had several restaurants. At two in the morning, they peeled out. I slept soundly until dawn, ran the 14 miles to Mountainair, and had two breakfasts before noon.

Four days later, the Texas border loomed. It marked the 1000-mile point of my journey. I'd told Matt Cooney of Channel 12 that I'd be "injury proof" by a thousand miles. Hah!

In 1980, the Interstate between Tucumcari, NM, and the Texas state line was not completed. Hundreds of cars and tractor-trailer trucks jammed the route I was running. The shoulder was covered with coarse gravel. Determined to run into Texas instead of protecting my feet and legs, I jogged the 18 miles from San Jon to Glenrio, cursing the rough footing and the relentless traffic. When I reached the TL2 Truck Stop on the border, my left shin was throbbing. I knew I was injured.

Two days later, I limped into Amarillo, the 63 miles taking two days, well under my 40 miles per day average. A local runner, Dan Moreland, took me to see his orthopedist who examined me and diagnosed a tibial stress fracture. I disagreed, and defiantly limped 16 miles the next morning before phoning Moreland. He delivered me to Johnny and Gerri Grill's home for a day-and-a-half rest. I iced, elevated, and rubbed my shin. I read their books and listened to Beethoven and Tchaikovsky records. The clock continued to run. I did not.

I needed to average 41 miles each day of the journey to eclipse Don Shepherd's 1964 solo time of 73 days, 8 hours, 20 minutes. Lying on a sofa in Amarillo, I felt my chances to break the record fading. On the morning of the second day, I was driven to my stopping point, Groom, and I resumed my run. I had fashioned a crude orthotic from layers of insole material. Lifting my forefoot and forcing me to land on my arch, the orthotic took pressure off my shin. That first day back on the road, I walk-jogged 32 miles. The next day, I managed 36. On the third day, I limped into Oklahoma.

A brutal heat wave had descended on the southern United States. Cattle were dying in the fields, roofers were passing out, and a streak of 19 straight 100-degree days (official Weather Bureau highs) followed me from Oklahoma City, across Missouri, Illinois, and Indiana.

Despite stops at every gas station and grocery store, I frequently ran out of drinks. Rather than dehydrate, I once drank from an irrigation ditch and another time from a livestock watering tank. My immune system rose to the challenges, and I never felt sick.

My shin continued to improve, but my pace had eroded into the 35 miles per day range. I was now more than a day-and-a-half (62 miles) behind Shepherd's record pace with only 700 miles to go.

I just want to go the distance

For the nineteenth afternoon in a row, the temperature had risen above 100 degrees. I ran the sidewalks east through Indianapolis and ducked into a McDonald's, more for the AC than refreshment. An hour away from the heat was not enough; within minutes of re-taking the road, I vomited a large orange drink.

I shuffled the final 14 miles to Greenfield, and then lay on the motel bed for an hour, too tired to eat. Finally, I rose to make my nightly phone calls.

"Matt Cooney here." It was the familiar voice of Channel 12's sports anchor, the one who had driven 20 hours from Jacksonville to visit me three weeks earlier in Tulsa, Oklahoma.

"Paul Cameron of Channel 7 announced last night that you're not going for the record."

I stammered my reply, "Well, I haven't really given up, not entirely."

The previous night's conversation was replayed in my mind. I had told Cameron that I was two days behind the pace required to better the 1964 transcontinental running time of South African Don Shepherd, 73 days, 8 hours, 20 minutes. How many times had I told reporters and host families the story?

I had recalled the pre-fight scene in Rocky, the 1976 hit movie. The boxer is unable to sleep, knowing he is going to take a beating. "No one's ever gone the distance with Creed (the champion). I just want to go the distance," he tells his girlfriend, Adrian.

Having Cooney repeat my words was an uppercut. "I still think it's possible," I told the reporter. "I haven't given up."

I would run 50 miles that day, to Richmond, or bust.

I didn't sleep much that night, July 16, 1980. As I stared at the ceiling, I knew that I was very fit. My injured shin had healed. After 59 days on the road, the habit was well-established: I would rise at dawn and get in ten to 20 miles before eating a major meal. Then I would push on in short stages until I reached 40 miles. I took long breaks when necessary, treated my blisters, slathered Shoe-Goo on the soles of my running shoes, and bought new socks. All I needed to do now was run an additional ten miles a day.

I left the Greenfield Motel in early morning darkness on July 17th. I would run 50 miles that day, to Richmond, or bust.

For the first time in three weeks, clouds formed and the temperature rose to only 85 degrees, a veritable cold front. I got to a cheap motel east of Richmond, Indiana, at 6 P.M. I wrote 50 in my journal, and got on the phone to home. "I ran well today. I hit fifty miles."

Excitement and optimism re-emerged, feelings that I hadn't experienced since New Mexico. I'd be crossing my home state of Ohio, starting tomorrow, and every town and landscape along US 40 was familiar.

The next ten days were the most productive of the journey despite the increasingly challenging terrain. I covered Ohio in four days, West Virginia in one, and Pennsylvania in five. My running totals were 54, 56, 56, 55, 59, 58, 58, 57, 57, and 56 miles.

<u>Highlights? There were many each day. These come easily to mind.</u>
>Ate a dinner of peanut butter crackers and Pepsi-Colas from vending machines at a rural motel in Illinois.
>Found a 50-cent piece on the threshold of my motel in Richmond, the evening of my first 50-mile day.
>Crossed the Y-bridge in Zanesville, Ohio on my 59-mile day, the longest of the journey.
>Slept on the lawn of a Holiday Inn, packed with country music festival fans in Youngstown, Ohio. A Mylar blanket from the NYC Marathon kept me warm and dry.
>Cried at Gettysburg National Cemetery in Pennsylvania where thousands of Union and Confederate soldiers had killed each other.
>Enjoyed a surprise birthday party in my honor in King of Prussia, PA.
>Treated to a movie (Caddy Shack) and a nice hotel room by Florida Times-Union reporter Greg Larson near Philadelphia.
>Accompanied for 20 miles by Dan Brannen as we ran toward the Delaware River.
> Crossed New Jersey in the rain.

July 29th was my last full day on the road. I spent the night in a shabby motel outside Newark, concerned about the final 31 miles to City Hall in New York City. Three major bridges were on my route, two with "No Pedestrians" regulations.

I hit the road for Perth Amboy, the southernmost gateway to Gotham. As Bruce Tulloh had done in 1968, I took my chances, under the cover of darkness. I slipped past the toll-booth attendants and in minutes, I was on Staten Island.

I had considered taking the Staten Island Ferry to Manhattan, but my advisor and encourager, Ted Corbitt, had worked a minor miracle: If I arrived at the base of the Verrazano-Narrows Bridge at 9:00 a.m., I'd be allowed to run in a closed lane on the lower level.

Not only did they let me cross the two-mile suspension bridge, I was given a police escort to Brooklyn. An hour later, I found the pedestrian access to the Brooklyn Bridge. In minutes, I would complete my run.

I strode across the classic span, paused briefly for a Jacksonville photographer, then punched the final half mile to Manhattan. I came off the ramp, jogged up the steps of City Hall and into a crowd of reporters, cameramen, friends, and my family. Wife Anita and children Bob, Scott, and Tammy had been flown to New York City.

Ted Corbitt signed my final witness card and penned the official time: 10:59 a.m., July 30, 1980. The elapsed time since my departure from Los Angeles on May 19th: 71 days, 22 hours, 59 minutes.

After an hour of interviews, Runner Magazine hosted a reception at their offices. By four in the afternoon, we arrived by train at my sister's home in Bridgeport, CT. The run was done.

Thirty-nine years have passed. Dozens more men have run coast to coast with backpacks, without crews or support vehicles. Amazingly, my time for an unaccompanied runner still stands at the time of this writing.
Excerpted from I, Alone: A Transcontinental Run *(1984, 2018) by Jay Birmingham.*

Addendum:
Postal card reports to Ted Corbitt:
150 W. 225th St.
NY, NY 10463

Postal card One
Postmark: Industry, CA
May 19, 1980
Dear Ted Corbitt—
   A start is made. Departed city hall shortly after 9:00 A.M. this date. [Exactly 9:15 AM PDT] Will keep you posted. Gary has approx. itinerary. Yours, Jay Birmingham

Postal card Two
Postmark: Miami, Arizona
June 1, 1980

Ted—This is my progress to date. Short mileage days have been due to lodging problems. Am treating every minor problem with care and feeling more fit each day. Have lost only 2 pounds through 5/30/80. Now climbing in altitude to 4600'. Jay Birmingham
May 19—LA-Pomona 34
      20—March AFB 34
      21—Palm Springs 48
      22—Indio + 10 mi. 40
      23—Desert Center 36
      24—Blythe 44
      25—Quartzsite, AZ 29
      26—Salome 38
      27—Aguila   29

28—Circle City 40
29—Phoenix 44
30—Kings Ranch 36
31—~~Superior (1 PM) 25~~
~~(will run more today)~~
Miami, AZ 42

<u>Postal card Three and Four</u>
Erick, OK
Dear Mr. Corbitt: Here is more recent data concerning my solo run across U.S.A. since Phoenix, AZ.

The final mile, July 30, 1980

    5/30 36 King Ranch
    5/31 42 Miami
    6/1   38 S. edge Salt Canyon
    6/2   28 N. edge Salt Canyon
                  (tough running)
    6/3   37 Lakeside
    6/4   51 Springerville
    6/5   49 Quemado, NM
    6/6   43 Datil
    6/7   36 Magdalena
    6/8   40 San Acacia
    6/9   31 Blue Springs (severe storms)
    6/10 36 Willard
    6/11 37 Encino   [Because of H_2O
    6/12 37 Pastura   scarcity, often carry
    6/13 36 Cuervo   5-6# of water & soda in
    6/14 43 Tucumcari pack]
    6/15 41 Endee (hurt R shin)
    6/16 27 Adrian, Texas
    6/17 18 Vega, +4 (easy day)
    6/18 30 Amarillo
    6/19 30 Conway
    6/20 16 Groom (leg worse)
    6/21   0 complete rest, built orthotic
    6/22 31 McLean
    6/23 43 Erick, Oklahoma

Feeling good again. Will keep you informed. Carrying 5-6# in pack now.

Addendum (on second postal card)
My notes indicate that you last heard from me at Sayre, OK.
Here are the missing days—
    Day 36>   Erick, OK   43 Shin pain acute

Canute	39	Medicine & ice	
Hydro	41	Improvement	
El Reno	40		
Okl. City	30		
Luther	34		
Depew	43		
Tulsa	46		

Stopped all medication and pampering as soon as symptoms eased.

Postal card 5
Somerset, PA 2605 miles
July 23, 1980
Dear Mr. Corbitt—The nagging shin pain of Texas and Oklahoma is completely gone with the help of a soft orthotic of my own construction, aspirin, and 3 days treatment with DMSO, starting in Oklahoma City. I've had to contend with the Midwest heat wave, over 100 degrees for more than two weeks. but am now enjoying cool, rainy weather.

Birmingham and Corbitt in New York City; pack under my arm.

Tulsa to Foyil, OK   46
(Day 44)
    To Afton   38
    To Neosho, MO 42
    To Marionville   47
    To Strafford.   43
    To Lebanon   46
    To Rolla   48
    To Stanton   47
    To Kirkwood   47
    To St. Louis and St. Jacob, IL 42
    To Vandalia   45
    To Woodbury   46
    To Terre Haute, IN 41
    To Stilesville   45
    To Gem (thru Indy) 41 100°

To Centerville   50
To Phoneton, OH   50   Cooler, 80s
To Alton   54   and 90s.
To Brownsville.   56   Cloudy at times.
To Middlebourne   56
To Claysville, PA 55   Rain and cool
To Acme   59   65-75°

Expect to finish around July 30.
Jay Birmingham

These postal card reports were recently returned to me by Ted Corbitt's son, Gary, following his father's death.

Chapter 4

LouisMichael Figueroa
1982 - 1996 – 2005
New Brunswick, New Jersey to San Francisco, California
Bangor, ME to San Diego
Perimeter of the US

My feet have traversed innumerable roads with many twists and turns.

There are some distances that cannot be measured. A marathon is 26.2 miles. In 1982, I ran 3,500 miles – I took a longer, southern route - across the US to fulfill a promise to a dying friend. When I had finished, I was the fastest and youngest ever to run across the US. I didn't know at the time that my publicity sound bite would be used in one of the biggest films of all time. In 1996, leukemia having ended my running career, I walked diagonally from Bangor, Maine to San Diego for local AIDS networks in honor of my brother who succumbed to three letters. There are songs which spring from country roads – and on that walk the symphony of my wife and children were born. In 2005, I started a 7,500 miles circle around the US for abused children. Halfway through, my illness caught up with me and I wouldn't go back to finish that walk until 2010.

(photo by Jose Galvez)

Through all of this, I have learned there are untold miles and stories between the training and start and finish lines…

Regardless of the fact that you're on a record setting pace across the US - when you're a 16-year-old male, you're nothing more than a giant hormone with sneakers. I'll come back to the hormones later.

My lead van had broken down outside of Brownsville, Tennessee. I had 6 days and 223 miles to get to Little Rock, Arkansas for an American Cancer Center benefit dinner with a guy by the name of Bill Clinton who was trying to win back the governorship of that state. Now in 1982, on a Friday night in Brownsville, you're told: "Ain't no way we 'all can get a new radiator for dat dere van til Monday mornin'." Not wanting to take an extra day and a half off, I told my coach and crew, "Look, I can go ahead and run the 64 miles to Memphis with the state police escorts." So that's what I did. My coach and crew went back to stay in Jackson while I went on to Memphis.

My biggest sponsor was Holiday Inn - my crew and I stayed at their hotels and motels across the US. Holiday Inns also graciously fed us. When we were in bigger cities we usually stayed at their larger, swankier hotels. It was a great photo shoot for Holiday Inn and we got a chance to enjoy luxurious accommodations. Now, in larger Holiday Inns they usually had a fancier restaurant in addition to their normal diner-type eateries that could be found in every one of their properties. This is where my crew and I were supposed to eat. At that time, Holiday Inn corporate headquarters and their flagship hotel was in Memphis. So, there I am, checking into the hotel when a girl walks into the lobby and gives me a glance filled with enough heat to raise my hormones to nuclear reactor type levels. Her name was Amanda. She was in Memphis with her parents and younger brother for her cousin's wedding in a few days.

Like any horny 16-year-old: I wasn't thinking. I was in pursuit of a conquest. I was filled with bravado and bragging. Somewhere in the whirlwind exchanges like this take place:

"I'm the kid, you probably heard about me, running across the US." "Holiday Inns are my sponsor." She asks, "You can eat wherever you want? Order anything from room service? And you just charge it to the room?" My reply: "Sure, babe."

This Holiday Inn top floor feature was a restaurant – Windows on the River. Second cousin to Windows on the World on top of the World Trade Center. And Windows on the Bay in San Francisco. You get the picture: 5-star restaurants not to be patronized by a kid and his date with the establishment picking up the check. "Steak and lobster?" Sure, babe. To make matters worse: the bartender was star-struck by meeting me and served my date and I alcoholic drinks (which he rang up as virgin coladas.) Sunday night, the bartender took me on a tour of Memphis. We climbed over the low-brick wall on the far end of Elvis' home Graceland. We were stopped by floodlights and security guards. One of the guards recognized me from a TV news report and we ended up getting a private tour of Graceland – including things that aren't on the regular tour – like the toilet seat the King died on - in the wee-hours of the morning.

Now, before we come to the part where I ended up in handcuffs, here are some background items you need to know in order to have a full appreciation of what took place.
1) When I checked in Friday evening the hotel's manager had already left home for the weekend.
2) I travelled with a crew of 3 people, so Holiday Inns always provided us with 4 rooms.

3) My coach and crew stayed behind in Jackson.
4) Remember, we were supposed to get our meals in the 'regular restaurant.'

The hotel's manager returns to work Monday morning, he glanced over his reports and a few details leapt off the page. One: there was only one room of the running crew occupied. Two: All the charges for the expensive restaurant.

The manager asks one of the desk clerks, "I thought there was a whole crew to this running kid, and what are all these restaurant charges for Windows?"

The desk clerk shrugs and says, "It's only the kid."

Just then, the manager receives a telex message from the Jackson, Tennessee Holiday Inn reserving rooms for the 'running crew' which will arrive tonight. He immediately calls the Jackson, Tennessee Holiday Inn. The desk clerk in Jackson didn't know that I had gone ahead to Memphis and told the Memphis manager that the "crew is here, they're having breakfast."

The Memphis manager thought: Well, if they're in Memphis, this kid is an imposter!

You can guess what happened next. I'm at the hotel pool with the girl who had just given me her virginity the day before. Amanda's face was as sunny and pink as the morning. Two Memphis police officers, a hotel security guard, and the hotel manager walk in a line as straight as an arrow and approach me as I am laid back on a lounge chair.

"Louis Figueroa?" a cop asks.

"Yes?" I reply, a question inquiring what they want and affirmation of my identity in one word.

The hotel manager's voice is filled with contempt and venom: "As I've told you; officers, the runner Louis Figueroa is in Jackson. I verified this with our people in Jackson 30 minutes ago. This boy is an imposter."

I am ordered by the cop whose manner was as sharp as razor wire to stand up, turn around, and place my hands behind my back. I'm cuffed and roughly turned around and frisked. My eyes fall on the girl whom I had spent the weekend romancing. Her face is sad. As I am being hauled off to jail, I scream: "I am Louis Figueroa!" many times over.

It was all straightened out five minutes after I arrived at the police station. My coach had called the hotel looking for me and then learned what had transpired. Because I was a minor, they wouldn't let me leave so I had to wait two hours by the sergeant on duty desk until my coach and crew arrived.

That day I was scheduled to run 50 miles to Palestine, Arkansas. The embarrassment and anger I felt fueled my legs that afternoon. Fifty miles felt like 10K.

"Let's keep going," I told my coach.

"How much further you want to go?" he asks.

"I don't know," I say, then tap the top of my right leg, "I think my legs are making the decisions today."

I run and run. Inside my head a persistent humming sound, like an electrical short buzzing in the rain accompanies each stride. Thirty more miles, west of Brinkley, Arkansas my coach and crew insist I at least stop so that we all can eat. At a mom and pop type cafeteria I was brooding so much that I couldn't taste my food. No one mentioned my arrest.

I told my coach I wanted to continue running. Near the van, my coach watched and listened as I stretched and raged at the audacity of the hotel manager for having me arrested.

I turned to look at my coach - his face was upset, conflicted with thought. He said, "I think you are angry with the wrong person. Let's look at what you did. First: that girl was nothing but a conquest for you – like winning a race. Women aren't medals or trophies. Second: Not only does Holiday Inn provide us with rooms, they also feed us. You took advantage of their generosity. Now it may not have been the bartender's best decision for knowingly serving minors, so you're not totally to blame for that. But I'm sure you used your charm and whatever star-power you think this run is giving you to convince the bartender to make a wrong decision. Fact of the matter is: from what I heard the bartender is going to be fired. And if the press had gotten wind that you were drinking, well; there went your good-boy image. If that had happened, we would have lost sponsors and that could put this run at risk. Seems to me that you brought a lot of this on yourself." His words hung in the silence like the sound of a slap. Never in my life had I been hit with such much truth. I became very still, and I could feel my face fill with shame.

My coach didn't say anything else. He got in the van and started my follow van's engine and I heard the transmission clunk loudly and reverberate through the floorboards when he dropped the gearshift into drive, almost like he had begun a mechanical process that would take on a life of its own.

I run and think about what I had done. I think about why I was out there running Intestate 40. The promise I had made to a dying friend whom I jokingly told I would run across the US for him if he fought the bone cancer that had insidiously invaded his legs. He didn't think I was joking, and I was reminded that I had promised. He died before I was scheduled to run the first mile. The press thought I was out of the deal. No, I told them – Bobby died fighting. He kept his side of the promise. Now I had to keep mine. The press ate up the story and my "Good Boy" image. Good Boy? I felt like a sham and hypocrite. I was guilty of all the things my coach accused me of. I wondered at the complexities and contradictions of that first scoop of soil that God breathed life into.

I asked whoever was in charge of the checks and balances in the universe to forgive me for my trespasses and continue to run. I run and I wonder if there is any way to adequately describe the bullshit that causes us to undo all the great gifts of both Heaven and Earth.

That day the sky was sealed with clouds – a bright sheen of silk steam but it offered no rain. My body was hard and sinewy as I ran inside a golden tunnel of mist that seemed to have been created just for me.

Miles later, the light went out of the sky and the moon rose like an orange planet. I thought I could hear the drone of mosquitos, but none settled on my skin – I was moving too fast.

Suddenly my stomach was roiling; my bowels were on fire. We were in the proverbial: Middle of Nowhere.

"What do you mean there's no toilet paper?" I'm incredulous.

My coach suggests that I've done 101 miles and maybe it's time to call it a day and to hold it until we can get to a gas station or Holiday Inn.

Yes, transcontinental runners do shit in the woods and use socks when there aren't any of those cute Charmin toilet paper bears around.

A few miles outside of Lonoke boat lights were shining inside the fog so that the fog looked like electrified steam rising off the water.

I arrived in Little Rock. I ran for 23 hours and covered 154 miles. I was finally tired. It was time to sleep. I stopped running and began to shake as if my bones disconnected.

After I slept, I was asked to take a call from a UPI reporter. Getting out of bed I felt like an elephant standing after a long siesta at a riverbank.

He started the interview with the same questions and in the same order as all of his previous interviews. The reporter used the word "detained" to describe my arrest. My coach had put out a press statement stating that I was mistaken for a runaway. Gaslight at its best. The reporter quickly moved on to the day's accomplishment.

The reporter asks, "So why did you stop at 23 hours and 154 miles?"

When I heard his question, I thought: Dude how much more did you want me to run? What I said was: "Well, I got to Little Rock and it seemed a good place to stop. Plus, I ran for 23 hours."

"You weren't trying for the 24-hour record?"

"Record?"

"The record for 24 hours on your running surface is 163 miles. You were on the 24-hour world record pace."

"I didn't know," was all I could say.

"You've been able to cover a lot of ground at a furious pace. What's your approach to running across the country?" the reporter asks.

A kaleidoscope of images over the past 3 days spin through my mind.

How could I explain to the reporter that I wasn't the "good boy" that he thought he was interviewing. That I had used a vulnerable girl for the sake of a conquest. I indulged in underage drinking and took advantage of my sponsors and participated in getting a hotel employee fired. I thought about the toll I paid in my anger, and inwardly laughed at the crux of self-reflection: I now understood my inner workings as well the outer form possibilities in the shape of 23 hours of running for a total of 154 miles.

"Look, it's not rocket scientist's stuff. I just put one foot in front of the other. And when I got tired, I slept. When I got hungry, I ate. And when I had to go to the bathroom, I went."

The press still called me a hero. A badge I didn't feel comfortable wearing.

****

It is 1996. A new disease which had been around for roughly two decades is so diabolical that it only needed an acronym to strike fear into anyone who had unprotected sex or a blood transfusion.

My brother Jimmy was dying of those 3 letters.

Once extremely handsome, his appearance brought to mind old photos of Nazi concentration camp survivors. Skin that appeared to be painted over bones is covered with lesions resembling leeches.

At the table across from us, an older gentleman who looked like a Republican banker with a stick up his ass, stared at my brother in disgust. His face seemed to say: How dare they let one of them in here?

"What the f**k are you looking at?" I yell, indignation spewing out of me like beer from a shaken bottle, spilling over the entire restaurant and silencing it.

"Take it easy, Louie." My brother's eyes were pleading that I calm my infamous temper.

"Take it easy? Look at the way that bastard was looking at you!"

"I get that all the time."

It was then that I saw the stigma that AIDS patients carried, and the loneliness and ostracism attached to the disease.

By this time in my life, I knew a little bit about disease, death, and dying. Leukemia had ended my running career in 1991. At Memorial Sloan Kettering Cancer Center, I made and lost friends as close to me as my blood. My wife, Jacqueline, had been killed in a car accident 3 years before I sat with my brother in that restaurant. Running wasn't as physically painful as the emotional pain of not being able to run like I once did. Plus, I had developed what old runners refer to as the Jessie Owens Syndrome – the nasty, self-destructive habit of smoking. I tried not to think about the fact that Jessie died of lung cancer because he smoked 4 packs of Camels non filters a day. I wanted to raise awareness to the disease, prevention education, and help local AIDS networks financially. I knew that my legs could still travel long distances. I wanted to take a different route, so I decided to walk diagonally across the US from Bangor, Maine to San Diego.

This time, I had no crew. I walked alone and with a 50-pound nap sack on my back symbolizing the stigma that AIDS patients carried. I learned early on in that walk that there were still a lot of ignorant people. After a local television interview in Lake Placid, my brother, who was supposed to walk the final mile with me in San Diego died. The next day as I was walking a white pickup truck filled with teenagers and young adults yelled, "Fag Lover" and threw beers can at me. Then they turned around and ran me off the road. I missed being hit by the front bumper by 3 inches and ran into a corn field and a farmhouse. I had to be escorted by police the rest of the day.

A caller during a radio interview vowed to kill me. Of course, he called in on a blocked number.

After a ton of media coverage, at night – the media held me up that day - on a dark and lonely road outside of Rochester, NY a battered pick-up truck pulled up ahead of me. I was totally isolated and a man who looked as if he stepped out of a Norman Rockwell painting approached me.

Oh, no! I thought. We were totally isolated.

"You that fella walking for AIDS?"

"Yes, sir." I said, trying to keep the rising panic out of my voice.

He pursed his lips and scratched the side of his cheek in thought. Then he said, "That's a horrible disease."

"Yes, sir."

"We need to do something about it."

Did he hear me exhale? "Yes, sir."

"That's what I'm trying to do."

"The news people said you like beer," he says, and reaches behind him for his wallet. In the truck's headlights I can see he only had 3 dollars and he handed them to me.

I protested, "No, sir, please send that to the Rochester AIDS Program."

"Son, I'd have to buy a stand with these 3 spare dollars I got. A quarter mile up the road there's a nice bar. Go in there and have a beer on me before you call it a day."

He shoved the money into my hand and walked back to the truck. The beer tasted extra good that night.

It was a girls' night out and they decided to have their palms read. When it was her turn, the Palm Reader said: 'You new love is on his way to you. But he is not coming by bus, plane, train, or car."

She said, "Well, he can't get here by boat – this is the desert. How's he going to get here?"

A few miles east of Benson, Arizona I had a gusher nosebleed – that's where the blood flows out at the rate of a slow sink faucet. I'm in the Benson hospital all day receiving platelets and coagulants.

The attending physician walks by and I ask, "Hey, doc, when can I get out of here?"

He gives me a sad smile and says, "One minute, I've got your hematologist on the phone. The nurse is bringing the phone to you."

I'm handed a cordless phone and after I say hello, I hear Dr. Burchenal of Sloan Kettering Cancer Center say, "You're grounded! How many little bruises and nosebleeds have you ignored?" He recites my blood counts. "You can't walk anymore. You're coming out of remission. You've got three choices – you can come back here or go up the road the Arizona Cancer Center in Tucson, or Moore Cancer Center in La Jolla."

I'd come so far. I didn't want to go back to New York. My superstitions told me that if I got driven to a suburb of San Diego I'd never finish the walk. So, Tucson it is.

Chemo can take months. I couldn't stay at a Holiday Inn (yes, they were a sponsor again) for months, so the Southern Arizona AIDS Foundation, better known by its acronym SAFE, puts me up at the home of one of their board members – David Cohn. David viewed himself as an underdog, he told me, "Society has got two strikes against me: I'm Jewish and gay."

SAFE asks if I can do some media and agree to a few benefits. "We could raise some much-needed money," the director tells me.

"Sure," I say, "so long as it's not on a Monday or Tuesday. I get hit with chemo on Monday and I'm still puking on Tuesday."

Her friend Phil tells her, "Hey, I met the Original Forrest Gump at a SAFE benefit, he's walking for AIDS."

She says, "Yeah, I saw him on the news. What's he like?"

"He's a nice guy. He tells a lot of funny jokes."

"That's cool."

A week later they go out to SIBS for Halloween. She doesn't mind accompanying Phil to Tucson's biggest gay bar because not much time had passed since she broke her engagement and she didn't want guys hitting on her.

Phil says, "Hey, that's the Original Forrest Gump sitting at the bar with the guys he's staying with – Dave. Come on, I'll introduce you to him."

I vaguely remembered the guy who introduced himself – I had met and shaken more hands during the benefits than a politician running for office.

"This is my friend, Paulina," he says. I shake her hand and thought: Too bad she's gay, she's got nice eyes and a pretty smile.

Later, "You're not gay? I'm not gay."

Even later, a dance in the moonlight as I softly sing Stevie Wonder's Ribbon in the Sky.

I achieved remission and went back to where I left off in Benson. It was easy to find the spot – there was still blood on the ground.

A media campaign was launched asking people in San Diego to walk the final mile with me.

Paulina walks the final mile with me in Jimmy's place and after that, down the aisle in our wedding.

****

The year is 2005. A 7,500-mile walk around the US for abused children. With each step I try to exorcise the demons of my being sexually abused as a child by our housekeeper. Ever since those horrid days I felt like an outsider. That's one of the reasons I ran – it was socially acceptable to do alone.

Now Kiwanis clubs provide a safety car while they document every mile.

In Savannah, Georgia I hold my press conference from the bench where Tom Hanks speaks my words. The news anchor mentions that I am a huge Winnie the Pooh fan. They also play the PSA my buddy Kenny Loggins recorded with me which features his hit Return to Pooh Corner.

The best moments in life are not the kind many historians record.

A few days later a burgundy family minivan pulls up ahead of me and my follow car. A man in his late twenties or early thirties approaches me and say, "Mr. Figueroa, may I have a word with you? My daughter caught you on the news the other night. During your interview, you said,

"'If there's a young person out there who is being touched and made to do things you don't want to do – tell someone. The person touching you is probably telling you to keep it a secret and if you tell your mom, dad, brother or sister or grandparents or best friend or dog will die. They are lying. No one is going to die and don't keep the secret.'" He took the kind of deep breath the someone does to chase away pain. "Well, it turns out her soccer coach was touching her private parts. He is now in jail. Word got around the soccer parents and another boy has also revealed he too was molested. My little girl heard you were a Winnie the Pooh fan. We shopped all over for a stuffed Pooh, but we could only find a Tigger. My little girl wants to meet you. My wife wanted to be here too, but it was impossible for her to get out of work today. Do you mind?"

How could I say No?

He goes back to the minivan and speaks for a few seconds. The side door opens, and he takes the hand of an 8 year-old-angel in disguise. Sunlight glints off her auburn hair and her blue eyes are watery.

"Thank you for saving me. You're a hero."

"I didn't save you. You saved yourself." I kneel to her level trying to catch her eyes. "You're the hero."

"Really? How?" She asks, her eyes not quite meeting mine.

"By telling the truth you saved yourself." I tapped my index finger against her heart, "and other children will be safe because that bad man is in jail and won't be able to hurt any more children."

She smiled and shoved a Tigger doll into my hands that today sits on my nightstand. (I look at Tigger several times a day.) Then she squeezed me so hard that it must've hurt. There was no other way to account for the tears in my eyes.

****

I've been all over this planet, but my favorite place in the world is The Towpath. The historic towpath runs along the main canal from Bakers Basin Road in Trenton to my hometown of New Brunswick, NJ. The canal was constructed in the early 1830's and its earthen towpath was used by mules to pull barges along the canal. On the other side the Raritan River rolls along its side. You walk over the cobblestone spillway to reach it, and as in life - sometimes you take a misstep and get wet. The huge River Birch, Pin Oaks, and Red and Silver Maple trees form a canopy of leaves. I always loved the way the branches moved in the breeze as if they were waving, "Hello."

This was my favorite place to run. When I ran fast enough, the sun squeezing through the branches became bolts of lightning. Seeing how fast I could make the bolts flash was a game I loved to play. Parked here at the edge of the canal, my father first asked my mother to marry him. It was where I brought Belinda, my first teenage love here. It was where I asked my first wife to marry me. I came there to celebrate. Heartbroken, this is where I would go so that the breezes could help me find some peace of mind.

I remember the last time I ran there. Leukemia had ended my running career and there was a gulf in my heart and soul that I had to traverse to find what's inside of me to do this one more time, in that dark place there was nowhere for me to run.

Sometimes I feel like I'm running in another dimension – my fears are actual ghosts who move without legs – sorta like the ones in Pacman only my ghosts have no colors, they are dark and have teeth. But I'm out running those little bastards. I run past the trees and the sunlight sweating through the branches and leaves once again become scintillating bolts of lightning. At times, it seems as if I'm running in other dimensions that appear in front or behind or parallel to the river or canal at my sides. I think of my friends that I had lost to cancer:

I see Brad and Rosie – two cancer patients with death sentences who fell in love on a cancer ward. Brad had wanted to be an artist. Near the end of their lives they went to Paris so Brad could paint. I see them in Paris or in the French countryside searching for a place to set up his easel.

A few more steps against the earth and I watch Kevin and Kelly greet each dawn with hope and love even though his prognosis isn't the best. The tumor in his brain can't stop the flow of knowledge pouring into it as he races towards his degree.

I run with power and hear breathing and music and laughter. The curve in the path is barely noticeable, but my body moves with it and after another group of flashes I see Jacqueline, my ballerina girl, who is the anchor of my soul here on this earth. I could never run fast enough towards her, I guess because her spirit is always dancing.

I head for the end of the path and the Landing Lane Bridge in the distance, my legs make scissoring shadows that cut the distance which remains until I run no more. I gather the people I love around me and head towards the flashes of lightning that mark my road because everything else is just darkness.

Chapter 5

Jim Starkovich
March 1 to May 28, 1994; 88 Days, 77 Days of **Running**
Fernandina Beach, FL to La Jolla, CA

Background

I started distance running long before jogging became popular. There were several motivators that convinced me to start working harder and doing longer distances.

One, a book on the NY Times best seller list titled ROYAL CANADIAN AIR FORCE EXERCISE PLAN FOR PHYSICAL FITNESS; the first phase only required you to exercise 11 mins. per day. It included walking and running. Another book, SELF MADE OLYMPIAN BY RON DAWS. Ron was an Olympic runner.

I worked for IBM Corp. for 24 years, primarily in Boca Raton, FL. My job involved a lot of travelling. Usually after checking into my hotel, I would run the streets, parks, trail or anywhere that seemed safe. So, 1 saw a lot of the country and many cities during my travels. During the week, at home and usually after work, I would run my favorite routes. As time went on, I was doing 30-50 mile weeks.

During vacations, we usually travelled internationally. Again, I would usually run the streets and explore the cities and countryside. In total, I ran in 60 different countries.

In 1976, we moved to Atlanta for a temporary assignment. During the late 70's, Atlanta was a hotbed of distance running. There were many top runners living there at the time. The most prominent being Gayle Barron and Jeff Galloway. Gayle won the Boston Marathon. Gayle and Jeff both won the Peachtree 10K which is Atlanta's premier running event. Jeff has gone on to become a renowned part of the running community with books, camps, articles, and running stores. I mention them because they motivated me to do more long-distance running.

When I returned to Boca Raton, a friend of mine and I decided we wanted to run across the state of Florida. We convinced my wife, Jo, to be our support crew. So, we dipped our toes in the Atlantic in Ormond Beach and 3 days later dipped toes in the Gulf of Mexico at Yankeetown.

I had read an article about people running across the Grand Canyon so I decided that was to be my next venture. I was living at sea level and the Grand Canyon is up in the 7000 ft. area. So I found an altitude simulator and trained with it. We drove to the North rim of the canyon. The next morning at about 5:30am I descended into the canyon. I ran on the Kaibab trail with a cliff on one side and a chasm on the other so I knew I certainly did not want to trip. I carried handteens for water with a plan to fill up at Phantom Ranch at the bottom; however, when I got there they were closed so I headed up without any water. Fortunately, there were day hikers coming down and I was able to beg water from them. Total run time was 6 hours. This was about the same amount of time it took Jo to drive around from the North Rim to meet me at the South Rim.

When I was age 44, I decided I wanted to run my age on my birthday so I did that for 9 years until it just became too tedious and difficult to keep doing it. Again, my wife, Jo was my Coach and Pit Crew.

Over the years, I trained and ran marathons. To date, I have run 14 marathons.

When I turned 55, IBM made me an offer I could not refuse. In the tradition of getting rid of older employees they offered me a year's salary and a lifetime pension.

Preparation for my Transcontinental Run

I studied the Rand-McNalley US Road Atlas to figure out which highways to use. I knew that Interstates were not appropriate nor legal for runners. I didn't want to do mountains.

I tried to avoid big cities but that wasn't possible without doing a lot of detours. I did not want to run in the summer heat. So, I finally picked Mar.1 as our start date and our route would be Southern US. I looked at the map of the US and planned the least distance it would take to complete.

I noted that most Transcon runners ran for a charity or a cause. I wanted to run just to see if I could. I didn't want to be delayed by having to give speeches or collect money. Also, I thought to myself, what if I can't make it; what an embarrassment that would be to me as well as a charity or cause. I wanted to run without constraints.

My wife, Jo, agreed to drive our support vehicle. We had a van (1986 Dodge) that was in pretty good shape. We worked with a person who built custom vans and he did the work for us. We cut out the roof so we could stand inside. We installed cabinets, sink, water supply and pump, microwave, TV and a queen-size bed. We bought a portable toilet from Target. Then I had the van painted. So, the vehicle and driver were ready to go.

I cranked up my mileage from about 60 per week to about 100 per week. I wanted to be well trained because I was planning to do about 30 miles per day during the Transcon.

Running

I planned to do 6-mile segments. So, Jo would go approximately 6 miles and find a place for Jo to wait for me. When I arrived, I would refresh and rest for a few minutes then off we would go again. For refreshment I drank Exceed or Gatorade and water; 1 gallon of each every day. I also would eat a pudding cup or a few cookies. In the morning, before starting, I would usually drink a SlimFast. We would usually start the day just before the sun came up and finish the segment about 11 or noon. After I had done about 30 miles, we would put up a marker and head out looking for a place to eat and a place to stay for the rest of the day and night.

Many of our markers were neon ribbon tied to a fence. That made it easy to know where to start the next morning. We didn't have cell phones back in 1994. Because we had no communication, we agreed that if one of us got lost, we would return to the last place we last saw each other. In Mississippi somewhere, I took off after refreshing but as I ran I couldn't remember Jo passing me. When I got to the point where I thought she should be waiting, she wasn't there. So, I ran back and she had not moved. She couldn't start the van and had no way to tell me. I cleaned the battery terminals and we were ready to go. We agreed that she would now leave first after each segment and honk as she went by.

The route had us staying on US 123 and into GA using US 82 then up to Montgomery and over the Edmund Pettus bridge in Selma on US 80. We traveled the same route followed by Martin Luther King Jr. in his famous march from Selma to Montgomery except we traveled it in reverse.

We decided that we would take 1 day off per week to let my body recover. We chose Monday (So, the final tally for the run was 77 days running and 11 days off). I would usually finish my day's run before noon. We would look for a grocery store and I would buy carbohydrates. Many times I would buy a cake and eat the whole cake in one sitting. This probably explains the reason I did not lose any weight on the run. I needed to pack on about 3000 calories for the next running day. (1 mile equals about 100 calories).

My highest mileage day was 42; This was coming down the mountain from Cloudcroft to Alamogordo, NM. My lowest mileage day was 22;  this was the day I had to hide in a culvert because tornadoes were hitting the area.

On one of our rest days, we detoured to Lubbock, TX to visit the Best Man at our wedding. While there, our friend called the local TV station which did a video on me. The newscast is now on www.youtube.com (Jim

Starkovich; there is more than one of us with the same name; I'm the one with gray hair; click on video VTS 01 1)

After 20 days in Texas (it is a BIG state) we crossed into Hobbs, NM (The local paper did an article on me (Hobbs Daily News-Sun; April 22, 1994). We picked up US 82 into Alamogordo, NM. Then over the Organ Mountains into Las Cruces and on to US 70 in Globe, AZ (This was the most desolate part of the entire crossing). Then US 60 to Phoenix and local roads to Tonopah, AZ. The map didn't show any roads to Blythe, CA so I ran up to Salome, AZ and down to Quartzite, AZ. I had to then run across the Colorado River on I-10 to cross into CA.

At Blythe, CA, I headed South through Glamis to Ramona, CA on CA 78. This took me through the Anza-Borrego Desert and a steep climb up to Julian. The only mishap we had on the trip happened just before crossing into Anza... I smelled gasoline and saw that my fuel pump was leaking so we high-tailed back to Brawley as fast as we could and, fortunately, got it fixed almost immediately.

In Julian, CA, I was refreshed because I could smell the ocean and I knew the finish was close. The next, and final day we traveled from Ramona, CA down to Poway and down Miramar Blvd. We crossed Hwy 101 and ran down to La Jolla Shores.

FINISH

<u>Observations</u>

I almost always ran against oncoming traffic. I noticed that I could see white-colored cars miles away as they approached me. Many brown and green cars I did not see until they were almost upon me. I decided that I would only buy white cars in the future. I recently checked with Google and a study of car colors verified my findings, i.e. white cars have less accidents than other colors.

Especially in Texas, herds of cattle would stand and watch me as I ran by. Then, suddenly, they would stampede away from me. With all those cow eyes watching me, I would run taller so I would look good for the cows. By contrast, horses would approach the highway fences as if I was going to offer them food.

We got our news from USA Today. In 1994, this paper was ubiquitous. There were racks in shopping centers, post offices, motels, on street corners, etc. The paper was 25 cents. Later, the price went to 50 cents, then $1. I no longer buy it but I think they are $2 now.

Along the way a dog befriended me. This was a problem because the dog would run out into the road and disrupt traffic. I got a lot of dirty looks and fingers from cars and trucks that had to veer, stop or slow down. I tried to shake him but he stayed with me for about 10 miles.

Addenda

After resting for a week in Oceanside, CA we drove to Anchorage, AK and then across Canada. I ran in ALL Canadian Provinces and Territories and several northern US states. I also completed running in ALL 50 US states. With my experience, I was hired by Marathon Tours. For 11 years, I escorted marathon runners to many marathons around the world (4 times to Antarctica).

I had the opportunity to talk to Sir Roger Bannister (first human to run a mile in less than 4 minute) several years after the run. He was more interested in talking to Jo, my wife, to hear how she supported me.

Chapter 6

Brian Stark
March 8 to October 31, 1998
Cape Henlopen State Park, Delaware to Point Reyes National Seashore, California following the American Discovery Trail

Dedicated to my father, Jim Stark, an adventure seeker and a fine storyteller, too.

Brian Stark, crossing a swift creek on Ohio's Buckeye Trail while following the American Discovery Trail.

Wait!

There weren't any cell phones in 1979, which was a shame because I really could have used one when my parents left me at a gas station in New Jersey and drove 400 miles away in the middle of the night. I was seven years old. We had just watched my dad run the Boston Marathon that morning and were driving through the night to get back home to Indiana for school the next day. Being the youngest of three boys, my hideout in the van was underneath the back bench. Like J.R.R. Tolkien's Gollum in his cave, I'd crawl under there next to the rear heater and hunker down in my corduroys and KangaROO shoes with a couple of coins tucked into the tiny zippered pocket of the left shoe. The future Eagle Scout in me was always ready for an adventure. We took long family trips to Florida and Connecticut and I wouldn't be seen for hours at a time in my cozy crawlspace. With the nearby heater and soothing music from our 8-tracks to lull me to sleep, I was content to listen to the melodies of *The Jazz Singer, Annie, Chorus Line* and *Grease* as the miles rolled by. Our specially equipped van had two gas tanks which allowed us to go twice the distance without stopping. My childhood was a happy existence, filled with good and kind people and a healthy dose of adventure.

When I felt the van come to a rest at around 11 p.m., I knew it was my one chance to go to the bathroom. My father was driving the late shift and as he wearily pumped the gas I told him I was headed to the bathroom. When I came out a few minutes later, I saw the van pulling away without me. Parents have the worst timing for forgetting their children. I started running and caught up to them, already showing track potential at an early age. My hand smacked the side but they didn't hear me and kept driving. The van entered the on-ramp, merged onto the interstate and disappeared into the black. Standing at the edge of that dark parking lot somewhere in New Jersey, with the wisdom perhaps not quite matching that of a young boy, I thought, "I bet I could walk home from here." I might have actually started on my way had I not been stopped by four good Samaritans in a Volkswagen Beetle. Many hours later, and one heck of a family detour home, I was eventually reunited with my family but what happened in that time was a true adventure that involved, among other things, a hike in the woods with a state trooper at dawn.

Knock, Knock

Fast-forward nineteen years later, having outgrown quite a few pairs of corduroy pants, I finished college and became a serious long-distance runner. I was on another road trip with my older brother Eric. This time it was March 1998 and rather than riding under the rear bench, I rode shotgun in his Honda Civic. One thing was similar to that family road trip long ago. We were heading east to the Delaware coast with the ironic intention of dropping me off and leaving me once again to fend for myself. This time, I wouldn't just be walking home to Indiana. I planned to run nearly 5,000 miles to California following the American Discovery Trail, a network of local and national trails connected by scenic backroads and winding forgotten paths. If I could finish this trek, I would become the first to run this new network of trails.

My corduroys had been traded in for nylon shorts and my KangaROO sneakers were swapped out for Saucony Shadow 5000 running shoes. Standing alone on the beach, wearing my running outfit and a ten-pound hip pack of meager supplies, I stuck one foot in the Atlantic Ocean at Cape Henlopen State Park and strode into the stiff headwinds on a cold and rainy spring day bound for California's Golden Gate Bridge, imaginatively floating on the horizon like a tiny red dot. The first ten minutes were a blur. Eric pulled up alongside me in his car, the window barely cracked, protecting himself from the cold rain.

"Are we having fun yet?" Classic big brother. "If you get cold and tired, just call me from the nearest pay phone and I'll come back to pick you up." It was a kind offer. Or perhaps it was meant to torment his 26-year-old baby brother.

The gravity of what I was doing set in as quickly as the cold rain on my bare skin. It was 40 degrees that day. The wind penetrated my thin shorts with ease. I ducked behind a pile of cement culverts at a construction site. Like Superman diving into a phone booth, I reached into my small pack and pulled out every piece of clothing I had: a thin pair of nylon tights, a long sleeve synthetic shirt, a Gore-Tex rain jacket and mittens. Not much more than the superhero, actually. Donning my entire wardrobe, I returned to the relentless wind.

Past transconners, or people who transit a continent on foot, say that part of the secret to success is to start off slowly and let your body adapt to the new lifestyle. I had decided it was good advice. After reaching the first town on my map I would stop early for a short first day. Long before Google and without even a cell phone, I hoped there would be a motel just seven miles after leaving the coast. A wet little 10k to start my eight-month transcon was just what I needed. When I arrived, soaked and already mentally exhausted, I learned the town did have lodging but it wasn't open. "Motel's closed," the owner informed me from his bedside phone where I finally tracked him down from a diner pay phone. "They tell me my blood's got no iron in it!" No problem. Just Uber a ride to the next town, right? AirBnb a private room? Couchsurf? All faraway dreams in 1998. I may have been older and wiser than that young boy standing at the edge of the parking lot all those years ago, but apparently the grown version of me was no different, still standing on the side of the road wondering what to do.

The printed county map I carried had my route carefully highlighted in yellow pen and secured in a Ziplock baggie. To lighten my load, I had trimmed away the borders of the map and planned to throw away pages as I finished them. Five hundred county and trail maps awaited shipping by my mother to predetermined post offices equally spread across the country along my route. I bought 12 pairs of shoes before leaving home and along with my maps, my mom would mail me a new pair of running shoes every three weeks. Using the distance legend on the map as a guide and a sharply bent twist-tie as my measuring device, I chartered the distance along my route to the next option. Redden State Forest with no listed services was 21 miles away. So much for an easy first day, I thought. Perhaps it would offer something to get out of the cold rain. The afternoon was miserable.

Every step forward raised another question. Why was I doing this? When would it start to be fun? After months of buildup to my friends and family and an article in my hometown newspaper, the first hours were nothing like what I had imagined during the year I had spent planning. My brother's words haunted me and I soon found myself scanning the horizon for a pay phone. He couldn't be more than a couple hundred miles away, right? He'd understand. It wouldn't have been the first time my family had to turn around to retrieve me.

I never found a pay phone that day and it's a good thing, too. If I had it's likely I also would have found an early end to my run. The temptation to use a cell phone, if I'd had one, would have been even greater. Somewhere on that stretch of wet county road, amid a vast sea of empty farmland with stumped crops in their winter slumber, a different type of question surfaced. Despite the misery and the cold and apparent hopelessness, a small voice inside bubbled up out of the thick pot of negative stew, "Who quits on the first day? You have to make it through at least one day, right?"

At dusk, soaked, hungry, and weary from shuffling 28 miles with my overburdened hip pack, I knocked on a house door at the entrance to the state forest. It was the manager's residence. A bushy-mustached man peered out as he greeted me.

My voice cracked with the pained control of emotion and I started in, a little higher pitched than normal, "My name is Brian. I'm a schoolteacher from Indiana and I'm running across America. This is my first day. Do you have a barn or a shed I could sleep in tonight?"

He just smiled and said, "Get in the truck."

I thought he was going to drive me into a nearby town where there might be a motel but instead we pulled out of his garage and drove across his backyard heading into the deep dark woods on a narrow track. I was no longer seven but the feeling of being led through the woods by a stranger was familiar. This time I had the wisdom of age on my side and my stranger danger radar was now springing to life. I restated, "You know, just a *barn* or a *shed*, anything like that would be great."

"Uh huh," he replied with a smile and kept driving.

Just then we came around a bend in the forest and saw an immense barn: two stories tall, all metal construction, windows, electricity, and all in fine shape.

"Ah, that would be great – thank you so much," I exclaimed.

The truck continued on without slowing. My driver said nothing.

Now I wondered what my driver had packed in the truck. Did he have a shovel, trash bags, and rope? I didn't have time to look around because soon the sky opened up and we emerged onto a blacktop parking lot adjoining a beautiful 1.5-million-dollar lodge. It was an immense thing built with stone and timber construction. There was a trail of smoke coming out one of the chimneys and a light on in a window. My driver threw the truck into park, his headlights shining on the front door in the dusk.

"Would that work for you?" he asked, the only sound in the air was the intermittent wipers occasionally sweeping watery specs from the windshield. His hand rested on the steering wheel and his forefinger pointed towards the sanctuary before us.

"Uh huh," was all I could manage, my mouth gaping at the turn of events. My driver, whose name was Lloyd Simmons, was what long-distance hikers refer to as a trail angel, people who seemingly exist simply to improve the lives of weary hikers with a small token of kindness when it is most appreciated. Lloyd explained that he was caretaker of the lodge and a yoga group had left earlier that day. The remnants of a fire still burned in the fireplace. The lodge, built as a hunting retreat for railroad executives in 1903, is listed on the National Register of Historic Places. It features a full kitchen, two fireplaces, and numerous bedrooms which can accommodate dozens of people. Lloyd surmised that my small pack likely didn't contain any dinner and he was right. My full pantry consisted of a half bagel and a granola bar. Hardly a feast for someone who just ran an ultramarathon in the rain while wearing a pack. He invited me to go inside and get cleaned up and then I could join him and his wife Sally for dinner at their house. I walked inside my new refuge, sat down by the warm glow of the embers at the massive fireplace and started to cry. I cried because of the tremendous relief I suddenly felt at the end of a long day. I cried because I was warm. But mostly, I cried because I knew sitting by that fire, I was going to continue to meet kind people like Sally and Lloyd who would help me out from time to time. I knew it would be difficult but that if I kept going, uplifting surprises like this were bound to happen again. And they did.

The imaginary red dot on the horizon that was the Golden Gate Bridge kept bobbing in my daydreams. Across the heat and humidity of Kansas in the summer where a constant swarm of grasshoppers attacked my legs from tall grass, over the Rocky Mountains in a vivid display of wildflowers, and the vast desert of Utah and Nevada with its basin and range topography making its own giant sized corduroy plane, it was always there, looming just over the hill up ahead. The thousands of miles rolled slowly by at five miles per hour. This was three years before the iPod played its first musical note. No earbuds, no podcasts, no playlists. If I wanted entertainment, I had to think of it. And I did a lot of thinking over seven and a half months of running about a marathon per day. I daydreamed about things that might happen during the run. Would I get pulled over by a police officer? Would I ever sleep in a fire station bunkroom, a church fellowship hall, or a cemetery? I often daydreamed about creature comforts: being taken in by a family who liked to eat doughnuts on the couch and watch movies. About a hotel giving me a free room for the night and then upgrading me to their suite. I even daydreamed about winning on a game show during my run. Throughout it all, my daydreams started to become real. Not just one or two of them, but all of them. Every single one of the above scenarios manifested itself, sometimes on the same day I had thought of it. Numerous people, seemingly out of nowhere, took me in for the night, filled my water bottle from their sink, or offered words of

Friendly police officers checking out whether I was all right in the middle of the Nevada desert – without a car.

encouragement and praise when I needed it most.

Thousands of miles matched by thousands of kind gestures later, the dot was real. I could actually see it across the San Francisco Bay calling me forward. Though it's nearly two miles long, no distance would have been sufficient to allow me to process the many thoughts I had that day as I jogged across it towards Point Reyes Seashore and my finish line.

My friends Ricky and Robert heard about my daydream to get on a game show and they took a short side trip with me during the run from the Golden Gate Bridge to visit a taping of The Price is Right in Los Angeles. This was back when Bob Barker was still the host along with his longtime announcer Rod Roddy. My friends had shirts made up to help improve my chances of getting on stage. Theirs said, "Friend of Runner" with an arrow pointed toward me while mine said, "Hey Bob, I ran 4,800 miles to hear Rod Roddy say, 'Brian Stark, come on down!'" The back was printed, "And I had my cat neutered," an homage to Bob's love of pets. It worked. I was called down to contestant's row and was finally able to employ a childhood of training for the show. I won a collection of stuffed teddy bears on a $1 bid as well as trips to Hawaii and Canada. Even better than the winnings was Bob's apparent admiration towards me. He stopped the show several times to ask me follow up questions about my run.

While churning out my millions of strides and gently trotting down the backroads and trails across America, I also thought of Lydia, my girlfriend. She came out to visit me several times during the run. Thinking ahead to what I wanted my future to look like after the run, I didn't know where life would take me but I knew I wanted her in it and I decided to manufacture a surprise proposal to her at the finish line. She said yes and we are now happily married. We have two wonderful children and we both share our love of adventure with them. That is a daydream that I now benefit from every day.

Since my run, I have found a rewarding career as an English teacher. Often, I hear teachers complain about how students daydream in class, are distracted from their lessons, or can't seem to focus. In schools, I wonder when are students allowed to be with their own thoughts? On my run, especially because I was alone and without electronics, I had nothing but my thoughts each day for 238 days. Perhaps my astounding luck in circumstances was just that. Perhaps I was benefiting from while male privilege, or it was the time before the caution following 9/11. But it is interesting to note that when I had the time to visualize very clearly what I wanted, opportunities presented themselves.

Friends Robert Webster and Ricky Sprague helped better my chances of being selected during a taping of The Price is Right.

At some point, we all face times in life when we look out into the unknown, searching for something we can't yet see. Going forward means taking a leap of faith without a guarantee of success. Go anyway and see what is beyond the horizon. Chances are there will be someone there to give you a hand along the way. Those four men in the Volkswagen beetle rescued my younger self from certain disaster had I started down the interstate ramp that night. Sally and Lloyd righted what surely would have become an early end to my trip without their help. Hundreds of others came to my aid over the next eight months. Like an underground railroad of trail angels, the kindness of the American spirit ensured I reached the other side of the continent. Their small actions changed my life and I've spent my time since then trying to pay back my debt. By sharing some of their stories with you, perhaps we can keep that train running just a little further down the track.

The complete story can be found in Getting to the Point. In a dozen pairs of shoes by Brian R. Stark. Available at Amazon.com or StatesRunner.com

The final miles at Point Reyes National Seashore, California, western terminus of the American Discovery Trail (photo by Robert Webster).

Chapter 7

Jim McCord
May 1 to November 1, 2002
San Diego, California to Washington DC

Photo of Maggie (our oldest daughter, Type 1 Diabetic since she was nine years old) and me at the beginning of my run in California.

My children thought I was going through some type of midlife crisis the day I told them I was going to run across the country. I was NOT a runner! Prior to this I had only run one marathon, the New York Marathon in 1997, to raise money for Cancer research. I clearly remember immediately after that marathon thinking, I'll NEVER do this again! I was thrilled that I had completed a marathon, slow as it was 4:38, about an 11-minute pace. The pain of my first marathon and for days later, convinced me that would certainly be my last marathon. What prompted my decision to run across the country was a way to help our daughter who, at that time, was struggling through her teenage years with Type 1 Diabetes. She was really struggling, which many Type 1 Diabetics do through their teen years. My father and grandfather had both passed away due to complications from diabetes. Running across the country wasn't something that just popped into my mind. I'd never have considered something like that, until I met Peter Fish!

It was June 2001 when I read an article about a 65-year-old man, Peter Fish, who was running from Kansas City to Washington DC for Sarcoma, a form of cancer that his daughter had. The article said he was running 20 miles a day and that he would be running into Cincinnati on Route 50 that day. Not being a distance runner I was amazed that any 65 year old could run 20 miles a day. I decided to go meet with him. I attempted to run along with Peter, but was in such bad shape that after about ½ mile Peter said "Jim, you can't run any longer, let's sit and talk." That's what we did for the next couple hours. We discussed his daughter's struggles with Sarcoma and my daughter's struggle with Type 1 Diabetes. I was so moved that at the end of the conversation I told Peter that next year I'd run across the country for Diabetes Awareness. I'll never forget, Peter said "Good luck Jim, you couldn't run 1 mile with me this morning." To this day, I'm grateful to Peter for his inspiration. He's in his 80's now and still running ultras! We stay in touch on Facebook and his running still inspires me!

Knowing I was definitely going to run across the country and well aware that I was in NO condition for the challenge (I was 248 lbs and couldn't run one mile with Peter that day) I realized I had to get a trainer. I met with or spoke over the phone with at least a dozen trainers in the Cincinnati area over the next month. Not one of them said I could go from the condition I was in to running across the country in 11 months. Frustrated because I knew I could if I could find the right trainer, I flew to LA, rented a car and drove to Death Valley in July of 2001. I figured if 75 people could run 135 miles in July in Death Valley (The Badwater 135), certainly they must have awesome trainers. I was hoping to meet one who was willing to take me on as a client. Fortunately, I met with Marshall Ulrich on his Four time Crossing of Death Valley. Marshall let me run with him briefly, which being so out of shape, was all I could do. I ran with him for about one mile and explained that I wanted to run across the country beginning next May and no trainer I had talked to thought it was possible. He said, yes you can and Lisa Smith Batchen is the trainer who can get you in that condition. Lisa was part of Marshall's crew and I met with her after my short run with Marsh. She asked me a few questions, then said, "YES, I can get you in condition to run across the country in less than ten months." Lisa Smith Batchen is an AWESOME trainer! She gave me a detailed program to follow, which I did to the letter. I did successfully run across the country beginning 10 months after I met Lisa. I had ZERO injuries during or after the run. Lisa, as of the writing of this book, is still training. If you or someone you know is looking for an Awesome Trainer, contact her! I cannot thank Marshall Ulrich enough for recommending her! There's not a chance I would have succeeded without Lisa's training program! My training began with long walks, short periods of runs, yoga twice each week, a weekly massage and a weekly visit with a chiropractor. Lisa gradually increased my running time and insisted I never run faster than a ten-minute mile. By that November, four months after I started training with her she had me run in the Toledo 24 hour run. I remember saying "Lisa, are you crazy, I can't begin to run/walk for 24 hours. I'll injure myself." She said she needed to learn, and so did I, whether or not my mind and body would hold up to distance running, and a 24-hour run was the perfect test. I ran/walked 71.5 miles during that run. It gave me confidence that I NEVER thought possible. Lisa is brilliant!

May 1, 2002 I left on my journey from a running store in San Diego. I chose May 1 because it was our daughter's birthday. It was quite emotional for both of us. New Balance was a sponsor of my run and provided all my clothing and shoes for the entire run. They wanted me to begin my run from one of their running stores in San Diego. John Ratzenberger, Cliff from Cheers, met me and my daughter at the running store. John had a son with Type 1 Diabetes and he had completed a cross country motorcycle ride for Diabetes Awareness just a couple years earlier. He saw on the internet that I was going to run across the country and contacted me to offer his help in any way he could. John also helped me get media attention and paid for a hotel room for my family upon our finish in Washington DC at the end of my run. I'm forever grateful for all John did for my run! The plan Lisa had for me was to run 20 miles each day and take every third day off completely as a rest day. The first day was exciting. It was a beautiful 75 degree, sunny, San Diego day. I completed my run with little pain. Day 2 was another beautiful day. My confidence was building. As planned, day 3 was a rest day. I had purchased a used RV and had a support driver with me most of the trip. My driver would meet me about every 5-6 miles and I could fill water bottles and get something to eat. We spent nights in the RV rather than in motels.

  That worked out very well for me. It's not easy finding people to drive support as that's a horribly boring job! I'm so grateful for all my support drivers, especially Ed Mason, a great friend who drove for me almost four of the six months of my journey. Ten other friends and family members drove for me at various times. All four of our children spent time with me on the run. While my kids were with me, they typically either rollerbladed, biked or ran alongside me much of the day to keep me inspired. These were awesome bonding times with each of the four kids. Maggie, the reason for my run, our daughter with Type 1 diabetes, visited three times and frequently ran much of those days with me.

  Running for Diabetes Awareness meant I wanted to get as much media as possible. I wasn't running to raise money, but awareness. Hours of my rest days were spent contacting newspapers, TV and Radio stations of cities and counties I'd be running through the next couple days. In those years, few people were running across the country and almost every media outlet I contacted was willing to cover the story. There were over 70 articles in newspapers (small town, county and major city), over 50 Television News stories and I was a guest on 15 radio talk shows throughout my run. In 2002 running across the country wasn't very popular, so media was easier to get!

  Rest days were a great time to catch up with the many emails I would get from people who were following my run. Rest days were necessary for me as mentioned earlier, I wasn't an experienced ultra-runner. I'd sleep late, contact media outlets in the cities and counties that I'd be running through in the next few days, do laundry and get plenty of rest which my inexperienced muscles needed. These rest days also gave me the opportunity to visit with the locals, which was so enjoyable, and to see sites that I would never have seen if I was not taking rest days.

  After two weeks of running with little pain and no injuries I felt like I could run 26 miles rather than 20 and run three days straight, rather than two before an off day. I spoke with Lisa, who agreed. From this point on I ran at least 26 miles each day, three days straight, and took a rest day, every fourth day. There were 3 exceptions where I took about a week off to attend our daughter, Molly's high school graduation, a wedding for a close cousin, Amy Dunn, and a week to take our daughter to University of Ky to start her freshman year.

Surprisingly, I discovered early on that this journey was more of a mental challenge than a physical challenge. The body will adjust to just about anything, provided you are in decent shape and you allow for recovery. The mind on the other hand was another story. The monotony of running so much, and rarely around people, gets old very quickly. My mind would think of things, crazy things, on a daily basis. Often reporters would ask what I thought as I was running across the country. My answer was usually something like this…. "You can't think of anything that I haven't thought of on this journey." Honestly, that's how I felt after a couple weeks.

Here's a brief synopsis from each state...
California - John Ratzenberger was there to see me off. Maggie flew out for the day also. We both were in tears as I ran away from the running store. Ed Mason, my loyal friend who drove the RV, cooked, cleaned and supported me for most of my run across the country was also there. Loved the weather, 70-80 most days, zero rain… I was quite nervous those first couple days as I really wasn't sure what I was getting into. Two days in and my nerves were settled. People were GREAT, my body was performing great and I was off to a great start. The highlight of CA was probably a "clothing optional" RV campground which was quite the experience.

Arizona - Running within sight of the Mexican border was really interesting for me. Every half mile or so there were 4 gallons of fresh water (I assume for illegal crossers, but I never found out for sure). The weather was brutal throughout AZ. Every day was over 100 degrees, three days were over 110! Still NO rain. A couple high school friends lived in Phoenix and it was AWESOME spending 5 days in their home, rather than the RV. I'd run my 26 miles then we'd drive back to Larry and Jan's for a wonderful dinner, a pool and a bed! The highlight of AZ for me was Salt River Canyon on Rte 60, spectacular views, but steep down and up going west to east. Show Low, AZ was also spectacular! We really lucked out as a HUGE forest fire overtook the entire Show Low area about a week after we ran through. Roads I'd run on just a week before closed for about 3 weeks during the fire. While running through Phoenix in 114-degree heat one day, I saw a homeless man sitting on a bench in the shade in a park. It was the only shade around, so I sat next to him to get a break in. We ended up chatting for over two hours! This conversation started a lifelong quest for me to speak with homeless people, learn their story and help them in any way I can. This was the first homeless person I'd ever spoken with. To this day, it was probably the most interesting conversation I've ever had. I've spoken to well over 100 homeless people since. Life-changing conversations. I highly advise you speak to some homeless people if it's something you've never done.

New Mexico - The heat wasn't nearly as bad in most of this state, 80-95 and finally rec'd some rain, but only one time and that was at night. Two great memories from NM. In the middle of nowhere, I hadn't seen a home in at least ten miles, I ran past a small house and a guy pitching horseshoes in the front yard. I was beat, he had some shade in his yard, and I hadn't experienced shade much at all since leaving California, and I love horse shoes. So I asked, "Can I pitch a game or two with ya?" He said yes, we pitched 3 games, I won two, he one, and he NEVER asked why I was running by his house, so, we never discussed it. My other memory from NM was spending Father's Day night on top of the RV on Rte 60 right in the middle of the Very Large Array! Our son Jimmy was my support driver at this time. We drank our first beer together that night. Luckily there happened to be meteor showers almost all night! No other lights in sight, no homes, no traffic, just my son and me on top of an RV watching meteors most of the night! Truly spectacular!!!

Texas - I ran on Rte 60 from Phoenix, through all AZ, NM, TX, OK... Brutal heat again in northern Texas and "Cattle Feedlots". Feedlots are where farmers hold tens of thousands of cows together and feed them to fatten them up for months before slaughter. It is BRUTAL running on a 100-degree day past feedlots! The smell is beyond anything I could put into words, so I won't try. What I can tell you is that I actually PUKED more than once! I never was good with handling bad odors. I did love going to two rodeos in small Texas towns and Texans were all extremely friendly. Spend the 4th of July in Clovis TX, near Cannon Air Force Base and saw plenty of jets and a pretty awesome smalltown fireworks display. My sister Peggy was my support driver at this time and we got to spend two awesome weeks getting to know each other even more so than we ever had!

Oklahoma/Kansas - Only ran a couple days in OK, through the pan handle into Kansas. Had two more high school friends, Jim and Ann Sexton, living in Kansas City and spent 6 glorious nights with them. It was always a nice break to sleep in a quality bed, rather than the RV, and spend time with great friends. I had what I considered to be the best story written by any media on my run while in Kansas. Thank you, Jim Sexton for getting Joe Posnanski to cover my run! Joe was from Cincinnati and a sportswriter for the paper. He met with Maggie and me, wrote an awesome story on the run, included numerous pics and it was on the front page of the Sunday sports section on a Sunday. I hadn't seen a Chiropractor the entire trip so stopped in Gary Koch's Chiropractic office. He worked on me for about an hour, said my left leg was 1 inch shorter than my right because of misalignment, adjusted me, and I felt so much better immediately! Yes, I highly recommend seeing chiropractors! My biggest health concern happened in OK... I had been feeling dizzy, sometimes even walking unsteadily for about two days. No way I was going to tell Ed and Molly who were supporting me in the RV as I knew they'd insist on taking me to a Doctor or Hospital. I was really concerned this dizziness could end my run if I went to a Dr or a Hospital. Well, Molly was rollerblading with me one day and said, "Dad, you pee too much. Maybe you're drinking too much water". Then she told me a story one of her high school teachers, Mr John Kelly, told them in class years ago. The story revolved around athletes who don't get enough electrolytes and drink too much water. I was desperate at that time, thinking my cross country run was over, so I listened intently to Molly. Immediately, I began drinking more gatorade, using more supplements and drinking slightly less water. The change happened that day. NO MORE dizziness! Eureka, thank you Molly and Mr Kelly! Our son Sam, 14 years old at that time, spent about 10 days supporting me, normally biking or running along with me. What a great way to bond with my children, spectacular memories!

Missouri – Much of the landscape and roads running through Missouri reminded me of my home state of Kentucky. While sitting on the steps of the Capitol building in Jefferson City taking a well deserved rest, a guy asked, are you going on the Katy Trail? I had no idea what the Katy Trail was and had never heard of it. Boy was I ever happy that he pulled a map out and showed me. It was an old railroad that was converted into a bike/running trail. Truly phenomenal running with no traffic at all for almost 200 miles! I ran the Katy Trail almost all the way to St Louis. I highly recommend the Katy Trail for cross country runners or bikers! I was fortunate to be a guest on two radio talk shows while in St Louis to discuss my run across the country and the underfunding of NIH research for diabetes.

Illinois/Indiana – I got phenomenal media coverage leaving St Louis. The Fox network in St Louis had a reporter interviewing me under the Arch just after sunrise. She asked a few questions, then a Fox photographer from a helicopter followed me running across the bridge over the Mississippi River into Illinois. They had a microphone on me and interviewed me from the helicopter as I ran. A friend who was my support driver at the time, R.J. Seifert, drove the RV (my support vehicle) behind me on the run across the bridge as there was no sidewalk and traffic was heavy. The next 10 days, I

had NO SUPPORT driver. No one was available to drive for me these 10 days. I'd run my 26 miles, then hitchhike (thumbed a ride) back to the RV at the end of my run. It was the first time I'd hitchhiked since I was a teenager. Some days I got a ride quickly but about half of these days, I was thumbing for over 2 hours before I got a ride.
I also experienced my only sickness while running through Illinois. Had a virus for 3 days, sore throat and fever. It was truly miserable to run a marathon, sick, then hitchhike back. That 3rd day I took a rest day and recovered in the RV all day.

Kentucky – It was just awesome running across the bridge over the Ohio River from Indiana to my home state of Kentucky. My cousin, Dave Neltner and his two children, Matt and Travis met me half-way across the bridge. I hadn't seen them since before the run started. Having been alone the past 10 days, this reunion was exactly what I needed. My best buddy and main support driver throughout my entire run, Ed Mason, also met me in Louisville. He would drive for me once again for the next 3 weeks. Without question, my favorite road anywhere in the country that I ran on was Old Frankfort Pike. It is a spectacular 2 lane country road from Frankfort to Lexington, Ky. There are miles of old stone walls lining incredibly gorgeous horse farms all along this road. One of the highlights of my run was the day I got to spend in Lexington, Ky. Our daughter Molly was a freshman at the University of Kentucky that year. She arranged for the University to have a "Diabetes Awareness Day" on the day I ran through Lexington. There were numerous speakers talking about diabetes and I was the keynote speaker. Needless to say, it was fantastic spending time with our daughter while there. Truly enjoyed running north out of Lexington on Rte 27 all the way to my hometown of Ft Thomas, Ky. Had plenty of T.V., newspaper and radio interviews about my run while in Ft Thomas and Cincinnati, Oh. Numerous friends ran with me through my hometown. My son Sam and the entire cross-country team (along with Coach Brad Dunlevy) from the high school our son Sam was attending, Covington Latin School, and my Doctor, Charles Eger, ran with me for a few miles from the largest running store, Bob Ronker's Running Spot, in Cincinnati at that time. Bob Roncker, the owner, had somehow convinced New Balance to sponsor me throughout this run with running shoes and clothes. I'm forever grateful to Bob for this!

Ohio – Running along Rte 32 east through Ohio was relatively flat and uneventful. I did have plenty of visitors, many who ran with me in western Ohio, because of the tremendous amount of media that covered my run through my hometown. The first day I had to run mainly in the rain was in eastern Ohio. 2002 was a drought year in the west and Midwest. It rained prior to Ohio, but mainly at night. Very rarely did I run in the rain until

Ohio. Then only for 3-4 days. I was incredibly fortunate to have dry weather for 90+% of my run.

West Virginia – I ran Rte 50 all through West Virginia. Truly spectacular mountain views, which meant a lot of uphill and downhill running. I always ran the uphills and walked all steep parts of mountain downhills. I had been told running downhill was bad for my knees, so I walked the steep downs and truly enjoyed that break from running. I'll never forget one night in a campground in West Virginia. We had seen a large black bear roaming the campground and the campground owners were warning everyone to be extremely careful. They said this bear occasionally roams the campground for food, hasn't hurt anyone yet, but wanted everyone to be careful and avoid the bear. That night I had a 10:00 pm appointment to be interviewed over the phone by a reporter from Scripps, Leo De Frank. It was possibly the most important of all the press interviews I had over the run because he said this article would be available nationwide in most major city newspapers. Well, I'm scared to death of bears and I couldn't get cell coverage from our campsite. The pay phone was about ¼ mile away at the front of the campground. The RV was plugged in so I had to walk to the pay phone. It was so foggy that night that I couldn't see my hand when I held it out 2 feet in front of my face. I took a flashlight, which was useless, and trembled all the way to the payphone. I trembled throughout our 45 minute phone conversation and all the way back to the RV. Truly, a night I'll never forget. Luckily, I never saw the bear that night! Ed, Dave and another buddy Bob Hengge, each spent time supporting me through West Virginia.

Virginia – The "Beltway Snipers" were the main story nationwide in October, 2002 as I began running in Virginia. The two men had been on a killing spree in Maryland and Virginia for the past 2 weeks. I had tons of messages and phone calls from home, asking me to pause my run until the snipers were caught. Everyone, including me at the time thought I would be a "perfect and easy target" for the two snipers. There wasn't a prayer that I would stop my running now. I was so close to the finish, Washington DC, and I was ready to finish my run. Fortunately on October 24, Mohammed and Malvo (the 2 snipers) were caught sleeping in their car at a rest area in Maryland. DRI, Diabetes Research Institute had handled contacting and setting up media for me for most of my run. They paid to have me and my support driver come to New York City in the last week of my run when they were having their annual convention. That was truly an AWESOME 3 days in NYC and a true pleasure getting to meet dozens of Doctors who had spent their entire adult lives researching a cure for Diabetes. I'm forever grateful for their handling media for me and also for their willingness to bring me to NYC for three days.

The finish in Washington DC – A great friend, Jamie Bernie and another great friend, Mary Lynn Cropper ran with me that last day into DC. It was an overwhelming day for me and I cried much of those last 9 miles into DC. When we ran through the Mall to the Capitol Building, I saw all four of our children, Maggie, Molly, Jimmy and Sam, along with my sister Peggy Maggio, nephew Mike Maggio, my Aunt Ruth Neltner, Amy, and Tim Dunn and Bonnie Keller waiting for me in front of the Capitol. Many other supporters and families affected by diabetes were also there to welcome me. It was over. I was done running. It was a phenomenal finish to an epic journey. Life changing doesn't quite cover it. Only those who have run or walked across the country could understand. Twenty five years earlier, at the age of 20, I bicycled across the country. That was also an epic journey. Running the country truly changed my life in so many ways. If you have the time and the interest, I say "go for it"!

Things I learned from this journey.
- You don't have to be a super athlete to run across the country.
- The mind and body are both far more powerful than most people think.
- Our mind and body will adjust to just about anything, given proper training and mindset.
- You'll find hundreds of unique things along the road.
- Speak to homeless people when you have time. Your thoughts on the homeless will change. Most of them are wonderful people who went through some horrendous times.
- Most people in our country are WONDERFUL people.
- America is truly a beautiful country.

This was truly a life changing and epic journey. One caution I'll add for anyone thinking of running across the country is this… I, and many of the crossers experienced depression soon after our finish. Mine lasted off and on for a few years. My thought on why I went through a depression after a crossing is this… Having had endorphins running wild in our bodies every day for months, then ending abruptly, seems to bring many of us into a temporary depression. Please don't let this stop anyone from pursuing your dream of a crossing. Just realize that you're not alone if you go through a depression afterwards. If I were to do it again, I'd have kept running 10-15 miles a day and gradually decreased mileage as I re-entered the real world.

Last day of my run November 1, 2002 Washington DC at the Capitol lawn...
Nephew Mike Maggio, me, daughter Maggie Painter, daughter Molly Hildwein, son Jimmy McCord and son Sam McCord Last day of my run November 1, 2002 Washington DC

A HUGE THANK YOU to each of the following people, who graciously volunteered to drive my RV support vehicle at various times throughout my run across America! Your support and generosity is forever appreciated! It would have never happened without each of you! It simply is not possible for me to thank you enough!

Ed Mason
John Grause
Terry Flynn
Bob Hengge
Cathy Wecker
RJ Seifert
Peggy McCord Maggio
Maggie McCord Painter
Molly McCord Hildwein
Jimmy McCord
Sam McCord

Chapter 8

John Wallace III
September 26, 2004 to January 27, 2005
Washington to Georgia

It's all part of the adventure.
Excerpts from the seejohnrun Official Footnote.
Additional information and photos: http://www.seejohnrun.com

5/3/04
  In five hours, I'm going to head out for the longest run I've ever done. 35 miles. After a month and a half of solid training, it's time to test out the nerves, muscles, tendons and blood vessels to their max.
  Personalized thank-you cards have been sent out to all of the generous donators and should be arriving at your door-step soon. The website is in the process of being updated again so check back there within the next week or so and of course as much as you'd like in the future. More photos will soon be added thanks to a fantastic deal I found on ebay for a 4-megapixel digital camera. The quality can definitely be seen when compared to the phonecam and digital video recorder images.

5/25/04
  Compared to the 35-miler on 5/2, this went 10 times better! I'm learning more and more each time I go out. In fact, I shaved off 2 hours from my previous 35-mile time. Getting in 12 miles before 10am is different because that's either when I get up on the weekends or when I start work on weekdays. The route/course was amazing. Even though it was an out and back type, the scenery still changes. The sound, however, did not change as the cicadas were deafening.
  Having water/porta-john stops every 4-5 miles was really great as I could refill my Gatorade bottle which I think I drank 140-160 oz. Along with plain old water and energy gels, my nutritional intake was far and away better than any previous long training run. The route was for the most part a very slight gradual incline on the first half and of course a very slight gradual decline coming back. It followed the Potomac River for the most part but was actually more inland than I expected. The tree cover canopy was a lifesaver because of the 'feels like' 93-degree temperatures. Every few miles I would run through an open area and experience the sun, heat and humidity.
  Several other hikers, bikers, campers, fisherman were spotted every now and then so I wasn't isolated totally from civilization. As far as wildlife, a wild turkey, scores of turtles (which are slow on land but practically

impossible to photograph on logs - they have some keen sense of hearing that frustrated me about 4 times before I gave up), a black snake, squirrels, deer, several birds and of course the insects. One problem with maintaining a slower, consistent pace is that the bugs can keep up with you. But it kept my arms stretched out from swatting them all.

No muscle failure following this run which was extremely well received. In fact, the leg muscles really have limited ill-effects. My feet took the brunt of the after-effects this time with puffiness and tenderness starting about 12 hours after finishing. My back was a little sore as well because of the extra supplies I had to carry in my pack.

6/21/04

I finally met my match. Words and photos cannot really describe the course of the Highlands Sky 40 Mile Trail Run. I'm not usually awed by a physical challenge but this really caught me off guard. Distance-wise, I was fine but terrain-wise I had no chance. I officially changed the state motto of West Virginia to "The state with no downhills".

We ran up and up and up over 4 miles then went practically straight down for a few miles or so before heading back up for another 3 miles. The word "Trail" is used very lightly as we were literally running upstream and downstream for much of the first half. The first few puddles of mud and muck you try to avoid and the same goes for keeping your feet dry when water crosses the course. After that you plunge straight through because it's too difficult zig-zagging the entire way. After each mud bog crossing, you hope a stream crossing is near to clean off your shoes. I think I had more water in my shoes than in my 60oz CamelBak hydration pack.

So the agony of defeat occurred at 1:25pm on Saturday afternoon. My first DNF or "Did Not Finish". To me, it also means "Did not Fail". I missed the cutoff by 20 minutes and 2 seconds but that last 14 miles over another 4.5 hours would have been as extreme as the first 26.6 miles in almost 8 hours.

7/30/04

It's been over a month since the last footnote update and a few months since the last webpage update. Over that time, I've been pulled in several directions, but this last month will be fully devoted to the trans-USA run. I've had some successes along the way thus far - strengthened my upper body, stayed injury free, accomplished distance PRs,
prepared mentally. I've also had some failures - 26 out of 40 miles finished in trail run, less mileage ran than expected during training, not as much sit up/stomach training up to this point. But everything has been a learning experience and my excitement for this to begin grows daily.

I've recently tested my iBook, cell phone and USB GPS unit to see if I can get remote internet access. It worked great around town here but may be questionable in remote western Oregon and other parts of the run. Waterproof and breathable jacket and pants were also purchased and will likely be used 33-50% of the days on the road and honestly if it rains every single day I will be a happy runner. I'm in negotiations to purchase/receive a jogger (photos posted online) and will be doing a practice run either this weekend or next.

I will be harnessing the power of the internet in the next 43 days to find lodging, maybe get a free pair of shoes or some bottled water, and receive well wishes from as many people as I can. Five months ago, everyone said "no way", four months ago it was "he's serious", three months ago many said "tell me more", two months ago others mentioned "I've been inspired", last month everyone was on vacation but this month you'll want to get back up to speed!

8/12/04

I've had an amazing response from so many people in so many different areas of the country. At the same time, I have a very hard time asking for any kind of assistance directly. The number of hours that I can devote to planning for this run are dwindling quickly and I will need some serious help over the next month. The main area is going to be lodging. I am going to post a list of cities I will be running near or through as well as a time period that it will happen. Hopefully, someone will know someone who knows someone near each of my nightly stops.

9/13/04

Has it begun, you ask? Nope, not just yet.

After much discussion, a little give-and-take, and a final 'put-my-foot-down' decision, the run will occur from my dad's birthday, 9/26/04, through my mom's birthday, 1/27/05. That will give me a few extra days and will bring the average to right about 30 miles per day.

I will be driving out to Washington next week and am going to try and drive part of the course in reverse to get a feel on what to expect. My last day of work was Friday so final preparations are being made both with the run and with our move west. I will be sending out individual emails to folks that have mentioned providing assistance along the way.

I'm lacing up my 'seejohnrun' running shoes, charging my camera, phone and laptop batteries, checking the jogger's tire pressure and preparing to meet the biggest challenge of my life!

9/25/04

Brand new updates to the web page with many photos added from the road trip from Maryland to Washington. **A note on the photos - if you click on the smaller, thumbnail images, it will open up a larger, detailed image. You can also use the "Next" link to view them all in order.** I'll try to have photos from the start uploaded right away tomorrow morning depending on the internet connection in Westport. Weather is going to be 51 degrees and cloudy for the start. Temperatures are expected to rise about 20 degrees by 4pm and the sun should be out by 10am or so.

10/9/04

The first footnote from the road! I'm currently enjoying high speed wireless internet access at an historic hotel in Condon, Oregon. After 40 miles in the sun, wind and rain along with some substantial hills and almost running out of water, Heidi and I decided the local park just wasn't good enough tonight.

Getting internet connections has been much harder than expected. Actually, my laptop battery life is more of the culprit. It has come in very handy on some tricky routes using the GPS and connecting online with my phone when it was plugged in. In addition to all of that, after running for 12-13 hours I am finding it is tough to write captions for photos, upload everything and still eat, sleep and relax before another long day begins.

Having one state under my belt feels really good. The scenery in Washington was amazing but the constant sun was too much. I will have to take a picture of my wrist with and without my watch on to show just how deep a tan one can get in 10-11 days. My ankles, soles and mostly my shins took a beating the first week but now with lots of elevation, cold compresses and ibuprofen they are much better. I still like to wrap them in ace bandages just for peace of mind.

Today, a man was particularly generous by giving me 3 liters of water because I had mentioned I was running low on the way into town. Every day I will chat with 2-5 people about the run and receive waves or honks by 5-10 times that many people.

The Forrest Gump beard is coming along quite nicely, and I'll have to do a good self-portrait soon. I had a little bit of a bobbed lip today due to too much sun yesterday and no chap stick. One of those things I actually didn't pack. The jogger is holding up after over 300 miles. I had to fix 2 flats and changed one worn out tire so far. The flats were actually caused by a strip of plastic that was supposed to prevent punctures but then caused it. The tire that wore down perplexes me because the other two are in very good shape and can go several hundred more miles at least.

10/28/04

Heidi and her dad arrived just in time to treat me to some great meals and track down Tony, the bicycle repairman. Tony revamped the jogger by replacing one of the wheels and bearings. Without his work, the run would have been in jeopardy and I appreciate his work immensely! In addition to his repairs, I shaved off quite a few pounds of gear that either wasn't being used or I just brought too much of. We arrived bright and early back in Hammett and I was on my way again.

It was great to see some familiar faces after a month on the road and Heidi made various attempts to shave the beard. It was spared though and will come in handy as I head into Nevada - high altitude Nevada. My arrival in Jackpot will be a rain/snow mix with highs in the upper 40s and lows in the upper 20s. The farther south I go the higher up I go and Wells forecasts a few snow showers with highs in the mid 40s and lows in the mid 20s. So that will be extremely interesting as I travel through Nevada. I'm hoping for an unexpected change in weather and maybe some kind of warm front to come through there. We'll see.

11/2/04

Just a quick footnote from Wells, Nevada. I was met today by another member of my support crew - David Barrett. David graciously accepted a plea from my parents to help me through part of Northeast Nevada. And let me tell you it is a cold and barren part of the country indeed. If the sun is not out, it is not warm. Period. So, over the last 29 miles and the next 73 miles, I won't need to worry about lodging because we will be shuttling back to Wells each night. After that I have 3 camping nights and then 4 more remote spots before the big city of Pioche. After 349 miles Nevada will be complete and I'll have a whirlwind 3-4 days in Utah which will be my 5th state of the journey. A couple weeks in Arizona after that with hopefully warmer temperatures and I'll almost be done with the mountainous portion of the country.

11/14/04

Well Utah has been a blur, but a very scenic blur! This morning I woke up in a state park boasting red canyons, volcanic formations, petrified woods and colorful sand dunes.

I hurried on into St. George, UT this morning to satisfy my craving for a Starbucks Gingerbread Latte. Luckily, it was easy to find and on the same road I need to get on to Hurricane, UT for the night. Unfortunately, they did not have wireless internet yet so I went over to the Ramada Inn to borrow some of their waves. After an hour or so, the manager was on his way so I had to leave. I went across the street to the Hampton Inn and finished up everything.

11/21/04

The cavalry (my dad) is about 4 hours away and we'll sort things out.

I was getting ready to get some breakfast around 7:30am this morning and on my way out the front door I noticed the jogger was not under the awning where I had left it last night. I checked inside to see if they moved it to a more secure spot. Nope, it was stolen sometime between dinner last night and breakfast this morning.

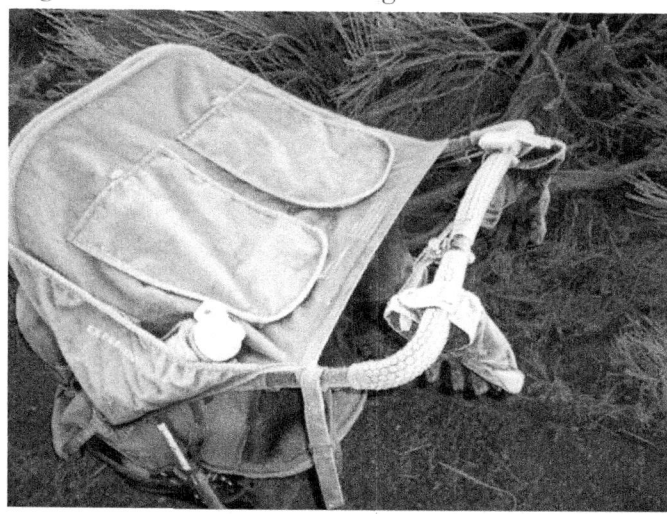

I immediately contacted the local authorities here and they have been on the lookout since this morning. It was probably loaded into a truck and is miles away from here by now. On the good side, if there is a good side, I have 95% of my gear. The only things I'm really missing are 2

Camelbak water pouches, an LED headlamp, various energy bars and some other odds and ends that fit into the upper and lower pouches. The only thing the thieves left was my hand water bottle with orange Gatorade still inside. They even took my reflective vest and bungee cords - I can't believe it!

So, my dad is still on his way for our Thanksgiving meeting. We'll sort things out and most likely have to track down a replacement jogger. That will take a big bite out of the budget and I'll have to second guess my hotel/motel stays for the rest of the run.

I wish I had better news to post but I'll keep everyone updated. This is definitely a twist I was not expecting but as I've always said - it's all part of the adventure...

11/23/04

It turns out this section of Arizona doesn't have any twin joggers. So, after a full day on the phone and visiting every big city and sports store in a hundred plus mile radius I had some help from Heidi who saw a model online at Amazon.com. Around 10:00pm we visited the local Flagstaff Comfort Inn parking lot, logged on (again - we had been online several times from here during the day) and found the new updated model of the jogger that was stolen. The only question remaining was - where can it get shipped to during a week with the Thanksgiving Day holiday.

The Police Department was our first stop and we tried to get in touch with the sergeant, but he was on emergency leave. Finally, a stroke of luck occurred and a lady by the name of Mary Begay who works within the law enforcement agencies there took us into her office and will help us out. The jogger will be sent in care of her overnight and hopefully will arrive tomorrow.

11/26/04

62 days complete, 62 days to go. We're finally out of Tuba City's grasp and will be into New Mexico sometime late this weekend. I started the day off early with a nice 19 mile run before we headed over to Gallup, NM. Cracker Barrel was having a Thanksgiving meal special, so we enjoyed turkey, mashed potatoes, stuffing, sweet potatoes, cranberry sauce and pumpkin pie. It was a tasty treat and we were still able to finish off a large popcorn and pop at the movie National Treasure afterwards. That completes my tour back into civilization and I'll be back in rural America again after this weekend.

The new jogger is still packed up but will make its debut this weekend. We just need to buy a new odometer and hopefully engineer it in much the same way as the last one was. It will be very nice to get the jogger back on the road because having access to everything I need was really convenient. Now I have to wait until wherever the van is parked in order to get water, my camera and so on. Running without the jogger has also increased my pace and sweat level so I am feeling the effects of that as well.

11/29/04

New Mexico, state number seven, was reached at 3pm MT yesterday and a full day of running 42 miles, having 2 great meals and sadly saying goodbye to my dad concluded around 12:30am MT today. His help was extremely timely and appreciated very much. We had a great time putting in close to 200 miles running and much more than that sightseeing.

Over the next week, I'll drop down another 2000 feet into Socorro, NM where I'll be hosted by a runner we met at El Ranch Motel/Hotel & Restaurant. Five days after that and another 1000 feet lower, I'll be in Roswell and it will be fairly 'flat & fast' the remainder of the run. Temperatures will also stabilize to a runner-friendly high in the 40s to 60s and lows in the 20s to 40s. It is 11 degrees right now under sunny skies in Gallup, NM and it's going to be chilly the next few nights. As long as it's mostly sunny and no more snow falls, everything should be fine.

The new jogger is fully assembled, reflective taping has been applied and a test loading will be performed in about 15 minutes. Then it will have to be folded down to fit out the door and I'll be on my way again. It looked like a small hill right away to start off with but I think it will be mostly flat the rest of the way.

12/10/04

New Mexico has been a very diverse state with freezing (-6 F) temperatures, amazing mountain views and now desert flatlands. I met up with my trans-continental bicycling friends Anja and Dirk coming into Socorro. We crossed paths near the North Rim of the Grand Canyon in Jacob Lake, AZ. Amazingly, 17 days later we met up again and had a great time with our host, Peter Romero who my dad and I met in Gallup, NM. So here we are again for one last meeting in Roswell before I head due east and they head due south.

I'm looking forward to my eighth state and third time zone when entering Texas. There are several local running club contacts and friends of theirs who will help with crossing Texas. My goal which should be attainable based on my current mileage is crossing Texas over the next month and arriving in Texarkana, TX on 12/30/04 in time to meet Heidi for New Year's Eve and Day. Texas is much more populated and settled than what I've been used to so hopefully I can travel as fast as I have been on the open roads up to this point.

One of my favorite photos to date is the head shot during the snowstorm coming out of Bingham. That along with the snow-covered jogger show the crazy day of running that was! I received no less than 12 offers for rides that day.

12/23/04

I've been starting later in the day the past week or so and have been enjoying the displays of lights at night. Texans sure know how to put on a good showing and my remaining week in the state should provide many more viewings. To go along with the decorations and lights there was an extreme Arctic Blast as the news station likes to put it. It was fairly impressive given it rarely snows 'down in these parts'. The day will rank up in the top five or so "Most Treacherous" days with the wind gusts, icy roads, bridge crossings and blowing snow.

I hope everyone has a Very Merry Christmas and a Happy New Year!! I'm hoping to finalize my Christmas plans tomorrow with some running club members north of Dallas. My New Year's plans will be spent relaxing with Heidi in Arkansas of all places and watching Michigan football. Go Blue!

12/25/04

Merry Christmas from the gracious and accommodating household of Wayne and Mandy Sueltz. They have taken me for the last two days and three nights during this holiday. I have really been made to feel at home and part of their family which includes newborn (12/21) twin girls in addition to their son. I thought my days were hectic and tiresome, but their days seem even more crazy and exhausting!

12/28/04

Today's city lineup is very interesting with Paris, Reno and then Detroit. I've had a couple of long mileage days since Christmas, but today's amount is 'only' around 32. Then it's another long 40 to New Boston before a very short 20 to Texarkana. The weather looks to be mild with a little wind today but temps hovering around 70.

Now that I am under 1000 miles to go and less than one month, thoughts about the finish are starting to fill my days on the road. The plan is to finish by sunset on Thursday, 1/27/05 still. Heidi has already booked my return flight to Seattle for 10am on Sunday, 1/30 so you can tell she is anxious to get me back into the 'real world'. I want to extend an open invitation to anyone who would like to be there for the finish or visit that weekend in January. Everyone that this footnote goes out to has played a role in helping me accomplish this journey so far and I would love to share it with whoever can make it to Tybee Island next month.

1/1/05

Happy New Year 2005!!!

Many NEW photos will be uploaded tonight after featuring my ninth state - Arkansas, Hope and Hot Springs National Park among other odds and ends.

Congratulations to my dad (and me too) for completing 15 straight years of running a minimum of one mile EVERY DAY. 5,480 consecutive days!

1/9/05

I crossed over the Mississippi River and entered my tenth state yesterday morning just before noon (11:55:45 AM) over a fairly treacherous bridge.

Another 25 or so miles later I arrived at my lodging for the night – Leroy Percy State Park. This is Mississippi's oldest state park and despite its age, has many modern amenities such as laundry, RV site hookups and a brunch every Sunday. That's right, I was able to enjoy a great meal just a bit ago before heading out on my marathon to Belzoni today. After that it will be another state park in the middle of the state before getting to Alabama in just a few days.

Welcome to the new footnote mailing list members. This email goes out to approximately 300 people now. The first footnote went out to about 30.

Arkansas seemed to go by quickly with lots of nice people and overly friendly dogs. I was followed for seven miles by one four-legged canine that was apparently named "Stay" or "Get Home" because every time I yelled those out, he continued to follow me! Southern hospitality is alive and well down here and I am a very happy and appreciative recipient. The media coverage is also starting to pick up with several small-town papers doing little interviews and photos. I seem to be getting 15 minutes of fame in each state. Arkansas was also the first state that I was not pulled over by law enforcement. What a change from Texas where I was stopped in the first three counties of the state!

1/14/05

First off, I'm about two weeks behind a much-needed congratulations to my mom for completing her first year of running without missing a single day. I know it is a major accomplishment having completed mine 15 years ago. She went above and beyond what I did my first year though covering about 150 more miles than I did with a total of 1187.7. She also ran one more marathon than I did, going to Chicago and Honolulu which are two of the largest in the world. I ran a small one in Milwaukee but being 14 it was still a major experience for me and one of my earliest running adventures. And finally, on top of all of this, she was named the 2004 Female Road Runner of the Year by the Upper Peninsula Road Runners Club in the region of Michigan where I was born and raised. These accomplishments are comparable in many ways to the trials and triumphs I have been experiencing on my journey across America.

1/18/05

My parents will be coming down in six days to see me through to the finish. It will be a nice show of support in addition to all their help from the beginning through today. There has been a lot of behind-the-scenes work done by my family and Heidi. Heidi will be flying in early on the 27th all the way from Seattle to view the finish (3000+ miles in a few hours rather than a few months). My Aunt who lives near Atlanta is also going to be part of the celebration at the ocean. If I can arrange it, there will be a time-delayed webcast video of the finish for all to view on the website.

1/24/05

I can't see or smell the salty sea just yet, but it is over just a few more hills and around just a few more corners. The final days will be under sunny skies and warm temperatures just like it began 120 days ago. There was a beautiful tailwind yesterday and there will be a bright full moon tomorrow night. I'm taking everything in because an adventure like this usually occurs only once in a lifetime.

I haven't said thank you enough to everyone following along and those who have helped me along. Thank you, thank you, thank you! For those that have been motivated even in the slightest degree - you have made the run a success. For those who have been inspired to someday achieve a cross-country run, there are many miles out there to choose from and I suggest straying from the course every once in a while. My greatest adventures within the adventure popped up at the oddest times and in the oddest places. In other words, get lost once in a while!

1/30/05

Sorry to leave you hanging over the last four days! It has been a wild conclusion to a wild adventure. Stay tuned all this week for details, photographs, video and recollections.

Covering the fourth longest route of the documented journey runners, I can now say "I ran across America!".

It's an amazing accomplishment and words truly can't describe the thankfulness I have for so many people across our country. But I'll do my best to capture it in some way and express it back to you all.

Wow! What a run!!

2/8/05

It's only been one week since arriving back here in the state of Washington. My mileage from 1/21-1/27 was 274 miles. My mileage from 1/28-2/7 was about 15. That's half of what I averaged (30.69) over the 124 days across America.

In addition to becoming homeowners, I have been slowly organizing all of the archives from the run. There are several newspapers with interviews and photos. There are scores if not hundreds of receipts. There are brochures, pamphlets, cards, stickers, magnets, magazines, guides, and many other paper products from various locations along the route. And of course, there are photographs (the finish was well documented), emails and video.

    I wish I could make this a daily/annual documentary with mileage postings, photographs and footnotes all year long. Whereas the Run Across America was my daily 'job', I just can't devote that same kind of energy to keep it up along with all my other activities. There will be postings and updates from time to time but much less often than what everyone is used to. There are still many exciting additions that I will be sharing with everyone over the coming weeks and months though so by all means stay connected!

Chapter 9

Helene Neville

May 1 - Aug 1, 2010, Ocean Beach, CA to Atlantic Beach, FL. (2,520 miles)
May 1 - June 15, 2013, Vancouver, BC to Tijuana, MEX. (1,560 miles)
May 1 - July 6, 2014, Marathon, Florida to Portland, Maine. (1,860 miles)
May 1 - Sept 5, 2015, St. Stephen, CAN to Ocean Shores, WA. (3,773 miles)
May 1 - Sep 23, 2017, WY to W.VA to Las Vegas, NV. (3,142 miles)
August 27 - Sep 3, 2018, the perimeter of the island of Oahu, HI (127 miles)
April 6 - April 30, 2019, Anchorage, AK to Livengood, AK. (442 miles)
July - August 17, 2019, Livengood, AK to Prudhoe Bay, AK. (426 miles)

Total running miles: 13,850 miles

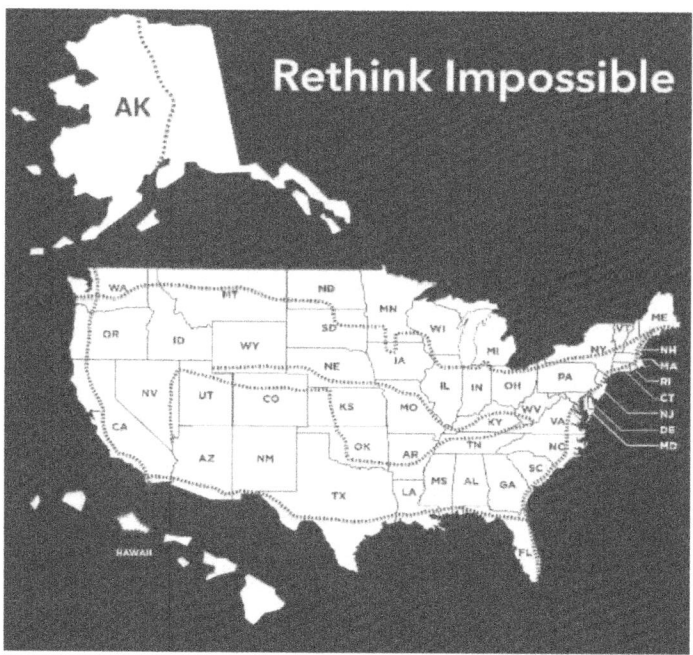

RUNNING AROUND THE UNITED STATES

In 2010, I would be turning 50...I had a dream of doing more for others...I am a connector of people, and love to run. I parlayed two things I am good at and ran with them...literally. I decided to run across America and to keep going until I transected all fifty states in the United States. It wasn't to be mindless meandering; I had a noble cause in mind.

I wasn't sure HOW to do it, or WHAT was needed to accomplish the run, I just knew WHY I was doing it. My WHY was clearly defined and I focused on it every day.

At age 31, I was first diagnosed with Hodgkin's lymphoma, and after chemotherapy, radiation and three brain surgeries, I tried everything they told me I couldn't do.

Imagine you survived cancer, endured chemotherapy, radiation and three brain surgeries. Then imagine running 25 miles, sometimes more, each day, without a roadside crew, surviving on whatever is in your pack for that particular day. All alone on the highways of America. And, after running those daily miles, you somehow harness the strength to visit hospitals, schools, and cancer centers to share your story…

On May 1, 2010, I embarked on my first transcontinental run across America. On May 17th my doctor called and said, "your tests are back, and your cancer is probably back." Imagine getting news like that! I told him, "I'm probably going to run to Florida, and I will call you in three months."

It was just me and thousands of miles of America to cross and conquer.

With limited resources - I wondered how I could get my message to "Rethink Impossible" out to others and live to tell about it.

Off I went to tackle a monumental run without sponsors or celebrity endorsements.

I would begin and end each vulnerable, in unfamiliar surroundings, to ask and receive help from strangers. Choosing to look for kindness in others rather than stay on guard expecting the worst. Mostly to "Rethink Impossible".

My plan to run again was put on hold when in late 2011 my cancer had returned, but that didn't stop me from running 1,560 miles from Vancouver, Canada to Tijuana, Mexico in 2013.

Three months before the start of my 2013 run, my 56-year-old brother unexpectedly died.

"He Ain't Heavy, He's My Brother" was my mantra. My brother always wanted to travel…he was going with me the rest of the way. I would say goodbye to him in a way I didn't get to before he died.

On May 1, 2014, I left Marathon, Florida and 68 days and 1,860 miles later, I ended in Portland, Maine.

On May 1, 2015, I started running from St. Stephens, New Brunswick, Canada and ran 3,773 miles in 128 days to Ocean Shores, Washington. On September 5, 2015, I finished running the entire perimeter of the continental United States. I ran 9,713 miles.

As a thank you to my community, I ran the Las Vegas Strip back and forth for 35 hours covering 135 miles. I pushed my limits beyond comprehension.

In 2016, I was sidelined by cancer and a messy divorce....and with a chemo port in my chest, I decided I would bring my brother home to our birthplace – Philadelphia, the City of Brotherly Love. I would run a marathon in his honor or die trying!

My Marathon of Love started at our childhood home, which is ten miles from the Philadelphia Art Museum, home to the infamous Rocky Steps. Those steps, known for the underdog, was the perfecting setting.

I spread some of my brother's ashes in our yard where we played as children and started running. I ran ten point two miles to the Rocky Steps and completed my Marathon of Love by running sixteen miles up and down the steps. It took me seven and a half hours, to run 384 times up and down the steps. Brotherly Love for sure. I intended to leave my brother's urn but decided that I would finish the final fourteen states, and he was going too.

On May 1, 2017, I started running the final twelve states across Middle America. My chemo port was removed two weeks prior to the start of this run. My first state was Wyoming. On day two, I was hospitalized for severe altitude sickness. The doctor said to return to low altitude or risk coma, or worse, maybe death. Of course, I didn't listen.

On day four, staggering, limping, and puking, I found a dirty and muddy stuffed bunny. Carrying it by ears, I staggered along the interstate. I was stopped by a cop who called into Evanston Mental Health facility obviously certain that I was an escaped mental patient.

Staggering along Interstate-80, and barely able to finish ten miles each day, people heard my story, hotels donated rooms, and many showed up and walked along the interstate with me. I finished Middle America in 147 days, covering 3,142 miles.

On Sept 3, 2018, I completed state number 49 by running the perimeter of Oahu. For a total of 12,976 miles for 49 states. Only Alaska remained.

Alaska, The Last Frontier, North to the Future, and one of the world's most inaccessible places. How would I get through Alaska? I decided Alaska would be run in two segments. I planned to run the first part, take a break to return and run The Dalton Highway, also known as the Haul Road, and is often profiled on the television show Ice Road Truckers, when the warmer weather set in.

I began Alaska with a Corneal abrasion, vaginal hemorrhage requiring surgery and thick smoke from multiple forest fires. I was running at the end of the earth. The Arctic Ocean. How could I run this mind-boggling event?

On my 59th birthday and on a road that literally ends and where life truly begins I completed the State of Alaska and jumped into the ice cold Arctic Ocean. It was glorious.

I reached the Arctic Ocean and became the first woman, and only the second person ever to run across all 50 states, and the only one to do it without a support team. Alaska was 868 miles. If I stopped, those who said I was too old, too sick, that it was too difficult especially for a woman - would be right. I went the distance to demonstrate to those needing hope and inspiration what's physically and mentally possible.

My brother's ashes traveled with me since 2013, I returned to the states I ran in 2010, and spread his ashes in those states too.

From my running, I have emerged with a renewed sense of purpose, determined to share my own awakening to improve the way we live and walk in the world.

Some think running is a lonely solo sport, and that couldn't be further from the truth. Even though I am alone on the road, I know I am never really alone, because people told me if I had the courage to run, they would look after me, and they did.

I used my personal vehicle as support and gear wagon. I played leap frog around the country, stayed in people's homes, and looked for people to drive or drop the car at designated locations for me to start and end my daily run… and having my own vehicle afforded me the opportunity to be immersed with people up close and personal. To become uniquely of the people. Sounded simple enough.

I ran into communities, often unannounced, introducing myself to strangers and asking if they could house or feed me for the night. And, despite suffering cancer, broken bones, an attempted assault, financial hardships, and the deaths of two family members, I continued running to show others that nothing should stand in the way of pursuing their goals and dreams. I ran where others said not to. I ventured into crime-stricken areas of major cities, desolate areas void of people and services, treacherous terrain, and isolated places with unpredictable weather conditions. People with nothing to give – often gave the most. People who have endured more than their fair share of devastation, destruction and poverty.

My run was as much about humanitarianism and athleticism. The most spiritual thing we can do is embrace humanity and connect with those around us.

I persevered and didn't give up, and beauty ensued. I allowed myself to be vulnerable and shared my hardship making another person feel at ease to share theirs.

What I want everybody to realize is that we can accomplish little by ourselves and everything together. My run is called One On The Run…meaning We are all ONE, ONE world, ONE team. And when we realize that we are one, we can do everything. We have the opportunity to focus on that which divides us or that which unites us.

I ran because I could. I ran for those who couldn't. I ran in honor and memory of those who are no longer with us. My run is not to realize my own dream but to inspire you to realize yours.

I ran to EXPOSE what's right with America! And what I discovered, while running, when I looked deeply, is that the world I am living in has more right than I ever imagined.

This run wasn't to realize my own dream, but to inspire others to realize their dream.

I have been sincerely touched by the generosity of people and the lives that have become a part of mine. It was a beautiful display of humanity and inspiration went full circle. This is the America I came to love; these are the people I came to love and admire.

Think about how many miles I traveled, alone, without support and no real plan, often showing up in towns unannounced, yet, I covered 13,850 miles on foot and was cared for, was loved, and was safely passed to the next person by road angels.

Chapter 10

Jeffrey Grabosky
January 20 to May 20, 2011
Oceanside, California – Fire Island, New York
3,702 Miles

How to Run Across America in Four Months

You picked up a book about crossing the country on foot. That choice reveals something about *you*.

The choice to embark on a journey of this magnitude reveals something about a *runner*. It might be confirmation that we are all essentially mad. But among all these authors, their stories, and their singular paths, you'll also hear notes of inspiration, perseverance, and achievement.

I've chosen to focus on the lead-up to my run: the WHY. It's a critical, stressful part of the journey that probably warrants more discussion than it gets. I say that based on experience...

Once I completed my trek and rejoined civil society, the conversations always turned to the granular – pace, mileage, diet, injuries, wildlife, detours, and close calls. To be sure, those details are important, because there's no other way to anticipate the myriad variables you'll face. It's not only helpful to hear about them, it also makes for memorable storytelling.

But I suspect any author here would attest that enduring a run of this magnitude calls for preparation that is mental as much as it is logistical or physical. You have to start answering tough questions long before you begin.

In the lead-up to the run, many will tell you it cannot be done. They are, of course, wrong. For the irrepressible, all things are possible, if you prepare. I'm going to help you do precisely that.

Saying "Yes"

I had been toying with the idea of running across the United States for a couple years, but there was always something that got in the way. A lifelong runner, I had already done several marathons and a couple 100-mile ultra-marathon races. Longer distances didn't put me off; I actually enjoyed the grind. I was competitive, but yearned for something more – some big adventure, unknown and awaiting my "hell, yes!"

The timing felt right. I was single and untethered. I loved my job, but knew I had other ambitions. It finally made sense to say yes. From that commitment – the biggest I'd made yet – I started to plan.

Up to that point, the most planning I had done for a marathon was deciding where I was going to grab my beers during the race. This was, to say the least, a level up.

Once you've embraced this extreme challenge, you must brace for every lame Forrest Gump joke known to man. That'll be the easy part. The hard part will be forcing your feet to move after running 20 miles straight into a sandstorm in rural Texas. At that moment, "Run, Forrest, Run!" will be music to your ears.

Why the heck are you doing this?

Fair question! Be ready to answer it many times over, and in different ways. Remember, not everyone has these seemingly unattainable goals. Communicating your "reason" is important not just for the people asking about you, but also for your future sanity.

If you already said "yes," you already have your purpose – one that will keep you moving when your mind and body are colluding to bring you to a halt at the nearest pizza parlor (or shrink). Those times will test your resolve, and you'll come to rely on your reason. So be honest with yourself from the outset. This will be the passion that sustains your inner fire and propels you forward.

My purpose stemmed from the death of my mother five years earlier. She was a devout Catholic and would often run while praying the Rosary, a series of prayers that focuses on the mysteries of Jesus' life. I set out to honor that as I ran, and I asked people to send me their prayer intentions. Not only would I have something to focus on besides myself and sheer distance, I'd have in mind thousands of others, from all over the world.

I chronicled that part of the journey in my book *Running with God Across America*, which was a title that barely beat out *Running, Pizza, and Beer*.

Bottom line: know what will push you through when you badly want to give up. Locate this, and you cannot fail. It's a strange surrender: not to pain or exhaustion, but to the singular purpose around which you designed this mission.

Mental Readiness

Whoever coined the phrase "Mind Over Matter," I salute them. All runners can recall a mental obstacle that hinders their development – or threatens to totally shut them down. It could be just getting past the first mile, or believing after mile 20 that they can push through another six. The "head game" is real.

Looking back on my cross-country run, it was the mental part that was the most challenging to overcome.
At the outset of training, I had imagined beautiful landscapes, rolling plains, and snow-capped mountains all there for me to enjoy while I plugged away on an empty road.

Those fantasies didn't last long.

Run on local roads and you'll soon realize some people aren't very kind. They throw stuff at you. They yell. Attentive drivers are the exception, not the rule. And weather can turn on a dime, completely changing your approach.

If I was to put my life on hold to undertake the unpredictable, there would have to be absolutely no way I could set out without reaching the finish. I'm stubborn like that.

To conquer the mental game, make a list of the reasons you'd allow yourself to tap out early. For me, it was only two things: 1) if I broke a bone that prevented me from continuing or 2) if I died. Short lists are nice, and I could remember those two things when I started questioning the feasibility of my journey.

Training

How could you possibly prepare your body for consistently running 150, 200, or 300+ miles a week for months on end? By taking each day as an opportunity to run a little farther, to train a little differently, and to face different obstacles.

I started training about five months out from my start date and did so in different parts of the country, which helped to acclimate me to elements that I'd eventually have to face. I gradually built up my mileage, so I became comfortable running 150-200 miles in a week. Comfortable, meaning I could wake up the next morning and somehow still move my legs for another 20 or 30 miles.

The physical aspect of training was the easy part. It was the mental part that forced me to overcome the obstacles that were more challenging than I had expected.

Try this out when you're training. Run a marathon a few days in a row over a long weekend while pushing a stroller weighing 70 pounds loaded up with supplies. Run in horrible weather. Run on backcountry roads where you need to watch for drivers. Run when you're tired or mad or hungry – or all three at the same time. And then when you want to give up, keep going, remember why you are training for your adventure and don't stop. Powering through these types of training scenarios are not easy, but winning the mental battle here builds confidence that you will also overcome the challenges that undoubtedly await.

The Nitty-Gritty Details: Route, Gear, Safety

This is where your journey will get real: months or weeks before you take that first step. And you *must* take this phase seriously. In school, many of us have aced a test without much studying, but these stakes are far higher. I was not going to be that guy running around in literal circles because I didn't take the time to map out where I was going, where I was sleeping, what I was eating, and what gear I was carrying.

You won't have the endurance to make it from one ocean to the other if you lack the stamina to plan through the logistics. There are three main categories: the type of crossing, the route planning, and the gear.

Solo or Road Trip Party?

This is the first step to planning your adventure. You have to decide if you're going it alone or if you'll have a crew with you. If the latter, you need to know whether they are friends who want to get involved, professionals whom you pay, or concerned family who want to help out.

If speed, safety, flexibility, and/or companionship is important, then having a crew with a vehicle to accompany you is the way to go. The ability to be picked up and dropped off at almost anywhere along the road is great for maximizing the distance per day. You don't have that option when you're solo. But the real benefit is not having to carry or push your gear for thousands of miles, which makes the running part exponentially easier.

With long road trips, there is bound to be conflict along the way. It's a 'road marriage' – there will be obstacles and disagreements, but as long as you are all committed to making it work, you'll probably not hate each other at the end.

If you would rather go it alone, imagine going on a cross-country road trip at five or six miles an hour. Running on your own is extremely tough, and hyper-awareness of your surroundings all the time is a necessity for safety. But at least there are no arguments at the end of the day when it is time to decide on where you are grabbing dinner.

I was totally self-supported, which made my survival dependent upon my own planning.

Route

Get a map of the country and study it. (It's big, right? You are going to cross that thing on your own two feet). The route you take will affect nearly everything involved in your crossing.

I am pretty sure I missed the day in school when it was taught that the shortest distance between two points is a straight line. I marked my map with dots on the cities where I had friends and family. That approach zig-zagged me all over the country, from California to Arizona to Texas, Oklahoma, Indiana, Virginia, New Jersey, and New York. There were some days (okay, a lot) I was cursing that decision.

Once I had those points, I looked at maps online, satellites, and Google Street View to figure out what roads could get me to where I wanted to go. Most states don't allow you to run on the Interstate highways (nor would I want to be within a couple feet of an 18-wheeler going 80 mph anyway). Sidewalks, wide shoulders on the road, and pedestrian or bike paths were all my friends. Dodging vehicles is a big deal when you're tired and, in my case, pushing all my gear. Winging your route at any point can be a dangerous proposition and you may end up pushing your rig on an ATV path through a mountain range for a couple days. No joke.

I wrote out each day's route on index cards ahead of time so if my phone didn't get a signal or died, I still had a good idea of where I needed to go. I planned out each day's mileage, where I would be staying (some nights I camped out but most I spent in a motel or with family and friends), and hopefully where I would be eating.

When you plan your route, it's imperative to take into account weather, elevation, and seasonal changes. I started in California in late January and made my way through the South where the weather was decent. By the time I hit the more Northern states, the weather wasn't as wintry and by May in New York, it was downright balmy.

Gear

Running gear can be fun to accumulate but not when you have to push it across the country.

If you're already a runner, you know how long your shoes will last. Factor that into how many miles you will be running or walking per day and figure out when you will need replacement shoes. Either mail them to your destination ahead of time or choose a place where you can pick them up when you need them. I only carried one extra pair of shoes and mailed replacements all across the country.

Since I went solo, I used a baby jogger to carry all my gear. This gave some people the impression of the world's most idiotic father pushing a child up desolate roads in bad weather. And yes, I got pulled over by police multiple times when people reported just that.

If you choose to use a jogger, upgrade the wheels. You are going to be kicking the crap out of them and need them to hold up. Carry a replacement set if they bust. I got into quite a jam when I couldn't fix one of the wheels somewhere in Missouri. The jogger company, BOB, was able to FedEx me the parts I needed overnight. Lesson: have the phone number of your jogger company handy and choose a good company. Also, bonus tip: don't wait until you are on the side of a highway to try your hand at changing a tire on your stroller.

For food and water, make sure you have enough bottled water and bring MREs for high calorie intake on the road. When I crossed the desert in California, I loaded up on as much water as I could carry and made it out after three days. It was nerve-wracking because it was extremely desolate, and I made it out with less than a liter of water to spare.

I chose to load up on my calories at night, usually shocking the wait staff when I'd order an appetizer, two large pizzas, a dessert and then finish

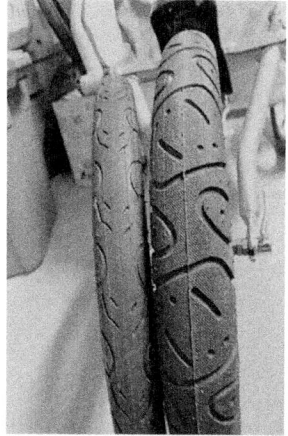

Standard vs. Upgraded Tire

every bite. They would be even more shocked if they knew I stopped at the gas station for a few additional bags of snacks on the way back to the motel. Yay, food!

Other gear that proved useful was a portable charger, a small tent (make sure the rain fly works), plastic bags, and large, empty plastic bottles for on-the-go potty breaks. Chapstick, a hat, and lightweight long pants and sleeves to protect from the sun were necessities as well. If you decide on a stroller, make the investment in a high quality one that will survive the demanding journey.

Body glide was used daily and having toilet paper at all times was a must. I also weighed myself as much as I could along the way to catch any issues early on. It truly is a balancing act to carry as little as possible, but also to ensure you have everything you will need.

Safety

Besides horrible drivers and bad weather, animals were at the top of my prep list. I had enough experiences in the past to know that dogs love to chase after runners and I wasn't about to become bait for bears or mountain lions or snakes along the journey either.

I invested in bear spray, a long knife, and a dog dazer (a device that emits a sound which confuses the canines). I used the dog dazer dozens of times, as more than once a pack of at least six chased me. When I came face-to-face with a mountain lion, I oh-so-casually reached for my knife before he decided to look elsewhere for food. Keep your safety gadgets close enough where you can reach them in an instant.

I saw tracks of who-knows-what animals when I was out running and tried to be as aware of my surroundings as I could. I never ran with music, ran on trails at every opportunity, often ran facing traffic, and avoided roads that were narrow and winding. The only time I'd change the side of the street was where there was a sharp left turn and no shoulder. I'd cross the street before the turn and then cross back over after the turn. I am pretty sure this saved my life multiple times. Use common sense: if something looks dangerous, it probably is.

My preferred running time was early in the morning to mid-afternoon and I was careful to not run in total darkness. If you choose to run at night, be lit up like a Christmas tree. People have been seriously injured and even killed attempting journeys like this. Be cautious – don't assume drivers see you.

A sobering tip – and one I took – is to create a will and prep letters to loved ones in case anything dire happens on the road.

Technology has come a long way - use it to your advantage. Make sure you have a tracker device on and check in with someone daily who knows where you are and when you should be getting to your destination. Have a plan with a friend or family member in case you get in trouble and don't have cell service – like if you don't call within an allotted time of when you are supposed to, your friend can call the local police or have someone go search for you.

Weather is a big factor when it comes to safety. Temperature, wind, rain, and snow are just a few elements that can impact your day. Regional and seasonal weather can involve thunder and lightning, tornados, hurricanes, and dust storms. Stay tuned to the weather forecast and if need be, change your route or take a day off to avoid dangerous weather.

Food, Recovery, Food

Next to the people I was praying for (and sleep), food was the one thing that I constantly thought about while out running. I was always hungry. But this is where it got fun.

I had to find food that allowed me to keep running and not cramp up or unload a meal on the side of the road or bother my digestive system. I managed to eat enough protein bars and have a decent breakfast to sustain me throughout the day.

But when dinner came, it was go time. There were many stops along the way where I had friends or family cook for me. Where I was alone, I'd gingerly walk into a restaurant, sit down and order a family meal and a beer. I managed to find one of those places where you could get your picture on the wall if you ate enough food in one sitting. It was *Man vs. Food* every day.

My body needed the nutrition as much as I enjoyed eating. I was averaging the equivalent of well over a marathon every day (and numerous times more than two marathons in a day) and nutrition was vital to keeping that pace.

But recovery was equally important. When I planned the route, I built in about ten rest days for recovery. I absolutely needed to give my body a break for the punishing work I was putting it through, so aligning days off to give talks, do my taxes, and visit friends was a great way to still feel engaged. By the grace of God, I suffered only recoverable injuries along the way.

By day three, a painful IT band issue surfaced that did not go away until more than 1500 miles later. In Oklahoma, I was facing an agonizing leg injury and stopped in the ER one evening to get X-rays. Fortunately, it wasn't broken, but I kept my mileage relatively low for a couple weeks to allow it to heal.

And by the time I got to Virginia, I had so much back pain that I couldn't walk down a small set of stairs at my sister's place. I was able to see a doctor there who helped speed along my recovery, but I extended my stay there for several days in order to recover. I even changed tactics due to my back problem and carried a backpack instead of a jogger for the final four-hundred miles. While I could move faster with the jogger, changing posture did help my back issue. After 3,300 miles with virtually no blisters, I ran the final 400 miles with bloody feet due to the extra weight on them. This is one reason why I advise against using a pack, even one that is relatively lightweight just from my personal experience.

I was mad at my body for slowing down and even more frustrated with the standstill so close to my destination. If I tried to continue too quickly, I was taking a chance on long-term damage to my body, which was definitely not part of my plan. This patience was a necessary part of winning the mental battle.

Take that Selfie

Technology makes it easy to announce your plans with the world. Do it. Either make a separate Facebook, Instagram, or Snapchat account for people who want to follow your adventure or just use your current page to do so. Heck, people have made money off of posting photos of their adventures to social media (more of a perk than a motivating force).

Not only did I have my family and friends who wanted to follow me but all the people I met along the way wanted to stay updated on my progress.

Social media keeps you accountable to your plan while laying the groundwork for an incredible network of people who can help bring attention to your cause. I had good fortune just before I started: a story ran online and was picked up internationally. That led many people to contact me from different parts of the world, and I even received help with translations of requests when emails arrived in foreign languages.

I had people meet me on the road because they saw my story posted online or featured on a local news station. I had people bring me food, offer me a room or shed, or just offer their words of encouragement. It made a huge difference to me that people were invested in my journey, that they were waiting for my daily updates, and that they were pulling for and praying for me.

Adventure Isn't Free

I'm not rich – and certainly wasn't at the time of the run. But I tried to put my resources to wise use. I sold things I didn't need and put that money away for my journey. I left my job in August to start preparing and planning. I lived with family members when I was training, first in New Jersey and then in Arizona, thereby saving money on rent.

I'm a numbers guy by trade so I used that knowledge to develop a budget for what I thought it would cost me for food and shelter. I worked at a running store and had a lot of running gear, but was fortunate to have my prior employer and a friend in the shoe business help by sending me shoes along the way.

I did the best I could to keep money out of the equation entirely by saving enough money so I could simply focus on my mission. I was not running to raise money for a cause, and while friends and family helped with some donations, I did not have a sponsor to foot my bill. Going solo also meant I wouldn't have to pay for a vehicle, gas, or the needs of the crew. The cost can vary greatly depending on how long you plan the trip to take and how often you want to stay in a motel versus being put up on someone's couch or camping out.

Unexpected Lessons

Runners can be obsessed about pace. But don't get in such a rush to get to your destination that you miss the beauty you encounter each day.

I look at a map of the United States today and I get a little thrill to think that I ran across it all alone. My dad, brother, and friends graciously met me at certain points along the way, but if my feet didn't keep going, my journey would have stopped.

Through all of the strain and setbacks, there were days of peace that had me in awe of the surrounding scenery. I vividly recall the landmarks, mile-markers, and people who left their mark on me.

I had strangers shout at me through their open windows as they sped by (probably telling me to get the imagined baby in the jogger off the road) but there were also people who stopped to give me some food and who bought me a beer in the evening. There were people of little means who insisted on giving me a donation. Despite designing a "self-sufficient" journey, I almost daily received some gesture of awe-inspiring kindness that helped me along.

For those days when you get stuck running in the rain, get sick on the side of the highway, or have stomach problems and wish you had a bathroom nearby, you learn to resolve those problems without losing sight of the bigger picture. Only by managing – and moving forward from – the daily issues can you fully celebrate the joys along the way.

Comedown

Remember how you felt after you finished your first big race or fulfilled your goal after months of training? Exhilarated. Empowered. Electric. That feeling fades away.

As with any grand adventure, there is an unsustainable amount of energy focused on the finish. Each of the millions of steps taken to get you from one ocean to the other is for the purpose of the last step. The elation, relief, and multitude of other emotions will sweep over you at once and it takes time to process it all.

I was so concentrated on the thousands of prayer intentions I received and felt connected with each person who reached out to me in some way. The sheer number of messages I received over my journey amazed me and I essentially became so focused on prayer and on taking my next step forward that I rarely thought of anything else. But the focus and goal vanish all at once.

This hit me hard. I had accomplished something amazing – and now it was over. I had no job, no home, no direction. What was I going to do with myself?

I found succor in the thousands of moments along the way that tested my understanding of myself, my country, and what was possible. The end marked a beginning. I was not the same person anymore – and that was a good thing.

A finish line is a symbolic goal, but it cannot be the pinnacle of your life. There must be some higher purpose underpinning your journey. Long after your run, you will continue to encounter experiences that push you to do more than you thought possible. In this way, the race only ends on your terms.

Let's Go!

I recall struggling to find any information on gear, logistics, or training from people who had completed a run across America prior to my own journey in 2011. I soon realized that anyone who did have information to share had different preferences and experiences.

My advice comprises personal anecdotes from a once-in-a-lifetime trek on a zig-zagging itinerary across the country. Thanks to the other authors sharing their stories, you may find some common threads and themes that bind these stories together. Inspiration abounds here.

But no matter how far you think you want to run, you must find your "edge" within. Whether you are tackling your first marathon or a cross-country tour on foot, it takes courage just to start moving. If you want to actually finish, know that you may fall. Embrace that your best-laid plan may fail you.

Only once you get beyond that fear can you devote yourself wholeheartedly. Whatever your calling, the journey waits for *you* to start.

Chapter 11

Milton Miller
Miami to Los Angeles
December 19th, 2010 to April 28th, 2011
Los Angeles to Miami: January 1st to April 17th, 2014

http://100DaysOfMadness.com
http://Facebook.com/100DaysOfMadness
Copyright 2015 by Milton Miller
<milton@100DaysOfMadness.com>
Excerpts from the 3rd Edition
Free download of the full book:
http://100DaysOfMadness.com/100DaysOfMadness.pdf

Departure

The stress during the days leading up to the departure was hard to manage and impossible to ignore, but everything that occupied my mind started to fade away the moment I left the pier. A clear and expected singularity of purpose emerged – a feeling that we rarely experience in modern life. There was now one clearly defined goal: making it to the Atlantic Ocean.

I was afraid. I was deeply afraid. But the moment I found myself alone running east, I felt a sudden sense of calmness. There are many forms of fear, and one that always haunts adventurers during the time leading to the starting moment is the fear of not starting. When I first started telling everyone that I was going to run across the country, I felt uneasy like someone bluffing at a card game. Then very gradually as the training progressed and everything got lined up to start, that fear was finally replaced with the anticipation of actually doing it.

Some of my friends were truly convinced that I had some loose screws in my head. I don't blame them. How many times in your life has one of your close friends told you "Guess what? I've decided to run 3000 miles later this year?"

Of course, most people just didn't take me seriously when I announced my first transcon in 2010, and I don't blame them, but nearly everyone believed me when I said I was going to do it again. Just a couple of friends questioned my resolve and my abilities, if not physical at least mental ones.

By the single reason of being there, puffing along the road, sweating profusely under the above average temperature for New Year's Day, and wondering if I brought everything I need, I felt truly happy. I was happy to be running. During the afternoon a little yellow airplane passed by going east. I like to imagine it was going to Miami, too.

I was happy but was also feeling lonely. I ran the first few miles with some friends, but I couldn't share my fears with anyone. I was challenging those who doubted and leaving behind those who believed.

A bit later in the afternoon, the yellow airplane returned, now going west. I guess he gave up; Miami was too far for him.

Life changes

Looking for the decision and the courage to commit to this, I was no longer satisfied with the idea of focusing on my career and making money. I had been inspired by some people who were chasing their true calling, or at least had the courage to try. I had friends who had fought with the seduction of money, pride, and novelty, but somehow overcame their allure. They broke away from the lockstep march to find the rhythm of their own feet. Nothing seemed scarier to me than the vulnerability and anxieties of seeking one's own identity and breaking out of the inertia that makes us be something we are not.

It is during the hard times that people change the most. Hard times often leave them no choice. People suffer through break-ups, bankruptcies, loss of loved ones, layoffs, divorces, evictions, and as a result they usually reemerge as better people, but in a way they would not have achieved with decision and planning. In 2010 I wasn't in a bad situation at work, financially, or in my relationships. Only one thing was bothering me and that was my body. I was a couch potato and my body shape left no doubt about it. Still, I could have joined a gym, started a diet, or done any of a hundred other things less radical than trying to cross the continent on foot.

Why are you doing it?

If you keep compromising, at some point your life becomes unrecognizable to you. Your life is not defined by what you want; it is defined by what you settle for.

The first time, in 2010, I wanted to change my life. I was tired of being fat, so I was emotionally motivated to do something about it and I took action. The second time, in 2014, the motivation was much simpler: I was missing it. It was that simple. I missed the experience of being on the road, connecting to people, transforming distance in time. Simple, clear, and personal.

Awareness

During the trip, the sky gradually started receiving more of my attention than the ground. Small differences in temperature resulted in big differences in performance. I kept track of the forecast carefully and would try to choose the right clothing and adjust the timing of my runs and walks accordingly. But most of all, I learned to accept the weather happily, no matter how it was, instead of complaining and bitching about it like "normal" people do.

Especially going across Florida and the deserts of New Mexico and Arizona, the land around me would at times seem to be the same for days. It changed, of course, but the change was so gradual. But the sky is telling a story that unfolds every moment. Every sunrise and every sunset were special and remarkable. Every storm was unique, and every day had its own story.

The vegetation along the road changes very gradually, but if you are paying attention you notice the differences from one day to the next, from one valley to another. I spotted many rabbits, saw thousands of deer, and I can remember every kind of thorn nature puts on the way to remind you that the land was not designed to be comfortable to humans.

You see things traveling on foot in ways that are different from any other. In a car you are always isolated from everything, being a passive observer in your own familiar compartment. On a motorcycle you are part of the environment and in contact with it all. The sense of presence on the road is overwhelming, but you are still going too fast to notice most things.

You see details while walking or running, but most of all you witness how life flows around you all the time. You can observe the happy kids in the back seats of SUV's going for the Sunday game. You see the stressed and unhappy suburbanites behind the wheel on weekdays, the beer drinking cowboys coming back from a hunting trip, and the profoundly distracted drivers looking at their cell phones while driving.

You always see plenty of animal life. Birds that you never noticed before, wild animals that run away when they sense your presence nearby, deer crossing the road in gorgeous long leaps, and hawks watching you curiously from the top of a pole without making any movement.

For years I have been on many of these roads without ever noticing any of it, thinking that everything between one city and another was a vast portion of nothingness. I thought that all the action worth seeing was in the city. I was blind to the diverse and interesting spectacle of life that happens everywhere.

The best of all

When I am asked about the best or most beautiful moment of this trip, I have a hard time answering. Not because I don't know what it is, but because it is difficult to give the answer without some long explanations and many details. I will attempt to give that answer now.

I experienced a deep happiness out of making distance turn into time. Time during which I learned to understand the amazing variety of feelings and experiences of running and the rich language my body uses to tell me what is going on with it. I learned to talk with nature, listen to the birds, and to embrace the weather without cursing it. I learned to appreciate every meal because sometimes I just didn't have any. I learned to transform fear into patience and patience into confidence. Most of all, I learned that to reach a very distant destination, you need to master your mind more than your strength.

During the months I spent on the road, I witnessed some moments of extreme beauty. Like the day I started my run earlier than usual, around 5:30 am, when it was still pitch dark. I was leaving a very small town and in just about 20 minutes I was traveling along a country road in the darkness, but the stars were bright enough to see the contour of the road so I didn't use my flashlight. While running, I saw a spectacle of several meteorites entering the atmosphere in quick succession. Their bright and fast lines in the sky were hypnotic and the darkness around me made them even more so. Moments like that are gone faster than you can think about them, and handheld cameras cannot capture their magic. So my memory will be the only one in charge of saving them for the future.

I felt in perfect balance with the world around me, like how I imagine the pioneers traveling to the west on horseback and on foot must have felt. Like them I was not in a situation in any way undefined or permanent. I had a clear goal: Reach the ocean.

The best moment of all was when I looked around and saw that I was not alone.

Nearly every day I met people that offered help, asked if I needed anything. Water? Food? Some gave me supplies, some gave me money, some offered rides. A gentleman in Florida offered me a bicycle. A lady who owns a campground offered me a place to camp for free. An old man that lives beside the road in Texas gave me beer. Hundreds of encounters like those. The displays of generosity and support I had along the way were so many and so intense at times that I never felt alone very long, nor did I fear being alone. I had plenty of time to ponder about the meaning of loneliness. Now I believe that loneliness is a state of mind that can happen regardless of distance or isolation. It is a void that the presence of people around you will not fill up.

Enjoy the silence

There are two kinds of people who don't say much: those who are quiet and those who talk a lot. I did a small experiment by talking less for a couple of days. Much less. While not talking all the time, for the first time I could listen to the voice and internal conversations in my mind. We don't listen very well most of our adult lives. We only listen long enough to determine if the speaker's ideas match our own. And when they do not, we stop listening and our minds rush to construct an argument against what we believe the opposing opinion to be. The same when talking to myself! The mind races with thousands of ideas and little conversations, and only when you notice that can you silence those as well. By not talking much, I give myself permission to listen more, to not attack other's ideas even when I don't agree with them. By listening fully, the speaker also feels free to fully speak their idea or position without fear of rebuttal in a way that I could not have imagined.

It was quite disturbing to notice how much chatter kept going on in my head after everyone stopped talking. Being more silent on the outside allowed me to notice how noisy I am on the inside. Drowning down this chatter will probably take a long time and may become one of the most rewarding changes in my life.

Throughout my whole life, I've made a concerted effort to give people a fair shake and understand different points of view because I felt that everyone had something valuable to offer, but it turns out most of what they had to offer was complete nonsense. I was recently struck by the grim realization that I squandered a significant portion of my life listening to everyone's bullshit. Until this point, I regarded my willingness to hear out the opinions of others as a worthwhile quality, and the result is that I probably wasted a few years of my existence being open to people's half-formed thoughts, asinine suggestions, and pointless stories.

So from now on you won't catch me pissing away my finite time on earth listening to grossly uninformed political opinions, nonsense about celebrity couples, how good or bad certain cars are, and why a particular sports team might have a chance this year. You won't retain my attention by talking about the weather or how bad allergy season is going to be. I will no longer be talking about the current news that I believe is pointless anyway, or reviews of products I have no intention to have.

Pain is a language

Pain is a feeling triggered in the nervous system. Pain may be sharp or dull. It may come and go, or it may be constant. You may feel pain in one area of your body, such as your back, abdomen, or chest, or you may feel pain all over, such as when your muscles ache from the flu. Pain is a part of the body's defense system, producing a reflexive retraction from the painful stimulus, and protects the affected body part while it heals, and helps avoid that harmful situation in the future. It is an important part of animal life, vital to healthy survival. Without pain, you might seriously hurt yourself without knowing it, or you might not realize you have a medical problem that needs treatment. Once you take care of the problem, pain usually goes away.

There is no such thing as one kind of pain. Pain is not something that is either there or it isn't. Pain is a language, a full spectrum of physiological information, full of nuances and details. When we resist pain and try to ignore it, we miss the many layers and insights being expressed. Pain is one of the voices of your body. Pain defines the current limits and edges of strain and injury. Some painful sensations tell us to stop, while some others are saying that muscles are being worked in ways they weren't used to, and that is great, so proceed carefully.

The body has many levels of awareness and self-consciousness. Sharp pain usually means the brain is trying to protect some injured part of the body to prevent further damage. At the same time, dull or gradual pain usually means a part of the body has been exercised and will grow and develop, but in our "pain- free culture" we tend to avoid that good kind of pain as well. You will grow and improve only when you learn to embrace the pain and appreciate it for what it really means.

During the last century, we seem to have confused comfort with happiness, while quite the opposite is true. Running teaches you that there is a difference between being tired after working hard and feeling lousy. Product marketing and advertising all talk about "making it easier" or more convenient. A life driven by consumption is dull, predictable, and boring. Challenging your body to the point of exhaustion makes it more aware and heightens the senses.

How to do it

Doing this takes total commitment. As soon as you make the decision to do it, tell everyone. Tell your Facebook friends, your co-workers, your running club, put a website on the air, tell your family, and tell your real-life friends. After telling everyone, you will have no choice.

Of all the challenges, all the difficulties, and all the things that will get in the way, the danger of not starting is the most significant. The day you start you will actually feel relieved for finally being on the road and not having to prepare for it anymore.

A winter transcon has its own challenges. The running part is usually easier as the temperatures will be nicer. But camping during winter is much more complicated than during summer. Choosing the right camping gear, especially if backpacking, is an art. Besides having an excellent tent and sleeping bag, I recommend an inflatable and ultra-light air mattress, a couple of emergency blankets (those aluminum foil ones), and a good waterproof running jacket. If you want to brush your teeth in the morning, don't leave the toothbrush outside the tent or it will be frozen solid during winter months. Instead, keep it inside the sleeping bag with you, along with all clothes.

There are many methods and training systems. All of them are partially right and partially wrong, but some of them can be useful to you. And everyone will have an opinion on how you should do things. The secret is to choose the methods you believe in and stick to them.

The worst kind of vice is advice, so be patient with those who give it (like I am doing in this book and trust your own instincts.

As much as possible, avoid doing anything new during the run. If you will be camping, then start camping before the run. If you will be eating certain foods, start doing that early as well. If you will wear certain clothes, then start wearing them weeks before the run.

I suggest you spend an entire month before the run living in conditions at least partially similar to what you will encounter on the road. Camp in your own backyard. Wear the same kind of clothes you will wear on the road. Eat the same things. All this will give you opportunities to adapt and to discover any problems or shortcomings that you can avoid, and still with time to make corrections to the plan.

If you will have a stroller, or a support vehicle, you will be able to use regular camping gear. But if you run with a backpack then you will need space-age, expensive gear used in rock climbing and other extreme sports. Every ounce is important when you have to carry it on your back. So do your research carefully and remember that you will get what you pay for.

A transcontinental run is an emotional roller coaster. You will feel every emotion there is, and you will feel them intensified by the physical effort, by loneliness, and by discomfort. Every time you feel bad, check all your gear. The ritual will calm you down and relax you. I guess that is what they do in the military. They know a soldier will be under tremendous stress, so they make him check all his gear. Repeating a ritual calms him down and helps him feel in control of his world.

Nothing pays off more than learning how to keep your feet free of blisters, relaxing at regular intervals, and sleeping as much as possible. Foot powder, good socks, and great camping gear are as important as your choice of running shoes.

In West Texas, New Mexico and Arizona I also switched sometimes from running with the regular running shoes to running in Huaraches instead. I improvised them using my flip-flops with an additional string from some old running shoes. It works very well in high temperatures as it keeps the feet cool and eliminates the occurrence of blisters completely.

Keep your mind occupied. Have enough music and audiobooks on your music player or phone to keep you listening for most of the day every day of your journey. Otherwise, you will be pestering your friends over the phone too often.

You will find hundreds of fences, gates, and walls along the way. Learning to choose when to cross, when to jump, and when to walk around is a skill you will develop. Lots of territory shown on the maps as public land are operated as private property, usually by energy companies, and you will have to deal with it. On each transcon, I had several encounters with private security (most of them friendly), had to jump hundreds of gates and fences, and had to find my way around a few broken bridges or otherwise unsafe locations.

Always run on the left side of the road, facing traffic. Use bike trails and sidewalks when possible. But if you need to be on the road, take the left side. Every time. No exceptions. Ever!

You will often hear on the news that another biker or runner got hit by a car he never saw coming. I don't trust drivers. I always look at the incoming traffic and I am always ready to jump out of the way.

Learn to spend your time in the most fun and relaxed way possible. A day running should be a day of fun. Otherwise, being on the road for months would be hell. There will be a lot of pain, but there is no need for suffering.

It is more important, and urgent, to learn how to have fun than to learn how to run faster or longer. If you are having a good time, everything else can be figured out as you go. But if you are feeling miserable, you won't have any creative energy or capacity to perceive the opportunities and good will around you. Being miserable, you also won't be able to focus on the task at hand each day, be that to improve your performance or anything else you choose to do.

Training

I put my focus on training my mind from the very beginning. By training my mind, I would be able to endure the long duration of a gruesome effort without quitting. Another benefit is that I would develop skills and capacities that would change my lifestyle afterwards.

Most people run to punish themselves, or at least to burn the calories after they ate too much. They have too many beers, or feel guilty about that bread pudding, and they go for a run. That is a very bad idea because it associates running with punishment.

It is also a bad idea because the sequence is all wrong. If they eat first, they process that food while sedentary, so some of it becomes fat. Next they run and then recover from the run. But the body doesn't recover properly and doesn't build as much muscle as it should, because now they don't want to eat properly after the run.

Instead, run or do any kind of exercise you like, as much as you can. With no guilt at all. Have as much fun as possible with it. Then you will be very hungry. Now eat whatever you want, even the bread pudding. Have beer. Now the body will recover from the run with food in the system.

In "normal" running, it is normal to eat a little or nothing significant before a run. Drinking water before is also common. But for the most part, runners drink a little bit of water during their runs and a lot after to recover. They also wait to eat after the run.

I couldn't do any of it while running across the country. From my first days of training, I always made sure I was drinking plenty of water before and after, but most of all during my runs. It felt weird at first, but to be honest, it felt weird to run at all in the beginning.

I also got used to dividing my meals in several small parts and eating while on the move. I would literally stop by a Burger King or pizza joint and order a big burger or a small pizza and eat while walking and jogging for hours. I would just make sure I ate very slowly. People looked at me really weird when I jogged nearby holding a pizza or a Big Mac in my hand and a big bottle of water in the other.

Short runs usually start when the body is relaxed. Most people do their runs early in the morning, right after waking up, so they are always starting their runs rested. Then they run until they feel tired, whatever distance it used to be for them, and the run ends. That is good training for the body, but it is not good training for the mind. You are telling your mind, "Run while rested, then stop when tired."

So I trained as tired as I could be. I would go out and dance or do whatever physical work I had to do around the house as late as possible in the evening. Then when I felt very tired, usually already sleepy, I would go out for a run. Most of my training for both transcons happened at night while everybody else was asleep.

I also made sure that I never stopped when I felt exhausted. I kept pushing ahead, even if I had to just walk. To make sure I didn't have any alternative, I would always run away from home for half of the goal distance for that day, without any money so I couldn't take a cab or bus on the way back if I decided to. This way I forced myself to walk back no matter how tired, in pain, or sleepy I was.

I was telling my mind, "Run or walk until the goal is reached, not an inch less."

Running long distances is like driving in hill country. You go through highs and lows constantly. Any experienced runner knows quite well the feeling of being tired, several miles into a race or training, and then feeling light and fresh again. That is when they push it hard again, stopping only when they feel really exhausted.

I did the exact opposite. If I was feeling at the bottom of my energy level, I would usually keep pushing forward until I experienced the next runner's high. Then I would stop! Because I wanted to tell my mind that being exhausted is not the reason to stop. Again, this is all about training the mind, not the body.

There is no rule written stating how fast you must run at any given time. So, run fast when you feel like it, jog easy when necessary, walk slow to keep moving forward. But no matter how slow you go, always look like you are running.

The reason for it is that your body has great muscle memory of how to walk. It has been doing it for decades. So if you get yourself into a pattern of motion similar to walking, that is what your body will fall into, especially when tired. But if you move as if you were jogging, even at a walking speed, you will be pushing your body into a different motion pattern which, very gradually, transforms itself into running.

Backpack

I decided to do the second run with a small backpack instead of a jogging stroller, like I did the first time. Even though I trained with the backpack for weeks, I couldn't tell with certainty if my back would hold up well under the extra stress. I had a Plan B: If my back couldn't handle it I would buy another jogging stroller and continue the old way. But I was really happy by the third day. I felt like I made the right decision and chose the best equipment.

Traveling with a stroller versus a backpack is a very different experience. A stroller required constant maneuvering around obstacles like potholes, curbs, gravel, and narrow spaces. None of those are problems for a man walking. I was using railroad tracks, narrow trails, irregular sidewalks, and paths parallel to the roads that would be very uncomfortable to push a stroller through, but just fine for walking. With a stroller, you oftentimes have to stay on the road, literally, where you are much more exposed to traffic. With the backpack, I used service "roads" that go along fences and utility lines, and sometimes I could even shortcut through paths that with a stroller I would have to go all the way around.

Camping

Once a location has been chosen, remove branches, pinecones, rocks, and any pointy or sharp branches or weeds from where you will place the tent. Cover the area with the house wrap. Raise the tent, put the gear inside, and close it! That avoids mosquitoes and spiders moving in before you do. Make sure the lines are all tight. If you expect rain, don't leave the house wrap hanging freely on the sides – fold it down under the tent so it won't collect water. If the weather is fine, I use the house wrap to cover the ground, but if it is going to rain, then the house wrap goes inside to form a "bathtub." Keep absolutely everything inside the screen, unless you like to find spiders, ants, and ticks inside your gear. Take the sleeping bag out of its compression bag soon and let it breathe. Sleeping bags always take on moisture, so the longer they air out, the better.

Tip: You get to a town and all of the hotels are full or too expensive. You are willing to camp but it's either too cold or heavy rain is coming. Solution: Rent a U-Haul van. Park it at some quiet place nearby and camp inside. You can lock the van from the inside. Return it in the morning and all you pay is $19.95 plus tax.

Another tip: You can take a shower at the YMCA, at most truck stops, at some gyms, and even at the firehouses if you ask them. House wrap is the best camping gear ever created!

I use house wrap to cover the ground before setting up camp. It protects the tent from dirt and protects the air mattress from thorns and sharp rocks. It also helps keep everything clean and organized, and for a guy with moderate OCD like me, keeping the camp clean is a must.

I also use the same house wrap, folded three or four times, to cover the ground when I want to lay down my backpack and gear to rest for any reason. This helps keep every piece of gear and clothing clean. When I want to sit down on a rock, cold bench, or on the rocky ground, the house wrap makes a good clean surface to sit on. House wrap is not very soft, and it feels a little brittle. At first I thought that would be a downside, but instead it is a great advantage, because once you fold it, it "remembers" the creases and you can fold it again in the same patterns effortlessly, even in strong winds. Try folding anything in the wind and you'll find it a frustrating experience, except house wrap. It nearly folds itself! I prefer to clean it with a rag because machine washing would make it too soft, and then it wouldn't fold as easy as it does now. It doesn't fray a lot, and it doesn't rip easily. It is also waterproof, and it helps isolate from the cold.

Jumping fences can be a pain in the ass. Literally. It can be a dangerous operation. But if you fold the house wrap 3 times and lay it on the ground, you can lie down and simply slide under the fence, and then pull the house wrap with the gear to the other side. It is so easy!

I keep it folded tight and hold it on the underside of my backpack with elastic cords. I can take it out and put it back without needing to take the backpack out. This way it also protects the bottom of the backpack if I put it on the ground for a moment. So even when I don't take it out and unfold it, the piece of house wrap is there helping out.

Mountains

In the face of adversity, we never step up to our ideals. We step down to our training. So, you better train right! I was about three days from El Paso, Texas, and standing right in front of me were the Guadalupe Mountains. They are more than eight thousand feet of elevation, but I only had to be concerned with about six thousand feet of its mountain pass on RT-62. I was at Salt Flat, which is nearly four thousand feet high, so it shouldn't be too hard.

The problem is that yesterday was the hardest day of this transcon! Last night the temperature dropped to around 20 degrees, and Salt Flat is... well... flat! There is nothing taller than a car in this desert and the sand here is as fine as sugar. By the end of the afternoon I couldn't find anything suitable to camp beside to protect me from the wind, so I ventured into the desert a couple hundred yards and chose two little hills, about as high as I am tall, and prepared to camp between them.

I didn't have anything to eat because I ran out of food in the morning, and the only store in Salt Flat where I could buy food was closed that day. The ground was all sand, and there were no rocks nearby that I could use to anchor the corners of the tent, so the sides were going to be exposed to the wind. Even worse, the wind was picking up, bringing with it lots of sand that was covering everything: the bag, the gear, the tent, and myself. I set up camp as fast as I could and got inside. I didn't even care to try to clean myself up or remove any clothes. When I sat down, I could feel and see that even the inside floor of the tent was already covered with sand. For a few hours I tried to sleep with my whole body and my head inside the sleeping bag. I cuddled my iPhone and iPad inside the sleeping bag with me to protect them from the fine sand.

The strong winds made some of the lines snap out of the stakes and the tent collapsed. Now I was wrapped with a flapping, noisy, chaotic tent, space blankets, gear everywhere, and several pounds of sand in a kind of high-tech sand and plastic burrito. It was terribly cold, dirty, and noisy. Well, I thought, it could be worse: I could be in the middle of a sandstorm.

That's when the sandstorm began...

Around 4am, tired and sleepy, shaking from the cold and thirst, I packed everything the best I could and went back to the road, nearly two hours before sunrise. I actually never even saw the sun all day because it was overcast, and as I kept going up the mountain the temperature never went above 25 degrees (-4 Celsius). At least the strong winds were gone and there was no significant windchill.

It took me six hours to reach the ranger station at the top, and another 6 hours to come down on the other side low enough that the ground was not covered in ice and I could find a good place to camp.

All the way I took great photographs and really enjoyed every minute. Knowing that I was crossing an important milestone made it easier, if not for my body, at least in my mind. I left behind the hardships and challenges of a tough territory that would test my patience and my resolve.

The last day

I had the impression that there would be an emotional buildup at the very end, that I would be feeling like I was about to explode with emotion, but that didn't happen. Instead what I felt was a very deep sense of calmness, of peacefulness. During the last few days, that feeling was so present I could taste it, I could feel it like the sound of water running down a stream that you can't see, but you feel its presence. I felt so profoundly happy and peaceful and now I think it's a much more durable state of mind.

I always asked myself, since I was a boy, what the best day of my life would be like. As time went by and I had so many great experiences, the idea of a "best" day was always confusing. Many days of my life could have been called the best day, and after having many of those I started calling them "another best day." While preparing for my second transcon, I thought another best day would be when I finally started and left Los Angeles. Instead, the start was a little improvised, and not the nice and smooth experience I wished it to be. Yet, I was happy with it. Crossing major milestones, like the Guadalupe Pass, or passing the half-way mark were good occasions and had plenty of significance, but in some ways they were days like any other, with problems to solve, challenges, and progress. But I still believed (or hoped) that the last day would somehow be special.

Now looking back I think there was a best day of all. There was one moment that divided my experience and changed everything. That day was during January 2011, during my first transcon. I was on the road for about 3 weeks, still in Florida but approaching Alabama. My body was already getting adapted to the routine of running and walking every day. I lost a significant amount of weight during training and since I left Miami, and my pace was improving. One day late in the afternoon, exhausted by the run, feeling cold and hungry, tired and sleepy, my legs burning, I believe the conditions were ready. Something important happened for the very first time.

I knew it! I had the clear realization that I was going to do the entire thing. Not just rationally, now I knew deep inside my heart that nothing would stop me. I was going to keep going until I saw the ocean. I knew I would do it or I would die trying! From that instant on there was only one way back home, and that way had to be through Los Angeles.

I cried, I cried of happiness, of some heavy and intense happiness that I never felt before and it came from the depths of my being, stronger than all my demons and ghosts that had been boiling for years in the inferno of my old memories, stronger than anything else I ever felt. I started screaming, a loud yell of defiance! Screaming expelled out of me not just sound but also bad memories, regrets, anger, disappointments, guilt, and residual drama. The sound was loud and long enough to carry out all my doubts and melancholy. It was a warrior cry, a challenge, the pure sound of uncensored happiness.

That state of mind never ended. It is the best because somehow it stayed with me and I can still feel it. It's a drug that keeps trickling into my blood every minute of my life. When all the tears and sweat came out, when the screams were so strong that snot and spit flew out in the air carrying the last bits of my doubts and regrets, feelings now alien to my body, I knew I could never again be the same man who left Miami. On the morning of April 17th, 2014, I started early from Fort Lauderdale and in the afternoon Joseph Mercogliano arrived to run the rest of the way with me. Joe covered the last 10 miles with me. We had amazing conversations and occasional beers along the way, and at this point I was so exhausted and beat up that any conversation, any pause, any distraction was a great help. Having people to run along is great any time, but that last day was special. By the time we got to Venetian Causeway it became a great party, with some 30+ hashers joining us, taking pictures, drinking beers, and celebrating.

I could barely hold a thought in my head. I felt free and relaxed, happy and hopeful, like only a free man can feel. Too many friends to list their names here. Also, I recollect things through a cloud of exhaustion. I have to see the pictures to know who was there. The only part I can remember clearly is how I felt. I remember the moment it all turned silent. All the chatter outside was ignored, and all the chatter inside my own head became quiet as well.

Passing by the New World Symphony, I saw they were playing some old movie in the outside projector, but I don't remember how it sounded, the world was silent around me. There were cars, there were tourists everywhere, but my mind was silent. I saw some friends running along. Joe was there, I was surrounded by love, surrounded by friends.

So that was it now. I could see it a couple hundred yards ahead of me. I knew people were cheering me along the streets and I think I waved at them, but I can't remember doing it. I could feel the smell of the ocean and the cool breeze touching my skin. Most of all, I could sense its proximity.

As I ran that last mile – easy, light, and fast – feeling more like flying than running, I had to clear my eyes every few moments as tears kept coming out. I was feeling perfectly well. Never felt better in my entire life. There was nothing else I needed to feel happy.

What else could a man want than to see the stars clearly at night, watch the sunset, and listen to the sounds of forests and deserts, and for about a hundred days have just one goal in mind, and finally reach it during a beautiful evening, surrounded by friends? What kind of life would be better than having the freedom and opportunity to be right there, at that moment? For those last few seconds, there was nothing in my mind other than pure satisfaction. The Atlantic Ocean finally there in front of me. And I ran for it…

In the dark, in silence, I was at peace.

Chapter 12

Chris Finill and Steve Pope from England
17th August to 5th November 2011. 79 days and 22 hours
Half Moon Bay, CA to Brighton Beach, Brooklyn, New York

THE TRIP

By 2011 I had run competitively for 35 years and Steve for 25. We were looking for a challenge beyond conventional ultras and had both been inspired three years earlier by reading Jim Shapiro's classic book 'Meditations from the Breakdown Lane' - his epic account of his own run across the US in the early eighties.

We were supported in our attempt all the way across by my wife, Julia who drove the support vehicle and by Ben Southern, a family friend who made a full-length documentary covering the entire trip (Youtube: "The 3,000 mile Men"). My daughter, Joanna joined us for the intense weeks into Nevada and Tom, my eldest son was on board from Pennsylvania for the last 5 days.

Our aim was simple: to cross the continent on foot from coast to coast stepping out of the Pacific, drying our toes on the beach and within 80 days to dive headlong into the Atlantic. The twist was to get there in time to run the 2011 edition of the NYC Marathon.

Actually, *doing* all this proved more complicated……....here are a few of the memorable moments.

CALIFORNIA!!!!!!

So, we were finally here at the start - sitting on the dunes at Half Moon Bay, just south of San Francisco, playing up our eccentric Englishman credentials for all we were worth as we chatted to Julia Reis, the friendly reporter from the Half Moon Bay Review who was covering our story. We chose Half Moon Bay as the starting point because we saw it on the map and liked the name.

Many times during long training runs, I'd imagine what it would be like to start our run. I'd always pictured a 'Baywatch' style backdrop of hot sandy beaches populated by scantily clad women. Somewhere in the background a radio would be playing Good Vibrations……... I couldn't remember visualising a grey freezing sea, nor a windswept beach whose only visitors were a few hardy walkers wrapped up in blankets. This was more like Bay City than Baywatch.

Once we started running however, the excitement of the adventure really came through. With grins as wide as the Golden Gate Bridge, we exited the Pacific reaching the beach road on our second attempt (early navigational error) and as the blacktop moved to our command under our shuffling stride we inched our way relentlessly Eastwards. It felt so easy and of course it was maybe because we had only gone a mile.

Running down a quiet lakeside road in the early evening sunshine, we locked into a pace of slightly over 6 miles per hour, a speed which would be our fallback pace for the next 79 days - fast enough to feel natural but, more importantly, slow enough to allow us the feeling that we were placing our feet on the road rather than landing on it- vital in keeping the dismal prospect of injury at bay.

A group of Californian cyclists, having finished their day jobs were now sporting their lycra, time trailing on expensive looking carbon fibre machines. Watching them, we failed to notice a young Chinese runner who silently ran past us. This proved to be the only time in the 3,000 miles that we were overtaken by another runner. We laughed as we speculated on what must have been going through his mind - probably the feeling of satisfaction that every runner experiences when overtaking another. In reality he was probably a pretty average runner and every reflex in my body wanted to blow him away with a flourish of sub six-minute miles - after all we were fresh, fit and faintly insulted by this tepid challenge. Instead, a different approach was needed. Surrendering our egos, we simply let him pull away into the distance consenting to his informal victory.

We had done the right thing. We had backed off to preserve and protect our bodies, not charged along ill-disciplined or recklessly. This fleeting but significant moment set the tone for the whole run - backing off rather than being aggressive in our running, trying not to mortgage the following day's distance by overexerting today and staying out of the Red Zone - a phrase passed on to me by Ed Roshitsh, a San Franciscan I had befriended on Facebook. Ed had failed in his trans USA attempt earlier in the year and as a single piece of advice had offered at all costs, "*stay out of the Red Zone*". Photographs of his swollen lower leg published on his Facebook page were testimony to the wisdom of this catchphrase.

If Day 1 had heralded the start of our run and Day 2 brought a sense of true departure, then Day 3 provided a watershed of a less welcome kind.

NEWS FROM HOME

An early phone call from Tom, back in England at the time, confirmed that my mother had died earlier that morning. This had been somewhat expected as she was 91 and had been in failing health for some time. I had realised two years before this that my mother dying either in the buildup to the run or actually during it was a possibility. She, the most unassuming person in the world, would never have wanted her death or funeral to get in the way of anyone else's plans. Although this was a super convenient way of looking at things it was actually true. Moreover, calling off or postponing the run would have been unthinkable. On the one hand this 'carry on regardless' attitude felt ruthless but on the other, pulling out would represent a bitter memorial to her memory. In the run up to the trip I had on a few occasions mentioned the trip to her and, in her dotage, she had beautifully failed to grasp the nature or scope of the challenge. Her response was usually littered with comments like "Ooh that's nice dear" OR "good heavens, why do you want to do that?" So now she was gone and the possibility of returning triumphantly and explaining all to her would never be. There is a part of every child that, regardless of age, yearns to please their parents. Alas, this was one outcome that would never come to pass.

And so back to the road, the master that summoned us to work and measured our self-esteem in miles and hours.

DESERT

With Yosemite behind us we were hugely relieved to make it through the searing Nevada heat, at its most testing between Tonopah and Ely - a stretch as physically and logistically demanding as anything we were to face. However, 16 days in as we approached Utah my leg started hurting. A stop in Delta after two days of walking allowed a referral to a physio. He diagnosed a stress fracture of the lower left tibia. In disbelief a second opinion was sought with the same result - a stress fracture of the lower left tibia….which was only going to get worse if I continued to run on it. My response of utter denial meant that I took one day off running completely in what looked like an irrational or hopeless attempt to allow healing. How could it possibly be a stress fracture? - I had been planning this trip for three years?!!

Maybe the diagnosis was wrong as walking 35 miles per day for several more days seemed to ease the 'fracture' - what I do know for certain is that while the 'recovery' took place my body steered all its healing power towards my leg. My hair, beard and nails stopped growing as if all resources were channeled into fixing the problem. It worked and the Delta physio, in a subsequent conversation, said I had 'dodged a bullet.' Had I been compelled to stop my run at that stage I would obviously have helped Steve with his solo attempt but my failure would have been an incredibly difficult pill to swallow. Thankfully, such a situation never arose.

COLORADO

Saturday 24th September, Steve's 45th birthday - we're on an isolated section of Highway 14 (which sections of this aren't?!) in Colorado heading towards Sterling. In the distance walking towards us was Chuck, a hobo making his way West. At this stage Steve and I had made it through the Rockies and therefore had over 1,000 miles under our belts. As Chuck was the only true pedestrian we had seen since the Pacific we took the chance to engage in conversation. We were feeling good about how far we had come but it transpired that Chuck was walking from New York to

California via the Dakotas - he had easily gone double our distance which was a bit of a blow……..made worse by the fact that he had walked from California to get to New York in the first place - therefore outdoing us by a comfortable 4,000 miles. Strangely, he was being followed by two goats which we assumed were his. This was disproved when we parted company - the goats, instead of continuing with Chuck heading West crossed the road and followed us East. This was a huge distraction as we couldn't shake them off and their lane discipline was tricky to deal with as they weaved, surged and dropped back as if they were Kenyans ganging up on us Ethiopians in the Olympic 10,000-meter final.

After five miles we were desperate to lose them and, passing farm buildings, coaxed them into following us up to a guy with a massive farm truck. We asked him if he owned them and he confirmed that he did, loaded them both on board and drove off at speed - we were less than convinced that they were his but the episode proved to be our get out of jail card for a difficult situation.

The next day we called in at a diner which like so many others had a couple of tables where one could sit with a cup of coffee and a doughnut. A group of retired men sat on one table whilst another put in their order at the counter. They were clearly old friends and the banter flowed between them:

"A man could die back here waiting for a coffee!" Called out the eldest of them from the table.
To which the fellow buying the drinks brilliantly replied:
"If I'd thought of that I'd have waited a bit longer!"

Laughing along, we asked to join them and spent some pleasant moments chewing the fat. These times were one of the things that made the trip for us. We always felt that having a 'purpose' to our being there - no matter how ephemeral or bizarre - gave us more of a lead into people's lives than if we were just travelling around. The guys insisted on giving us $25 towards our parallel quest to raise money for 'Help for Heroes', a UK charity similar to the Wounded Warrior Project. None of them was wealthy, they just summed up the generosity of the average small town American.

INTO THE MIDWEST

Through Nebraska we plodded on along 92 East, noticing how things were starting to change as we headed East. The Rockies seemed to be more than just a physical dividing line. West of the mountains it seemed to be the law that all households must have at least half a dozen items of junk in their front gardens including a gently-rotting vehicle. Once you get East of the dividing Range however, everything is tidied up and although you can leave your child's bike outside with no worries about it being stolen, things in general are much tidier.

Cars also started to get smaller as we ran East. Giant pick-up trucks were slowly replaced with smaller and often European cars. There were fewer houses that had been abandoned and left to fall down. Everything was becoming somehow less wild and frontier-like. Steve and I missed the West as we felt a bond with it, ourselves being also quite run down and gradually falling apart.

Navigation was becoming slightly trickier, simply because there were more roads. Rather than the Google Maps printout simply telling us to "Stay on this road for 142 miles," we had to keep our wits about us more.

Julia was absolutely invaluable here, checking our route against her Sat Nav and constantly looking for shortcuts that would save us a mile here and there. Sometimes in towns she would drive ahead and stop at intersections that might not be well marked. The result was that in 3,100 miles of running, we only went a few hundred yards out of our way

INDIANA

Monday 17th October - Route 30. On yet another beautiful sunny morning, through Chicago Heights, we crossed from Illinois into Indiana. The border sign proudly announced that not only was the State proud to be 'The crossroads of America' but also 'Lincoln's Boyhood Home'. State pride seemed downgraded from Illinois which had previously weighed in with a more upbeat and bullish 'Land of Lincoln'

"I really need a new pair of running shoes" I declared.

"We haven't seen a running shop in 1,800 miles and we're not going to see one now are we?" Steve replied dismissively. "You'll have to go to somewhere like Walmart and get some big luminous basketball boots with flashing lights." He then added, "You can go in the car one evening whilst I relax in the motel. I'm not detouring one inch from our route."

Five minutes later we passed a running shop.

Steve and I, both being UK size 9, had traded running shoes all the way across as a means of minimising the risk of injury. That said, the collective stock was becoming knackered and we seized this opportunity to stop at Fleetfeet Sports in Schererville - effectively running into the store as if it were a pit stop in a Grand Prix albeit at a less frantic pace. Misty Renee, a serious runner herself, ran the shop and took a keen interest in our story to the extent that she was kind enough to allow each of us a free pair of running shoes. This was another example of the generosity of spirit extended to us throughout our journey across.

SUPPORT FROM THE SOUTH

Early on the morning of Tuesday 25th October we met Jim McCord in Ohio close to the Pennsylvania border. He had journeyed up from Kentucky to support us. He ran with us for a few miles close toward the Pennsylvania border. Running with him we found a working watch and a screwdriver. There is a mathematics, a law of averages and pattern to the certainty with which one comes across assorted crap and general rubbish on a run of this magnitude - in our case several wrenches, a discarded calculator, a saw, over $10 in cash and (most scary of all) a beautiful, sharp, gleaming carving knife just outside the gates of an Illinois Elementary School.

As we took a break with Jim in a coffee shop complete with Redhatters on the next table, he gave us the benefit of his experience of crossing successfully in 2002. Speaking to Steve and I he made the point that we actually had it easy - we were, as we had to be, completely focused on the run whereas Julia and Ben, in their supporting role had to hang around, kill time and organise the mundane day to day aspects of the run. Never a truer word spoken.

BACK OF THE DINOSAUR

October 26th saw us crossing into Pennsylvania and the border sign had been reduced to a small green placard dangling from a lamppost!

We would now face some real hills for the first time since the Rockies. The small undulations that we had first noticed in Ohio had hinted that our climbing ability would shortly be tested again.

One passing local cheerfully described the state's roads as being 'like the back of a dinosaur!' which did not exactly help our morale.

As we approached the end of our run (it seems crazy but this mode of thought gained currency about 400 miles from New York) there was no hiding from the clock. Each and every day we must cover our 40 miles in order to finish in time for the New York Marathon. There are insistent landmarks to be passed - 20 miles by noon is good, less than that by 1pm and we know that we must get our skates on. It is getting dark earlier now, so we aim to be off the road by 5.30pm - a time portrayed to us on bright days by our elongating shadows ushering us East as we ran.

For days the sensible young man who earnestly read the weather forecast had been scaring me each morning with threats of an imminent cold snap and possibly even some unseasonably early October snow. I could tell by his voice that his concern for us was genuine and he probably helped old ladies across the road and volunteered at the local Scout Group. His warnings became ever more dire and on October 29th, as we ran through Clearfield, the weather had obviously decided to go along with the nice young man.

We started off with a cold grey sky and things 'progressed' from there. We climbed steadily and before long, small flakes began to fall and the thick dark sky assured us that there was plenty more where they came from. Soon we were in driving sleet and being soaked by every passing vehicle. Most tried their best not to but couldn't really help it. The breakdown lane where we were running rapidly turned into a skating rink as the layer of hail, snow and mush began to freeze. We started to slip and slide. The day turned into a battle to stay upright and avoid freezing ourselves.

The weather had played a huge part in our trip. It was a unifying force, giving us something new to complain about each day, something we could both share by condemning our collective misfortune. A family was building a snowman so we stopped to take a photograph before passing through the aptly named Snow Shoe.

Mid-afternoon we spotted a roadside bar which didn't look too welcoming from the outside, but we were past caring. We just wanted to be inside and warm for a few minutes. Things didn't immediately improve when our question asking if they did coffee was met with a shake of the head. As we had discovered on so many previous occasions in this country, a bit of banter soon brought out the best in Brenda, the owner, and she ended up making us coffee with two large plates of chips. We had a good laugh with her and a couple of locals who insisted that they were 'Rednecks and proud of it.'

Apparently, the term only has negative connotations when used by city dwellers. To these people it simply meant that they were hard working, could live off the land, look after themselves and didn't need Government help. She also told me that 'Mums 'were local shorthand for chrysanthemums - another cultural mystery solved.

When she saw Steve trying to dry his gloves she insisted on giving him a pair of gardening gloves before refusing to charge us for any of the food and drink! I don't know whether it was Brenda's hospitality, getting warm again or the beer, but, by the end of the day, our spirits were soaring with the overwhelming feeling that if we could cover 40 miles in these conditions then nothing - absolutely nothing - could stop us from reaching New York.

That early season snowstorm had wreaked havoc across the Eastern Seaboard. Parts of New Hampshire and Vermont received over a foot of snow and an inch fell in Central Park - the first October snowfall there since 1973. Back in Pennsylvania, the leaves were still on the trees so the weight of snow that sat on them brought down dozens of power lines across the state.

NEW YORK, NEW YORK

Forward to November 5th, and dodging multi lane traffic never designed with pedestrians in mind we crossed the George Washington Bridge and officially entered New York, our final state. Tiny boats passed below us and the latticework of the steel tower in front grew steadily larger. All the cyclists were leaving the city but all the runners were entering it. We took a couple of left turns to make our way to the Hudson so that we could run along the river path.

We stopped off for coffee just to get a feel for this city. It was strange to see so many people. For an hour and a half we ran along with the river to our right, with a constant stream of joggers coming the other way or occasionally passing us. Leaving the quiet path and running through central Manhattan where we were surrounded by people was amazing. We had run 3,000 miles through small town America and to suddenly be dodging people and cars was bizarre.

At the Marathon Registration we asked where the press room was only to find that it was based at the Hilton Hotel a couple of miles back along the way we had just come. Nothing for it but bite the bullet and run back there. Confidence is the key and the immortal phrase *"We've been told to come to the press conference, can you show us where it is please?"* works wonders.

Fortunately, nobody ever asked the question: *"Just who exactly told you to come here?"*

One of the ladies serving the food at the Press Centre recognised our accents and announced that her son had married an Englishwoman followed by, *"I bet you drink tea? Would you like a nice cup of tea?"*

Seizing on this opportunity like drowning men we were introduced to the man in charge and allowed into the race reception for elite athletes. There we explained our adventure to Kathrine Switzer but our stomachs soon started to rule our heads.

A large smoked salmon caught our eye and to our shame, as tiny Kenyan athletes nibbled away at slivers that would not satisfy a mouse, we simply started hoovering up food by the plateful.

Buffet devoured and with numbers for the following day in hand we realised that we had better get on the road again for the last 10 miles to the Atlantic. Has anyone ever run further than 3,000 miles to pick up race numbers?

Brighton Beach turned out to be a lot further than we had hoped. The sun was going down and we were starting to get worried. Plunging into the sea in the pitch black didn't sound appealing.

BRIGHTON BEACH

Having not put a foot wrong in over 3,000 miles, Steve managed to trip over the curb 100 metres from the Atlantic and slam onto the ground. With blood dripping from his wrist he looked up to see my brother-in-law Jim, who was waiting patiently to guide us onto the beach. We ran through the 'finish line' banner that he and Sue, my sister, had rigged up and plunged into the water. To our relief, it was much warmer than Half Moon Bay had been back in August. Emerging to a stunning sunset, we finally noticed…… Jim Shapiro.

Quiet and dignified, he had cleared his diary and looked so happy to see us. Despite the fact that he did not know us at all, the bond of the event somehow transcended all the usual social norms. Steve was unable to resist pointing out that Jim was to blame for the whole thing - but beyond that this was one of the most profound moments of my life - the realisation of a dream which had essentially been all my adult life in the preparation and utterly exhausting in its execution.

"It does change you." Jim said, *"You won't realise it straight away but it will."*

EASY DAY - 26.2 MILES

And so to the New York Marathon - luckily we had only run 280 miles in the week building up to it. I had never felt anything like this before the start of a race. With the combination of a hard day yesterday, champagne, beer, cake and hardly any sleep, I could barely walk. We started cautiously.

"Shall we push it a bit harder for the second half?" I asked Steve at 13 miles. "Better leave it for a really fast finish" Steve replied.

"Ready to give it some now?" At 16 miles. "Let's go at 23 eh?"

Into Central Park, winding and hilly.

Most of the runners around us were slowing with accumulated tiredness to around 9 minutes per mile pace whereas we were now running as if possessed. We must have added on half a mile in distance weaving in and out of people. Despite this we ran the last two miles in less than 12 minutes.

We finished in 3.38 and wandered through the Autumn sunshine towards the park exit and from there to my sister's home in nearby Princeton. The whole thing was over, over and done.

A Retrospective view from Steve

People would often ask us after our return, whether we actually enjoyed the run. My answer always surprised them. I genuinely enjoyed about 98% of it. Most people find it hard to understand how such a long hard sustained effort could possibly be described as pleasurable. The ones that 'got it' tended to be those who had been on long mountaineering expeditions or who had done extended bike rides. They understood the simple pleasures of a drink of cold water on a hot day or how good a cup of tea tastes when you are soaking wet through and cold to the core.

To the more sedate, the run would remain a mystery. Someone summed up the problem quite neatly:

If you find yourself having to explain 'why' to someone then you are wasting your time.

Harsh but true.

The other questions that I was asked a lot, mainly by radio or newspaper interviewers were:

"How did you deal with the monotony?" And "What did you do when you ran out of conversation?"

The truth is that it was very rarely monotonous. If you examine anybody's daily routine, 90% of it is exactly the same as it was yesterday, whether you are a nuclear physicist or a bin man. We got to see new places and meet new people every single day and our regime of running was broken up every hour when we arrived at the car and more frequently, when we stopped in diners or simply had a quick chat with an inquisitive passerby.

The other thing that might surprise you is that we never ran out of conversation. We both share a questioning nature along with a desire to learn how things work, what they did and how they were made. We share an interest in America - its history, geography, politics, social structure. We could have a conversation about most things, I was keen to learn from Chris about subjects he knew more about such as music, economics, philosophy and politics. Likewise, Chris was fascinated by my encyclopedic knowledge of PG Tips tea cards from the 60s and 70s.

I can honestly say that we never exchanged an angry word during the three months we were away. This must have been partly because we had a very big shared goal which we worked towards together, but I think also that our temperaments were broadly similar - we were both fairly laid back (although Chris is maybe less laid back than me). I think also that our approach of dividing up the tasks before and during the trip worked well because we could both play to our strengths. I am an early morning person and have no problems leaping (or more accurately staggering) out of bed at 5.45 whereas Chris - to put it mildly, is not. Therefore, I would sort out morning stuff. Chris had the sense of direction whereas I could get lost in my own house. Chris would have to save the day by navigating us faultlessly to our motel armed only with a huge scale state map and the light from my phone, when the Sat Nav was insisting that we ploughed on through a swamp.

The after-effects of our run were similar to those we would experience if we had raced a marathon hard. We didn't feel particularly tired and didn't sleep any more than normally; we just had a lack of elasticity in our legs and no great desire to run long distances. We ended up raising about £15,000 for Help for Heroes. Four weeks later Chris raced a 5k about a minute slower than he would have done before the run and I reckon I'm about the same. I think that it will take many months before we can run at the same pace we could before the trip.

More importantly, we can both honestly say that we wouldn't have swapped the experience for all the World. Some people may have run across America quicker, some may have raised more money than we did, but I don't believe that anyone had as much fun as we did.

Thanks to Julia, Ben, Joanna and Tom for making the journey possible. Steve and Chris

Chapter 13

Doug Masiuk
May 28th to December 22, 2012
San Francisco, California to New York City, New York

    Old worn asphalt and patterns carved into the tarmac: dull, grey, compressed. Roads like these change the sounds from approaching tires. Behind your shoulder low and long not high pitched, shrilly from worn asphalt. Here in Nevada there are twelve posts marking every mile. In Illinois there are 20. Each state has a pattern then loses its thread. Rust snapped off that reflector from a post. The ground washed away and two markers before mile marker 260 is missing.
    The contours of the landscapes slowly changing with each step. 1880-foot steps for every mile. 12 markers for a mile. The green tabs with a mile number on the posts slowly adding up. Do you know that the rumble strips vary on different roads? Why wouldn't they? This shoulder is wider. On some roads non-existent. You can see a slight crowning of the highway in the center of the lanes. This is intentional so that gusting winds keep vehicles in their place not pushing cars, trucks, busses into each other or maybe you. Here the white lines are flat grey. This is just past the Naval Air Station Fallon. I'm on Interstate 80. These are far-away places that you never knew existed.

Four days before coming off the long slope from the Sierra Nevada's past Carson City and further into the continent the winds began to swirl around. The sky was a deep wonderful grey. It was cold. I knew it was snowing way above. The flakes getting lost between up there and down here. 30 Mile an hour head winds. Part of my planning, start on the west coast. You will have the wind at your back. Tradewinds move west to east. Out here you have to acknowledge things like this, details changing. This was a reality. The wind can come from the east. It is its' will. You are only a pedestrian.

It was dusk and for the better part of a day I was running upward on a slight incline. Before me many miles forward was this ridge. It ran perpendicular to the road where the road and the range intersected the planners had sliced a gap to allow the road to follow. Between me and the range no trees just these shrubs. Bushes no higher than a waist. Red dirt soft like talc underneath. Each step floating up and the feet driving forward. Dust would stick on the shins creating a hard line between socks and leg. A reference of "yes there was work done." This was one of the ways to gauge it. Dirty legs, mile markers passed. Proximity to a geological feature. If you were standing far enough away and were to look down it would seem like nothing. If you were to track it on a map, nothing. In the moment running towards the range where the road cut through it would feel like you were cutting across the universe eclipsing milestones and devouring distances. Then not really. Hour after hour seemingly forever, a ridge.

No matter where I am, what my mood may be when asked about my experience running across the US this is one memory that always sticks out. This nameless valley. Dusk and light fading fast. The hillside way off in the distance painted in a hard dark red light. Brick in the dark.

A tractor trailer was coming. You could hear the sound from the 18 tires from way back. Then the subtle vibrations of the side of the road. You were a pro knowing and learning passing vehicle sounds for weeks now. This one was different. With no cars in front of me, trucks would sway way out from the shoulder that I was running on sometimes hitting the horn when they passed kind of an acknowledgment that they knew what you were about. No one just runs in the middle of nowhere. You're on a mission. Passing vehicles and their passengers knew this in a passing instant.

As the truck was approaching, I could hear it slow. Then the lights caught the vary corners of my peripheral vision. The sounds of 70,000 pounds of truck and freight sliding to a stop. A football field length in front of me half on the shoulder, half in the road, a truck at rest. The running lights up like two eyes, red, orange, afire, glaring back and something mechanical not natural like the plants, red dirt, range and worn tarmac in front, to the side and beneath me from the first days light until now.

Me running towards the truck, hard gulp, intimidation. No one had messed with me yet. The state trooper who drove up while I was peeing on the side of the road. No issue. The dog that had followed me for ten miles while I ran on the dirt service road that hugged the highway. The broken-down gypsy van, "Keep going, here's some water." "Where you running to?" "New York City" When you are in this position you think of life in all sorts of ways. Highest of highs, oh the so very lows. You think in mythological terms and then the best self-loathing, questioning fearful ones. Manic. Over the course of 1 hour you can be many different versions of yourself. Heart pounding, running so clean, smooth perfect you think you can feel the earth turning beneath your feet. Others, your legs are an inch long and if you cry you may die from dehydration. Then a mileage sign, "300 Miles to Salt Lake City", a billboard, "5 miles to a gas station." Your thoughts, progress. These miles don't run themselves.

The door opens. A man lumbers off the side of the truck. It is dark. He is walking towards you. "I've been looking for you all night." This is the end of daytime. Me thinking, "All night?" Trucker "I heard you on the radio yesterday in Elko from the HOGG radio station." Me still scared, confused, part this is what it is and when you stop running for hours on end, just a speck moving towards something always in front and out of grasp, it takes a while to register anything. An untied shoe that's laces have been slapping your ankles for an hour. Your crew trying to talk with you. You are so lost, placed in that head space, divorced from most anything. Everything else almost alien. Remember you are a human being too.

I am face to face with the trucker: "I heard you on the radio and I wanted to find you to say thank you." Someone would do this for you, I thought? In the middle of nowhere all alone, hours of thought just on this mission, aim, objective, goal… dream. A constant daydream punctuated by real hard facts from unchangeable details. This is a path and you are running it. Winds can blow in any direction out here.

"My brother was a type 1 Diabetic. He died twelve years ago. As kids he always struggled. He was sick. He died at 31. It broke my family's heart." "When I heard you share your story about being a Diabetic, how you wanted to show others that if someone with Diabetes could run across the US, anything is possible." Moments of silence. I can see my support vehicle slowly approaching down from the range. "I hate Diabetes for what it did to my brother, to my family.… I don't have the sadness and anger that I have felt forever. It can be something more than pain and heartache" A pause, "Do you need anything? Me: "Im good." He got back into his truck. Hit the horn and easing off, gone, as quickly as he came.

I took maybe ten steps then felt this punch in my guts. I started to cry, at mile marker 261, Interstate 80, at dusk, getting cold and falling blood sugars. One more mile. Even if they are not there someone is watching. So run. Run for that family. Run for that Diabetic. This is your gift, your feet.

Use it no matter how much it will hurt, disrupt a regular life, what it means to others is immeasurable. This is who you are now and why you are here.

When I began there was this oh so vague idea of what this would look like. It's success is measured in getting there. So coming off of Kit Carson Pass the first of four mountain ranges that I would be passing over it was about moving quickly. Friends and friends of friends and family and their family friend covered us giving us places to stay. By the time we got out of Lake Tahoe and were crossing into Nevada we had no idea what to do. Being a Diabetic, call the local American Diabetes Association. Reach out to the Juvenile Diabetes Research Foundation. Ask. It goes something like this "My name is Doug Masiuk and I am a type 1 Diabetic. I am currently running across the United States. I am doing this to share with others that anything is possible with Diabetes." From those initial calls my crew and I learned a lot. People came forth to keep the project going.

During my run across the US we did over 100 events in communities across the country. There were radio interviews, articles in newspapers, in magazines, on the television. Events with Diabetes organizations, at schools, universities, hospitals, town meetings, met Congresspeople, you name it. With the media the story was shared to over 30 million people. This was my version of a run across the US. Running is

inherently self-centered. You, your feet, a route. It can be something more. So many people, health groups, doctors, scientists, politicians, philanthropists chose Diabetes as a fight to get behind. I was the recipient of their choice. They are why I am here today. Why I exist. This is what you could contribute.

Our schedule was getting stretched way beyond what we planned for. 4 Months became 5. With a rotating crew there was a point where I was going to be by myself. I was south of Chicago. I had a friend that I stayed within the city for a couple of days to regroup. Plans can fail. Adapt or give up. My friend was an avid cyclist. "Well, you can quit or just get a bike and figure it out." We found a bike.

The plan: find the milk jug on the mile marker post that marked my stopping point from the night before. Drive for twenty miles. Drop the bike off, chain it to a tree or toss it in a ditch. Look around hard. Photograph it in your mind. Drive back to where you ended the day before stopping along the way to drop off snacks and water. Remember where you put them. Run towards the bike. The hours between a hurtful nervous energy. Uncertainty. What are you going to do, quit? This is your best effort. No one guarantees that it should be easy. This is your journey. Still, the fear. Not a lot of safety but there was progress and me moving further across the route across the country.

The first day it worked! You ran and rode a bike for 28 miles. You did it. One of the greatest sense of accomplishments that I have ever felt. I was not a bike rider but this was what was needed. To be, to do this thing, to run across the United States. The second day, catastrophe!

Somewhere east of the Illinois, Indiana border on secondary roads cutting across the state the wind picked up. First stage completed, ran then rode back the twenty miles on the bike. Do it again. These swaps of running then riding then driving took time. Your body is one form of the clock and the sun is another. If you don't move, sunset comes fast. In November it comes quickly.

Drove the bike and put it between a row of trees between two fields. There was a hard right turn 1/4 mile from the main road that you would be turning onto. Remember this space. Mark it on the phone. Drive back. Run towards the bike. It began to rain. It was 3 o'clock. Get on the bike. Ride to the car. It is dark. It is pouring now. It is Sunday and no cars out there. It is getting colder. Your phone died. You are in a rural farming area. Small lights faded through the mist from far away farm houses. Massive fields in-between. You lost the car. Your hands are frozen, fingers stuck. A huge wave of panic then the Diabetes math: How many carbs do you have? You've exercised for how long? Were those fast miles ran? Your blood glucose meter frozen now. A brick. When you are emotional as a Diabetic it is difficult to best guess your blood sugars. Do you eat or are these spasms from you being frozen? You are alone.

A car turns into a driveway down the road. You follow it as fast as you can turning into the driveway.

Knock on the door. "Hi my name is… I am running across the US. Currently I am doing this by myself using a bike to get back to my car. I lost it. Please, I need help." Standing in their foyer, soaked and the water leaking from shoes, draining down your tights and from underneath your cuffs, Shivering. There is a picture of a duck on the wall. They were built for water. Not you. 10 pairs of eyes looking in disbelief. A voice, "I'll go look." Maybe their grandmother, "Here is a blanket," passing it to me. I sit on the floor. Don't you dare sob. The older man, probably a dad. "Here's a battery for your glucose meter" reaching down to pass it to you. "My nephew's a Diabetic." There are about 30 million of us in the US. Your hands too frozen to milk out a drop of blood for the test. The tack not going in far enough. Eventually it flows once the hands register the heat and the blood rises to the surface. It burns.

"Your car is at the end of the driveway across the street" from the man who went to find it.. Another hand passing you a sandwich. Someone helps you up. There is a hug from the grandmother "Thank you for doing this."

Every reason to quit. There are so many. Sometimes there is only one reason to continue, to do your very best to make it. You as the runner, singular. How you get there, takes many, plural.

You do something like this a world will come forth revealing just how amazing it truly is. How generous, thoughtful, supportive we all can be. The only way I had made it across was from support from strangers. From every hotel I called along the way that gave us a free stay. Every restaurant that fed us. A Ford dealer changing your oil. Someone like Amy Holmwood giving you their SUV to use. My friends and crew that dropped everything to prop me up to keep going. You will have more cheerleaders, a new extended family, a world that will do what they can to keep you going or something as simple as finding your car.

So stop now? No because, that towel, that floor under a roof with a duck painting on a wall, a battery, this comes forth because people know what you are doing is amazing. Ridiculous, reckless but being done to float for a moment on that line between what cannot and what is possible. You are something more than a person, this vessel, that is simply running, you are now a cause. You are proving something. To those before you who were not fortunate. With the accumulation of moments like this, the people that you meet along the way, they for me became a reason for my "why." The countless 1000's that supported, cheered, waved along the way. There may be a million reasons to back it up and book a ride out of there. It is the moments and memories of the people that gave themselves so that you could do this creates a strength to go on.

The storm breaks and the next day is cool and dry, still fumbling with how to process how close it all crashed the day before. The phone rings: "Hi, I'm Jim McCord. I met with Rae Ainsle, the girl running across the US barefoot. She told me you crossed paths in Colorado." Smaller world even though it is taking you forever to run across it. "My daughter is a type 1 Diabetic and I ran across the US to share with her, to get her to take care of her Diabetes... I understand that you are by yourself?" I tell Jim what is happening. "Can I come out and crew with you for a few days?" he asks. Salvation.

Jim McCord is a legend in the US crossing world. Yes, he ran

across. He knows everyone that has ever done so. He is known to drop everything and come out and meet fellow crossers at their starts, at their finishing points, sometimes in-between. I was in Indiana. I had someone coming to crew for me in a week's time. Jim would save me in between.

When Jim arrived we met in a hotel lobby. His daughter Maggie and her husband were there to drop him off. The plan was that I was running just north of his home in Cincinnati. I would have Thanksgiving at his house. Again, a world would take you in. They would do whatever they could to make your journey better, safer, less impossible. Celebrate a holiday.

The first day: We drove out to where I stopped the day before. "What do you usually do?" I told about the biking. The necessities of Diabetes was something that he was familiar with. Something that he was not used to, the amount of Nutella that a person with Diabetes should be eating. I ate lots of it. I was also emaciated. When you ran this much, having unhealthy low amount of body fat, glucose from meals immediately goes right into the blood stream. As a Diabetic you want to be in a range. With me I was scraping the bottom. A better example of this comes from another project. This is an example of how trying Diabetes management when running like this and riding a fine line between just getting by and completely crashing can be.

In 2019 I tried to run across Australia. An ankle sprain led me to favor the opposing leg and the muscle in the quad tore, ligaments turned to noodles. A leg rendered useless. I had to quit. In the month that I was there I ran 950 miles in 28 days. It was hot, breaking temperature records and breaking me. My day would go like this: Blood glucose at 5:30 AM: 80. Eat a peanut butter jelly sandwich and a glass of juice. Run for an hour. No insulin to cover the meal (you don't do this as a Diabetic). Get back in from the first run. Blood sugar: 58. Eat a bowl of cereal in the shape of a mixing bowl, another glass of juice. Run another 7 miles. Meet up with the support vehicle after an hour. Test blood sugar. It's 48. Eat 4 slices of french toast with lots of jelly and butter. Another glass of juice. Run for another hour. Come back in. Test blood sugar. 51. Eat another peanut butter jelly sandwich. Two more glasses of juice. Run another hour. Mile count so far for the day, 22ish. Somewhere in there, slice of turkey and mayonnaise. Blood sugar, 40. Juice. Temperature outside climbing, 115. Break for the afternoon. Insulin for the AM, none. Zero. Calories 4000 or so. Weight, losing, 120 pounds. My healthy weight 130. Rest then run again when the sun began to set.

When I was running across the US it was just as challenging. Run 30 miles a day. Eat, lose weight and be chronically scraping the low blood sugar range. Being a diabetic since 1977, having run far and having done so often I was familiar with this. Having bailed on training runs with low blood sugar. Eating proteins, carbohydrates, fats, fast sugars and in numerous combinations and pairings of them. You learn what will work. This balance between exercise, diet and insulin. These cause and effect relationships. Sometimes Diabetes has a mind of its own. You expected one number and you get something completely unexpected. The frustration. Start pushing really demanding inputs at it running thirty plus miles, a headwind, hills, or you just are having a bad day, and all of these can throw the unexpected at you. Diabetes hated this.

So running across a continent, or when I biked across the US, yes I have done this too but so has Jim McCord, here comes the variance. Diabetes loves routine,. It loves something very predictable. It always will but this is not the life we live. This is not what I want nor do others. If I could run like this Jon and Jane could see, and of greater significance Jon and Jane's parents would know that anything could be possible with Diabetes. Those kids could be on soccer teams and go forth and live to their potential regardless of having a failed organ.

On the side of the road in Ohio Jim dropped me off. "I'll see you in hour." Stands of oak trees, branches bare, leaves underfoot. No wind yet. The sky, a grey. 58 more minutes until the next mark. Footsteps in-between. A red mark way off down the road. You moving to it. It moving to you. It's a person. It's Jim. When was the last time you caught yourself smiling while running? I don't remember anymore. It happens sometimes. A recognition of emotion. A moment you acknowledge for the impact that it is making upon you. This time, grateful. Of course, grateful. It is not a bike tied to a tree.

"Thought I would come out and run a few with you." Jim passing you water. "The cars just down the road." "Called a radio station in Cincinnati. They want to interview you this afternoon." Your job, easy, just run.

Then one of the greatest gifts that I would ever receive: "You know there are so many people that would do anything to be doing what you are doing right now. They are in hospitals and can't walk. Here you are running." This changed my life forever. Through all of the uncertainty. Wet feet, sunburnt everything, out of money and not sure how my crew and I would be able to afford to eat those tomorrow's, the simplicity of an idea. No, a fact, that you were indeed fortunate. You were in good health and running. Never take this for granted. For more than simply supporting me on the side of the road, for crewing, for taking me into his home to celebrate Thanksgiving with his family, for calling hotels, radio stations and newspapers, something greater. That yes, you were here, able bodied and not a statistic. One of the millions that have health complications from this chronic illness. You are a person with Diabetes running across the United States. Something that no one has done before you. You are lucky. Never forget this.

A long time ago in a waiting room at Moses Taylor Hospital in Scranton, PA my parents sat in a sea foam green tiled room. My father had sideburns. My mother was sobbing. A man stood in front of them. His white doctor's coat smelled like cigarettes. It was November the first, 1977. This was one of my first memories. My parents heartbreak. The day I was diagnosed.

Something happened in-between. A mom took it to heart, unwillingly blaming herself. It became a reason to drink more. I would remember her saying 'if I could I would take your Diabetes away and give it to myself. As a six-year-old in a hospital room I knew that this would never happened. This was mine. In time alcoholism would kill her.

The Barbara Davis center is one of a few type 1 Diabetes facilities in the world. Their research, care and expertise makes them leaders in making the lives of Diabetics better. When I was running through Denver I was invited to come to the hospital to share with them about the run across the country. I was a person who was simply on the move, running across the US getting people to take notice. To share with this community was an honor.

After the presentation one of the people in attendance asked if I had a few minutes. There was a patient and their family downstairs who was just admitted. The patient was 9 years old. She was on a family trip with her siblings, parents and grandmother. The news of her diagnosis was a shock.

They had no history of Diabetes in their family. This would be one of the hardest days for a parent in their lifetime.

The staff person checked with the family and I was led into a hospital room. A child sat on a bed. An IV hanging from the anchor, its needle pierced through the inside bend of a little elbow. A grandmother sat in the chair in the corner. The dad by the window arms crossed looking down, dazed. A mom beside the child leaning forward, eyes the widest of wides staring past the door as it opened. The child ready to adapt whatever the mood changed too from the adults in the room. I know what this felt like. Speak from the heart. Their life may depend on these words.

"I have Diabetes just like you. Right now I am running across the US. I was diagnosed at the age of three…" Then on. The conversation went on for an hour. The mom's eyes wrapped in tears. The dad listening. "If I can run across the country with this disease your child can go forth and do amazing things. Anything is possible with Diabetes. You are lucky to be here at the Barbara Davis Center. This is the best place in the world to be a Diabetic." The words, more of them, then they ended. Not a victim but someone starting off on their life's journey.

In the doorway a nurse, an endocrinologist, a marketing person. There were bright smiles and tears in eyes. A doctor's hand reaching for mine "this is the best gift a recently diagnosed family and child could ever receive." Because I was running across the US was the only reason I was in that room. Because I was a type-1 doing the seemingly impossible people wanted to hear. Because I was a person with Diabetes this would make the run that much greater. Because I was a Diabetic I only had a chance because places like the Barbara Davis Center existed. This is what I could do to make Diabetes better. Run and share. It is not any harder than that. Move your feet then speak. It meant a great deal to me, to a memory of a deceased parent, to a strange family in a city far away from home, to a trucker teary eyed rolling across the flats outside of Elko, NV, this was my version of running across the US.

Running down the canyons of Mid Town then into the low rises of Hell's Kitchen across to Union Square then into the Village. More than ten years before I used to walk these streets. I went to school at NYU. When I was younger I smoked cigarettes about two packs a day. Lived off of a trickle of sugar and milk from coffee. I had very little but I did have the most amazing opportunity to be a student at an amazing institution. Diabetes was barely an afterthought just taking my daily injections, never testing, seldomly visiting a doctor or getting blood work done. I was fine. I would make it. Denial is beautiful like that. This is no way for a person with a failed pancreas to live. It was suicidal.

Running past NYU and the entrance to Tisch School of the Arts I stopped, opened the front door, stepped inside. It was a Sunday morning early. There was no one around. I looked around thinking of that time, those people, remembering what was inspiring to me. For a moment getting so caught up into all of it but then pulling back. No still the same. These are hopes, desires, choices. Anything is possible. This is always true. Diabetes or not. So much is possible. 7 more miles and your run across the country would end.

A few blocks later, then crossing a bridge, then running through Brooklyn then the ocean. A family, friends, fans waiting. I was still a person with Diabetes. I am a runner. I believe that within all of us there is amazing potential for greatness. We live in a world where things like this are possible.

To that patient and family that is learning of a diagnosis today. Anything is possible with Diabetes. We are USA crossers, CEO's, Supreme Court Justices, Doctors, camp counselors, Diabetes organizations cheerleaders and supporters, grandparents, parents, children, families and so much more. We are in the 21 century and like no other time in history, this is the best time to be a Diabetic and it is only getting better.

You don't have a reason to give up, give in, or simply stop. If you ever have doubts, need a reason to cross a continent, feel like it is impossible, look up the patron saint of crossing continents Terry Fox. If Terry can, what is our excuse? Terry has inspired so many to keep going. Doug runs the nonprofit www.outrundiabetes.org OutRun Diabetes.org creates 1 Mile events to get people to move 1 mile to better and prevent Diabetes.

Chapter 14

Rosalynn Frederick
March 23 to August 15, 2013
Grover Beach, California to Norwalk, Connecticut

California, Arizona, New Mexico, Texas, Oklahoma, Kansas, Missouri, Illinois, Indiana, Ohio, Pennsylvania, New Jersey, New York, Connecticut. That was the route I took, the states I traveled through for at least a few miles.

My calculations were that the route was approximately 2,995 miles. I started in Grover Beach, California, and ended in Norwalk, Connecticut. I covered almost all of the distance on foot. There were about 120 miles from eastern Missouri to western Illinois that I did not cover on foot. For those 120 miles I hitchhiked, took a taxi, and even rode one public bus. Details on that later.

For the last several years, every time I've attempted to write my story, the inspiration and the adventure of it all have fizzled out when I think about the 120 miles. I could have done it all. I *should* have done it all. As I write my story now, it's my hope to find words that carefully balance the line between speaking my truth and acknowledging that every story has two sides.

The idea to run across the country was born in me in 2011. I was a high school Spanish teacher at the time but knew that wasn't the best path for me. I had also just had a very difficult break up with my boyfriend. I was feeling lost and looking for direction. A friend of mine recommended a psychic she had worked with in the past who had helped her a great deal. Of course, I was skeptical, but I was also curious, knowing this wasn't the type of psychic that you drop in on at the fair to read your palm. Ultimately, I called her. I was eager for even a hint of insight regarding where to go from where I was and if there was any chance of mending the relationship which had just fallen apart. Along with minimal discussion about relationship topics, she spoke a great deal of athletic pursuits, about the topic of travel, and about a book in my future, none of which I had expected or even desired to discuss at that time. I took it in, though.

Something I had not told the psychic when we spoke was that I have a passion for travel. I've traveled to or lived in Canada, Mexico, El Salvador, Belize, Costa Rica, Chile, Spain, France, England, Portugal, Niger, Cameroon, Ivory Coast, Tibet, Nepal, Hong Kong, and Brazil. When I was a Spanish teacher, I traveled with a group of students to Costa Rica and loved it!

Another thing that I had not communicated to the psychic was that I had a love of long-distance running. By 2011 I had run the Big Sur,

Newport, and Mohawk-Hudson (2Xs) Marathons. I was also regularly running 5ks and 10ks. Running made me feel free and healthy.

Travel and running. These were things I loved. Now, here was this psychic who, out of the blue, started talking to me about a future which included athletic pursuits and travel!

It was the discussion I had with this psychic that sparked my idea for running across the country. It created a desire within me to seek out a running adventure and inspired an idea for a new professional direction, a nonprofit that would assist young people in traveling the world for educational purposes. The Youth Travel Fund. I decided to run across the country while at the same time getting the word out about and raising money for youth travel.

On Saturday, March 23, 2013, after about 10 months of planning and preparation, I waded in the ocean at Pismo Beach in the town of Grover Beach, CA. At 12:00 PM, I hit the road. Oh. My. God. I was doing it.

Being on the open road in California was incredible. Sunny blue skies and perfectly warm days. Besides a glitch in the route on day #1 which took me down a dead-end road about 10 miles in, the first 4 days were smooth. I ran about 20 miles each day and spent the first 3 nights burrowed in my sleeping bag (the nights were chilly), sleeping upright in my car on the side of the road. Miraculously my muscles did not rebel. I was thrilled to feel so successful.

I fell in love with jogging alone on long, winding roads surrounded by hills and fields and old-fashioned oil pumps; one small person in a vast landscape, moving at a relative crawl compared to the cars and trucks that whizzed by now and again. The desert landscape I became immersed in once I got further from the coast was beautiful. Along my travels I found that many people think deserts are uninteresting, but there's something about the subdued colors and openness of desert landscapes that fills me with a sense of fullness and calm.

On March 28, 2013, near Arvin, CA, I excitedly embarked on my first off-road experience. After running along paved highways for the previous few days, I welcomed the dirt path ahead of me. The plan was for me to spend the day on what I have dubbed "The Tehachapi Hills." (I don't actually think that is what they are called but since the town of Tehachapi is at the top, it's felt like a logical name to me.) The hills were beautiful, remote, and there was no cell service for the entire route. I looked forward to the quiet hours ahead that I would share with mother nature alone. The grassy fields on each side of the path were dotted with gnarly trees and wildflowers and fenced in with charmingly dilapidated and weathered barbed wire fencing. I breathed the natural beauty in and out. I was in my element.

It was 14 miles to the top. I climbed all day. One foot in front of the other. Up, up, up, zigging and zagging on the bumpy, dirt switchblade path. A never ending, upward bank ahead of me and an ever-increasing descending slope behind me. I used the upward slope every so often to prop my toes up while I stretched my calves. I did this more than usual, assuming that my calves needed it due to the constant contraction of an upward jog.

Many hours passed before I emerged from the solitary ascent at a spot where the dirt road simply ended- cut off by the paved road. It was mid-afternoon and I felt tired, but good. My support driver had driven up on the paved road and was at the top waiting when I arrived. I had no idea when I started jogging up the hills that day that upon reaching the top I would be presented with one of the biggest personal challenges of the entire run experience.

As I was resting and eating my post-run snack, we had the fortune to cross paths with the owner of a house directly across the street from where we were parked. He was a professional adventurer (literally) who was returning from a bike ride. My support driver struck up a conversation with him. In the course of the dialogue, the guy asked my support driver if I was "his lady."

Apparently, this question made my support driver want to push the guy and his bike over the edge of the steep hill we were standing on. His explanation to me for this reaction was that when the bike guy asked that question he had to face the truth and admit to himself that I was not, in fact, his lady. The reason this bothered him so much was, he told me "I'm falling for ya."

Anger is the best word to describe how I felt when I heard this message. We had discussed this. He had agreed. This wasn't what I wanted, he knew it, and I didn't want to deal with his emotions. It complicated things in my mind. I wish I could say I was able to process it and move forward from a place of loving-kindness, compassion, and equanimity- basic principles of the Buddhist path I had recently committed myself to by "taking refuge" after participating in study and practice for multiple years, but I wasn't able to.

In retrospect, the best thing for me to have done in the face of this revelation and my intense emotional reaction might have been to part ways with my support driver and completely rethink my timeline for the run. Maybe even to consider going it alone. At the time, however, it didn't seem an option. I put faith in the hope that things would work themselves out over time and allowed the momentum of the months of preparation to propel me forward on the path that lay before me.

That night, we stayed in the home of the bike rider we had just met. We had a nice meal and an enjoyable evening with him. When I woke up the next morning, I got out of bed and noticed that I had a golf ball sized lump sticking out of my left outer calf, right above the ankle bone. It was painful to walk, but I was determined not to let it slow me down, if possible. Enter the ARP.

ARP stands for Accelerated Recovery and Performance. The ARP is a technology meant to be used in the event of an injury. It consists of a metal box with wires and sensor pads attached. The pads are used to find, then treat the injury.

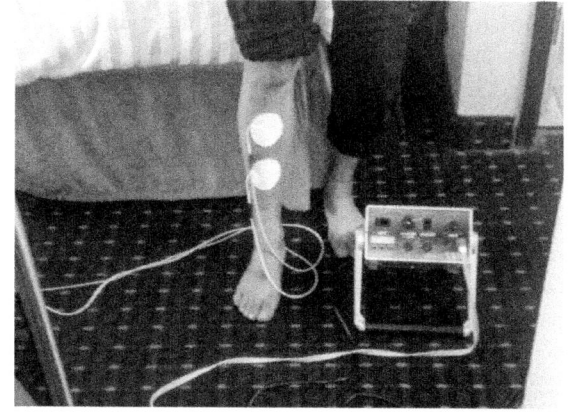

The most basic explanation of the process, as I understand it, is that the machine sends out electrical currents to identify the origin of an injury and then uses electrical currents to address nerve and circulation issues to seemingly magically, and extremely painfully, heal the injury. It doesn't just kill the pain or mask the symptoms, it heals the root cause of the injury.

My plan after discovering my injury that morning was to try to run through the injury and if that didn't work, to try the ARP. I quickly discovered that running was very painful, and I was worried that if I continued, I would worsen the injury. A couple of miles away from the place I had spent the night, there was a small municipal airport. The person on duty that day was kind enough to let me use a room in one of the buildings to try out my ARP for the first time. I have to say it was one of the most excruciating things I had ever experienced but I was prepared for that. I had been told that I needed to blast as much electrical current as I could stand to the injury. The advice I had gotten from my trainers was to scream, swear, bite down on a piece of wood, do whatever I needed to do to push it to the highest level of pain I could tolerate. My understanding was that the more electrical current I could tolerate, the quicker the healing would be. After my first session of ARP treatment, I started running again with less pain than I had experienced that morning and finished my route for the day. Unfortunately, the next morning, the pain was back. Again, I tried to make do, but the pain was too intense. At this point, I was just outside of Boron, CA.

I spent about a week and a half recovering from my injury between Boron and Barstow, CA. My recovery plan was as follows: 1) Don't run, and 2) Use the ARP every day. It was during this recovery hiatus that my support driver made a realization that would benefit us for the remainder of the journey. He discovered that hotel managers were willing to donate rooms where we could stay for free! It sometimes took a little haggling on the part of my support driver, but in the end, we only paid for one or two nights in a hotel over the 5-month period on the road. Best Western Desert Villa Inn, in Barstow, was the first hotel to donate rooms. Hats off to them.

For the next 5 months, I spent the majority of my nights in free hotel rooms. These hotel rooms were supplemented by camping, sleeping in my car, and, my favorite of all the types of lodging - but not to diminish any of them - was being welcomed into the private homes of generous strangers. How truly wonderful that people in communities all across the country opened their homes to the two of us. I have so many wonderful memories of people who, after hearing about what I was trying to accomplish, were willing to give me food, shelter, and, in one instance on a chilly damp evening in Texoma, Oklahoma, the use of a jet stream bathtub with Enya blasting on the CD player. In addition to free accommodations, it's important to mention how many restaurants along my route donated free meals. Words can't express my appreciation for this generosity and for the steady persistence of my support driver in making this happen.

On April 22nd I crossed the border from California into Arizona. After my extended stay in California, it felt incredible to be in state #2. The canyon lands of Arizona were one of my favorite parts of the route. There's something indescribably awesome (in the literal sense of the word) about the ancient, still, majesty of the canyons. They seem undisturbed by modernization. As I jogged by them for hours on end, I could almost imagine seeing dinosaurs roaming at their bases. I felt like an explorer of new lands, or maybe even other planets, in the desolate canyonlands. I loved the unique sense of being that I felt as I was surrounded by these giants.

On May 8th, I arrived at the border of the Navajo Nation. An interesting bit of information that I learned as I told people I was planning to cross through the Navajo Nation land was that this was a route not widely taken by transcon runners. I heard that the local Navajo police did not take kindly to travelers lingering on the land, and here I was planning to cross slowly on foot. My support driver and I considered the options and decided to risk taking this route since it was definitely the shortest way to where we needed to go. It was a true adventure seeing signs in a different language and going without a shower or bathroom for 3 days since there were no hotels or restaurants along the route I took. And contrary to what we had heard, we were welcomed all along the way. We were provided with places to sleep for 3 out of the four nights we were there. One night in a church, one night in a room in what had once been an orphanage, and one night we camped in the backyard of someone's home. We spent only one night sleeping in the car on the side of the road. The night in the car I woke up to the police flashing their car lights and shining flashlights at me. After what I had initially heard about people passing through, I have to admit I was a little nervous about what would happen next. Gratefully, the police stated that their intention was simply to make sure we were doing alright, not to discourage us from being there. I feel fortunate that my journey enabled me to experience the Navajo land and so grateful for the support along the way.

By May 13th I had reached New Mexico. The day before my birthday, on May 26th, I hit the 1,000 mile mark near Albuquerque. I had completed approximately one-third of my journey across the United States. I silently celebrated this milestone by standing still for a moment, looking around at the nondescript scene, and feeling the joy of my accomplishment somewhere deep inside. I still remember exactly what that scene looks like in my mind's eye. By June 2nd I was leaving New Mexico headed north west, crossing a small corner of Texas. I felt sad to leave the southwest behind. It felt like I was saying goodbye to an old friend. Maybe I felt attached because, being the first part of my run, the experiences somehow felt momentous. Whatever the case, as I turned north and the landscape changed to green grass and trees, a new phase began. Although I still had a long way to go, my surroundings felt more familiar and I felt closer to home.

From Kansas to Missouri, the humidity hit me like a ton of bricks. Although it had been hot in the southwest, it was dry. I had been wearing black spandex to protect my legs from the sun since the middle of Arizona. All of a sudden, it was so humid I felt like I was suffocating in my spandex. There was one day in Kansas that I had to cut the day short. I called my support driver almost in tears and asked him to pick me up early so that I could rest indoors in a cool place. My spandex were no longer a staple of my wardrobe from that point forward.

It was in Missouri that things took a turn for the worst. The 120 miles that I mentioned earlier? This is where they began.

It's difficult for me to write this part of the story because while it's not my desire to feel negativity regarding my support driver, six plus years later, I still do. However, I would be remiss if I did not acknowledge that while there was ongoing tension between me and him, the work he did to cut the budget of the food and lodging for the trip to a fraction of what I had imagined it would be was incredible. I am forever grateful to him for that. In addition, his driving skills were second to none. Some of the "roads" he drove on in my old Ford Focus, without 4-wheel drive, in order to find me the shortest route between two locations called for technical driving skills that the average person does not possess. If these logistical components could have been the crux of our relationship, what an amazing pair we would have made. Instead, what defined our time together ended up being guilt, jealousy, power struggles, possessiveness, manipulation, control, and resentment.

While seeing past my own selfish perspective about the conflicts he and I grappled with has not been easy, it has become clear to me over the years that I too played a role in the drama that unfolded. It takes two to tango. While I feel my ultimate motivation in most of my interactions with him was to create and hold personal boundaries, I realize this more than likely came off as disdain to him. We had gotten ourselves into a holding pattern that caused us both to suffer.

There was a moment in Missouri when the conflicts between me and my support driver got so heated that I thought he was going to walk away from the commitment he had made to my run. At the same time I was very close to telling him to leave. Things escalated to the point that I could feel the words on the tip of my tongue, "I'm done. I'll figure things out without you from here."

A mutual friend we were visiting at the time argued strongly for us to finish the journey together. My guilt at the thought of leaving him stranded in Missouri with no money and no plan and my uncertainty about what my own plan would be if I did this, along with our friend's advice, caused me to bite my tongue and suck it up. Kind of.

On July 6th, I started moving eastward again. I was not in a good place. I suppose I felt trapped with someone I didn't want to be with. I was also experiencing intense pain in my hips. I started taking multiple doses of ibuprofen each day to ease the pain. It seemed to help with the symptoms. My beloved ARP had begun malfunctioning by this time. Unfortunately, it had taken a severe fall off of the roof of my car onto really hard concrete and the insides got shaken up pretty badly. From that point forward, it didn't work the way I knew it should and I had no option to replace it.

Below is an excerpt (slightly revised) from a blog post I wrote on April 25, 2014, eight months after reaching the east coast and "finishing" my run. The title of the post was "An important truth about the USA Run for Youth Travel." It begins where my narrative above left off and explains the initial details of the 120 miles.

On July 6th, the first day back on the road after my week off, I wasn't recovered. I wanted to run and I tried to run. I made it a few miles, but I was still in severe pain. I was also feeling a great deal of pressure (from myself) to keep moving forward. I was stressed about being behind schedule and was running short on funds and emotional strength. This is when I made a decision that I will always regret. Instead of calling my support driver to come pick me up and telling him and everyone following my journey what was going on, I hitched a ride for a good portion of the mileage that was left for the day. Yes, I rode in someone's car for about 10 miles. Then I lay in a secluded area of land for several hours elevating my feet and hoping that taking it easy for one extra day would give me the rest I needed to heal. I told myself that if I did this, I would be in better shape to go back out on the road the following day and cover the planned mileage.

At the time I was not really thinking logically and was scared that my injuries could cause permanent damage to my body. I also knew that if I delayed my trip any longer that there was a good chance I wouldn't make it to the finish line. I couldn't bear the thought of adding anymore extra days to the length of the journey and I felt like I would quit before I took anymore time off.

What I wasn't willing to say in 2014, that I feel compelled to say now in order to fully express myself is that what I actually couldn't bear the thought of was spending any additional time with my support driver. I couldn't bear the thought of depending on him or of letting him in on my personal struggle. The thought of spending multiple days with him in a hotel room recovering made my skin crawl. It's very clear to me now that this was not a logical way to approach the situation, but at the time, I was not clear minded.

On July 7th, I got back out there again- eager, hopeful. Again, my body rebelled. Again, I secretly hitched a ride, trying to convince myself that that was all I needed- one more day of rest to heal. I intended to get back on track the next day. I felt horrible about what I was doing. I knew it was wrong. I knew the brave thing to do would be to tell everyone what was going on. But I chose not to. I honestly can't remember how I convinced myself that what I was doing was acceptable. I think desperation had taken over. I had lost perspective on my values and my sense of self. I was so overwhelmed by my emotions that I was willing to lie to avoid dealing with them. I was so disappointed in myself, yet I kept doing it. For 10 days, I went out in the morning hoping to be able to cover the planned mileage on my own and ended up hitchhiking, calling a cab, or taking a bus for a portion of the mileage...and I didn't tell anyone.

Finally, something happened that shook me out of my state and inspired me to stop what I was doing. This something came in the form of an incredible human being who was doing a solo crossing in the opposite direction I was going. It was July 16th when I first spoke to Jack Fussell. He was somewhere in Texas that day. After talking to Jack, I knew I couldn't keep on doing what I was doing. I was ashamed. He had been on the road since January and he was hurting, too. During the first conversation we had he said, "Rosalynn, if you could get a feel for the pain that I have felt at different times along my run, you would break down in tears feeling sorry for me." After speaking to him one time, I was inspired by his strength and determination. The next day, I completed all of my mileage. How did I do it? I walked. The entire way. I don't know why it hadn't occurred to me to do this earlier, but it hadn't. I honestly don't remember even considering it. But from that point forward, I told myself if my friend was on the road each day sweating it out through his pain, I could do the same. I spoke with him every day from that point forward for the rest of the journey.

For the last month of the USA Run I walked 30 miles almost every day. When I finally made it to Norwalk, CT on August 15, 2013, a small crowd of fans: family, a few friends, a reporter, and some random bystanders, were gathered at the edge of Calf Pasture Beach awaiting my arrival. I crossed the symbolic finish line made of yellow and green party streamers and continued straight into the water, immersing myself for a moment. It was over. As I walked out of the water, I celebrated but in my heart I knew I was living a lie.

One of the things I've questioned frequently since I finished my run is why I took it so seriously. Why did I decide to keep going on the days when I struggled mightily, sometimes emotionally and sometimes physically? There was no one forcing me to keep going. I was doing this because I wanted to. Why did it feel so urgent?

Two things come to mind: momentum and purpose. Momentum is one thing that made this experience increasingly compelling and kept me going each day. Another way to describe it would be the snowball effect "...a process that starts from an initial state of small significance and builds upon itself, becoming larger (graver, more serious)..." (wikipedia) The cumulative amount of energy that I expended on accomplishing this endeavor increased with every passing day. Over time, it became my everything. Somewhere in the middle of the journey it felt like maybe I lost connection with my past and my future. I experienced it like a forgetting, a loss of perspective, of the "big picture" of my life. My reality was pounding the pavement; it was gingerly finding areas to place my feet amongst a sea of low lying cacti that adorned the pathless ground my GPS was guiding me across; it was running in fields with cows; slowly and determinedly running up an incline of 3000 feet in 2 hours; encountering my first rattlesnake; 100-degree days with 80% humidity; a whirlwind of new faces and places every day. It was wonderful, beautiful, liberating and at the same time intense and emotionally arduous due to what I was experiencing with my support driver in my "off hours," when I was not running.

I once described to someone that the days running in the heat and humidity of the midwest were "some of the toughest days of my life." When I think back on that now, I almost feel foolish. With all that is going on the world - sickness, war, poverty, hunger, wildfires endangering the lives of people, animals, and the environment - it makes no sense for me to describe spending my days on a jogging adventure, fulfilling my dream, as any kind of true hardship. In the moment, though, that was my truth.

It's now been almost six and a half years since I crossed the finish line at Calf Pasture Beach. I've had a lot of time to process my five-month journey. This story conveys where I am with it right now. I know there will be more processing and evolution of my perspective with every passing month, year, and decade. I find myself wondering what someone reading this will take from it. I guess there's no real way for me to know that at this moment. However, if I'm to trust myself and my intuition, which I am constantly striving toward, I have to believe that there's something important to convey with the words I have chosen. So, finally, I am giving myself permission to tell my story in the most honest way I know how. Thank you for reading.

Chapter 15

Benjamin Lee
May 18, 2013 to December 1, 2013
San Francisco, California to Cape Henlopen, Delaware

I spent 6.5 months of my life walking 5523km/3431miles! It is equivalent to completing two marathons every three days for 6.5 months. Not something I could have imagined doing. Looking back on it now, I still wonder how I did it.

I would be frequently asked, "Why would anyone choose to do such a thing?" The answer differed for every cross-country walker. Some wished to raise money or spread awareness, some just wanted to do it because...just because! I wanted that big adventure, something incredible that I could tell my future grandkids. A challenge to explore a country in a way I had never tried before.

The USA had always been near the top of my list of places to visit. I had just graduated from University and was free to go for that adventure before embarking on a career. After briefly considering hitchhiking across the country, I decided to walk from ocean to ocean – West Coast to the East Coast. Prior to this adventure, I had almost always been a couch potato. I had never been involved in any sport and was far from being fit but the fitness struggles I would have, never popped into my head. This was the adventure and challenge I was looking for and the more I thought about it, the more I knew I was going to stop at nothing until it was accomplished.

I received a lot of mixed reactions from those I told: "Why? How?

You're insane! Too dangerous!" At the time, I didn't think it was that crazy. I decided it was a great opportunity to link the trip with supporting a charity. I selected Oxfam, a charity that fights against poverty and injustice around the world, as the organization I would raise money for. I set my target to raise AUD$10,000.

I also decided that I wanted a travel partner in this great adventure but no one I knew personally was even remotely interested or crazy enough to join me in such a journey. I had frequently turned to online travel forums in the past to find travel companions as most of my friends and family weren't interested in traveling to the places I wanted to go nor for the length of time I had planned. I do enjoy traveling solo, but also love having someone alongside me to share in the joys and memories that traveling brings. Whilst this can be a risky approach, you can get lucky. Through such a forum, I found Lindsey, a lovely Canadian woman who also loved the idea of the walk and wished to join me.

Although I do recommend training to prepare for such a trek, my training was non-existent. I did try to prepare with long walks but early on, I strained a thigh muscle, which prevented much preparation. The training would have to wait for the trek itself.

At the airport, I was calm and excited, but my mom was the opposite. Knowing she wouldn't see me for at least half a year and with the risk and uncertainty of the journey ahead, she teared up while saying goodbye. I left my home in Melbourne, Australia and flew to San Francisco with a pack full of camping equipment and little knowledge of what lay ahead.

I met Lindsey in a hostel in San Francisco as planned. She was lovely, but I can't say we ever really "clicked." We spent a couple of days sightseeing around the city and picked up last-minute supplies. I needed some sort of cart to hold my equipment, food and water as I didn't want to carry it all on my back. I couldn't find much and ended up buying one of those pull-along shopping trolleys which were available for $5 from Target. I removed the canvas bag that was attached and just strapped my backpack to the frame. I knew it wouldn't last but it was a temporary solution.

On the 18th of May 2013, we began our walk. I was incredibly excited to get started but the whole day was full of mistakes and confusion. Our plan was to begin the walk from the north end of the Golden Gate Bridge. To get there, we needed to take a bus, but we ended up wasting an hour by going to the wrong bus stop. Eventually, we arrived with the sun shining and not a cloud in sight. The bridge was impressive and everything I had hoped it would be.

We followed the coast all the way to the east coast of San Francisco. We couldn't walk on the bridge to Oakland, so we had to take the BART (San Fran's train system) across. This would be the first of only two times along the whole walk that I would take some form of transportation. Both times were to get across a body of water that didn't have a bridge that I could legally cross on foot. I was adamant that I had to walk all the way. If I ever caught a ride to someone's house, I would always make my way back to the same spot that I was picked up from. No exceptions. Anything other than walking all the way would be cheating and that was unacceptable.

Without a working phone, we had no GPS and got lost many times. Also, college graduation meant all the hotels were booked, so a lot of time was wasted looking for a place to stay. What did I learn from day one? We were poorly prepared and had a lot to learn.

Unless you've done some long-distance walking before, there's bound to be a big learning curve. As you begin your walk, you'll continuously learn new things that will help you along your way. That's one tip that I could give you if you're planning a similar trek. Don't be too concerned about not knowing everything. Everyone works differently and as your journey progresses, your methods will change, your routines will change and you will change.

The next month or so was incredibly challenging and memorable. Many strangers opened their homes to us as we searched for safe places to stay. We stayed on a houseboat, a pear farm and even in a giant mansion that had been taken over by a squatter. The squatter even told us he had killed his best friend! Our makeshift carts eventually fell apart, so we purchased jogging strollers. We constantly had flat tire after flat tire that was moral sapping. We also had what we thought was a bear come through our camp to feast on our trash.

We walked over the Sierra Nevada's and through Nevada during peak summer. Nights were freezing but days were unbearably hot. It got so hot during the day that we were forced to rest during the day and walk throughout the night just to conserve our water supply. It was almost impossible to sleep during 50 Celsius/122 Fahrenheit days as you lay in a pool of your own sweat, waiting for the cool relief of the evenings.

Lindsey became sick, so she caught a ride to the nearest town. The town was about 60km/37 miles from where I was, but I told her that I would walk through the night and be there in the morning. Prior to this, the furthest I had walked in a day was about 35km/21 miles. Walking alone, in the pitch black of the Nevada desert for hours without seeing a single person or even a light, was an experience I will never forget. Every little sound would make you worry that something was in the shadows following you. I started walking at 5pm and didn't arrive until 5am the next morning. When I eventually saw the sign for the town, it happened. I broke down in tears and sobbed uncontrollably. I don't know why I did but I guess it was due to physical and mental exhaustion, mixed with pride and happiness with what I had done. I've spoken to many other walkers who have done similar treks and every single one has reached that same breaking point. They all had different reasons for reaching that point, but they reached it, nonetheless.

Lindsey had come down with bronchitis and had reached her limit, so she decided to go home. I tried to change her mind without success. Moments after arriving in Delta, Utah, her parents came to take her home and they offered to drive me to the airport so I could catch a flight home too. They tried to convince me that continuing alone wasn't a good idea but the brief, final conversation between us did not end well. I was disappointed and angry to lose my travel partner, which left me with only two choices: quit or continue my journey alone. I never wanted to do this alone and after what had been an extremely difficult first month, the thought of continuing alone for the next five months was hard to deal with. I had never quit anything in my life though and there was no way I would allow this to be the first time.

The following week was extremely difficult psychologically. I needed time to get my head in the correct frame of mind which ended up giving me too much time to think! I started overthinking things and this led me into a dark place I had never been to before. My head became filled with negative thoughts and I'd become overwhelmed by it all and would frequently burst into tears. I tried to talk to anyone I could to try and lift my spirits and sought for them to convince me that I needed to continue. Many told me that I should just go home and that I could lose my mind if I pushed on and spent so much time alone. I felt completely lost more so than ever before. The self-induced pressure on my shoulders was immense. I had told people I would complete this walk and donations towards my charity had been made. How could I quit now? I didn't know if my pride would ever recover if I took the easy path. I would regret it forever. At my lowest point, I wrote a text message to my family saying I was coming home. Thankfully, I never sent that message.

One of the few bright spots during that week was meeting David and Sharon. They were a gorgeous retired couple that had driven past Lindsey and I while we were on the road. They were curious about my trek, so they invited me for a chat. I ended up spending the whole afternoon in their RV telling them what we were doing and that Lindsey had returned home. They realized I was going through a difficult time and invited me to join them for their 4th of July celebrations that evening which involved enjoying a demolition derby. I pretty much spent the whole day with them and I can't tell you how much it helped me.

Despite my fears and anxiety, I decided to continue the walk solo. My worries disappeared, and I focused on taking one step at a time. I realized I could do this. I would do this. The further I walked, the more comfortable and happier I became. I loved being on the road and I embraced the time spent by myself. I met some incredible people along the way. Some took me into their homes, bought me lunch and others just drove up whilst I was walking to hand me a cold drink or money. This happened throughout my whole adventure and it still amazes me just how generous and kind people were towards me.

In Colorado, I started hearing stories about another man that was about a week ahead of me. He too was walking across the country and I became excited. Maybe I could find this guy and we could walk together. I spent multiple nights trawling through Google and Facebook, hunting for this person. I found him! It had to be him. I looked through his Facebook page and he had just arrived in Steamboat Springs, which was about four days walk ahead of me. The man's name was Joe Bell.

Joe was walking across the country for a very sad but incredibly important reason. Joe's son, Jadin, was gay and had been the target of immense bullying. Sadly, Jadin took his own life. As a grieving father, Joe wanted to make sense of it all, find solace from the experience of losing his son and try to make the world a better place. He decided to walk across the country to share Jadin's story and the devastating effects bullying can have.

I sent Joe a message and we met up in Steamboat Springs. He was middle-aged with grey hair, a moustache and a goatee and had a friendly smile. We sat for a couple of hours sharing stories and experiences from the road. We immediately clicked and went to a cinema later that day to watch *The Conjuring*. That's when he shared his story of the Red Vine Licorice. Whenever Joe and Jadin went to the movies, they always got Red Vine Licorice. After Jadin passed, Joe continued the tradition. He would buy a packet and leave one piece of Red Vine Licorice on the seat next to him for

Jadin.

After the movie, I brought up the idea of walking together and he agreed. I attended a talk Joe gave at the local school to a group of 12-years-old students. You could feel the emotion and passion as he spoke, and I knew he was going to make a difference to the people he met.

The next three weeks that we spent walking together flew by. It was great to have someone alongside me again. We went to the cinema a number of times, we hired a boat and went fishing at Grand Lake, we relaxed in the hot springs at Hot Sulphur Springs, we hid from the authorities as we stealth camped in the Rocky Mountain National Park and we spent a night at The Stanley hotel that inspired Stephen King to write *The Shining*. We had fun and we enjoyed this all too brief partnership.

Eventually, we made it to Boulder, Colorado. This would be where we parted ways. Joe was going to spend some time there to try and organize as many speaking engagements as he could. On my final night in Boulder, I got to meet Joe's partner Lola and their son, Joseph. He was a bright, funny and incredibly likable young man. Joe, Joseph and I ended up having dinner with three other people who have played a major part in my walk: Nate

Damm (walked across America in 2011), Jonathan Stalls (walked across America in 2010) and Lacey Champion (she and her family helped me incredibly over the next few months). It was a great evening spent sharing stories and adventures.

That evening, I said my final goodbye to Joe. To be honest, I wasn't that sad or upset. Joe had always joked that he had wanted to make his way to Florida and wrestle an alligator. Privately, my plan was to finish the walk and then head down to meet him there. I knew I would see him in a few months, so it wasn't a goodbye but a see you later.

I had gotten over the mountains and now was left with the task of hiking across the Midwest. Nebraska, Iowa, Illinois and Indiana were all extremely flat and filled with wide-open fields and farms. I could now push myself and walk for longer distances and in far quicker time. I already got through Nevada in peak summer and over both the Sierra Nevada and the Rockies, so these flats should be a piece of cake!

The main roads and highways were a mixed bag to walk on. When there was a nice shoulder along the road, there was no issue. I could follow that for hours without worrying about the traffic. Often though, the shoulder would either disappear or shrink to a few feet. This meant that I was forced to walk inches away from speeding traffic or on the road itself. It was either that or walk on the dirt and sand which was incredibly difficult. I was constantly on the lookout for side roads and walking or cycling paths. Most of the time, my route would depend on where the next cycling path could be found. These cycling paths were often wide, paved and flat, which was the perfect surface to push my cart on. Sometimes these paths would go from one side of a state to the other and that was gold for me!

During the second half of my walk, people often offered to pick up my cart and drive it to the next town. Walking without the cart made things easier, safer and allowed me to cover a greater distance. Without the cart, I could easily walk on the grass, dirt or sand alongside the road. A big thank you to the many people who helped me in this way. One incredible family did this for me during my entire crossing of Illinois. I basically only had to push my cart as I entered Illinois and as I left.

Illinois became a very difficult and emotional time for me. On October 10th, as I was waiting for the train to take me to Chicago for a bit of rest and relaxation, I scrolled through Facebook and saw a post made on Joe Bell's Facebook page. While walking along the road the previous evening, a truck driver had fallen asleep at the wheel and veered into Joe, killing him instantly. In disbelief and thinking that this must be some bad joke, I continued to scroll through my feed and found more posts from people expressing their sadness and offering condolences. I then started to get phone calls from people who knew both Joe and I. They called to pass on the devastating news. He was gone. I spent the next hour on the train to

Chicago in tears, unable to keep my mind off the tragic news.

When I got back onto the road and started walking again, things were different. I felt a far greater sense of worry and danger when walking alongside the road. This was partly because of what happened to Joe and the fact that people back home kept telling me to be safe and to watch out. I remember one section of road that had no shoulder whatsoever and there was also a large ditch that ran right alongside the road. It was impossible for me to push my cart in this ditch, so I had no choice but to walk on the road and just pray that the drivers that passed were paying attention and driving carefully. I knew that any of these vehicles that passed inches away from me could potentially hit me. This stretch of road went on for a couple of miles and the longer it went on, the more stressed and panicked I became. With the constant sense of danger, thoughts of quitting crept into my mind.

The other major concern was the weather. I needed to finish before the snow arrived, otherwise, I would be in trouble. I wasn't prepared to trek through snow or to sleep in my tent in those temperatures. I knew it was coming though, so I kept increasing my daily walking distance to make up as much time as possible. While camping along the hiking trails, I began to wake up to find my water bottles completely frozen.

I eventually made it to Parkersburg, West Virginia. This point had been a milestone since the start. I knew that once I got to this point, a massive portion of the remaining walk would be on hiking/cycling trails, which meant I would rarely have to walk on the road. From here, I would be taking the North Bend Rail Trail, the Chesapeake and Ohio Canal and the Washington and Old Dominion Trail. Combining these three trails would take me all the way to Washington DC with a few bits of road in between.

About a month before I was due to complete the walk, I contacted my mom to ask if she or any of my family would be flying over to be with me when I finished. I had always assumed that she would be there, but she told me she wouldn't be able to come. She had recently had a hip operation which made it impossible to spend 16 hours on a plane. I was devastated. This would mean that I would be walking onto that beach by myself with no one to hug and no one to celebrate with. I never envisaged that I would be standing there alone, giving myself a pat on the back.

When I made it to Harpers Ferry, West Virginia, I met up with a lady called Mary and her lovely daughter, Abby. Mary had been following me on my journey through my Facebook account and offered to help. She met me on a cold evening outside my motel to pick up my cart and took it home to enable me to slack-pack for the next two days until I reached her home just outside of Washington DC.

I continued along the Chesapeake and Ohio Canal and the Washington and Old Dominion Trail, all the way to Mary's house. I arrived late evening and was greeted by Mary's entire family. They were a lovely family and made me quickly feel at home. I got the entire downstairs to myself, which had been turned into an entertainment room. I enjoyed a wonderful dinner after which Abby, Mary and I played a fun card game.

The next morning, I decided to just relax in the house. Mary came back home and asked if I would give her a hand with unloading the shopping. As I opened the trunk of her car, the only thing I could say was "What the f**k?!" My brother, Jon, was lying there holding his phone, recording my reaction. I was shocked and all that came out were more swear words! We gave each other a big hug. I hadn't seen any family or friends since I left Melbourne six months earlier, so it was great to see him. Since my mom couldn't be there, she had contacted Mary secretly to plan for Jon to surprise me instead. The plan was that he would walk with me for the final week.

The next day, Jon and I began our final leg to the finish. It was going to be a short 17 miles / 27km day on nice walking trails into Washington DC. Short for me at least. Jon was not prepared for what lay ahead as he struggled to walk the distances that I had become so accustomed to. He required far more breaks and quickly developed blisters on his feet. I could certainly empathize with his pain as I went through my fair share of blisters during the last six months.

After a cold but pleasant evening spent sightseeing in Washington DC, we continued towards the Chesapeake Bay Bridge. I would normally cover the distance in a day, but we needed to take it easy on Jon's legs and feet. Three days later, we reached Highway 50 that crossed the bridge. This bridge was a major road and pedestrians were not allowed on it. This would be the second time that I would have to take a vehicle on the trek. The plan was for Mary to meet us at the start of the bridge, pick us up, drive us across and drop us off at the end of the bridge, where we would continue to walk. With our rain gear on and the rain pouring around us, we headed towards the bridge when we heard a vehicle behind us, honking. We moved aside as much as possible to allow the vehicle to pass but it didn't.

It continued to slowly follow us from behind and honked again. We stopped and turned around and as the vehicle came closer, I could see a familiar face in the passenger seat. It was my mom, Pauline. My initial reaction was quite different from when I saw Jon. There was no swearing this time! As the vehicle came to a stop, Mom jumped out and we embraced in a big hug. It was incredible to see her after all this time. She had been the one who had given me the most support throughout the whole journey and was the person I most wanted to be there at the end. She admitted that she would have always regretted not being there to celebrate the end with me, so she secretly organized everything with Mary.

When we reached the Chesapeake Bay Bridge, we jumped into Mom's car and drove to the other side. For the remainder of the trek, she would take our backpacks and drive ahead to the next motel, so Jon and I could walk without any packs each day and meet up with her at the end of each day. We were now down to the final 76miles/122km and this would be covered in four days. Jon's feet were getting worse and at the end of each day, he was in a lot of pain.

My final day arrived, and it was going to be a short one as we had finished the previous day only a few miles away from the town of Lewes. It was the final town I would walk through before reaching Cape Henlopen State Park and then finally the Atlantic Ocean. As we walked through Lewes, we met up with Mom and Mary, who wanted to join us for the final few kilometers of the 6.5-month adventure. It was odd; it just felt like any other day. I wasn't sure what to expect but I had run this moment through my mind almost every day since I had the idea. In my head, it went a little like this:

The sky would be blue, and the weather perfect. The sun would shine on my back as I made my way towards the sandy beach of Cape Henlopen State Park. My family would be following close behind me and there would be a great buzz of excitement between us. I would be excited and pumped. I was about to experience the greatest feeling of accomplishment I've ever felt. I would walk over that final sand dune and look out over the great big blue ocean; my eyes would fill with tears. I'd drop everything and walk out into that final point that I'd been dreaming about since day one. With one final deep breath, I would step out into the cold water, overcome with an intense feeling of happiness, pride and accomplishment. I would hear my family clapping and cheering behind me. After taking a moment, I would splash my face with some water and then turn to embrace those who had supported me on this adventure. I had done it!

So, that's what I had imagined which seemed like a logical end to me. It didn't quite go like that though. The sky was overcast and grey. There was no sun. There was, however, a definite buzz of excitement between Jon, Mom and Mary though. To me, it felt just like another day of the trek. As I walked over the final sand dune and set my eyes on the Atlantic Ocean, I certainly had a big smile on my face. My mom was holding her phone up, recording the final moments. Jon was trying to keep up whilst enduring the pain from the many blisters he had developed. He was nursing a noticeable limp. I dropped my shoes onto the sand and finally waded into the cold water up to my knees and raised my hands up in triumph. I could hear the group clapping and cheering. I placed my hands onto my head and then thought, *"Now what?"*

I didn't feel anything. Sure, there was happiness but there wasn't the intense sense of accomplishment I had expected. I had spent 6.5 months doing this and had been through some tough times. Now, I was finally here, yet there wasn't the level of euphoria I had anticipated. I felt a little…empty. Just thinking about this moment during the trek would make me emotional. Now that I had arrived, there were no tears. I kind of just stood there, looking out at the ocean and wondered: *"What should I do now?"* After a few moments, I turned around and gave my brother, Mom and Mary a big hug. I tried to force some tears because I wanted to cry. They just weren't there!

We stood around chatting, taking photos and sharing some champagne for a while and then I pulled out two pieces of Red Vine Licorice. I stuck them into the sand and let the waves wash them away. I needed to honor Joe and Jadin because they had played such a big part in my journey. They deserved to reach this point too. I did tear up a little bit as the waves washed them away and I said my final goodbye to Joe. Despite all the tears, trials and tribulations, the 6.5 months spent on this crazy adventure was the best experience I've ever had and one I think about each and every day. I experienced unbelievable generosity and kindness from complete strangers, I uncovered a world of beauty that can only be seen at walking pace and I found an inner strength and determination that I didn't know I had. I hope my story and the 26 other incredible individuals have inspired you to follow your dreams, no matter how crazy. Don't let anyone tell you that it can't be done. You can do anything you set your mind to. I will end on one of my favorite quotes from the late Avicii: "One day you will leave this world behind. So, live a life you will remember."

Chapter 16

Newton Baker
January 16, 2015 to June 2, 2015
Huntington Beach, California to Washington D.C.

Dedicated to MARK BAUMER, Transcon Friend of Earth,
killed by car, Transcon 2016

    Why do this? "... to do something peculiarly difficult to such a perfect pitch that we catch the universe, understand it, ride it, and live." William Stafford
Race Background by Assistant Professor Cara Ocobock:
    "In 2015, a team of athletes ran across the United States. RaceAcrossUSA, was developed by the 100 Mile Club® to spread awareness of and combat childhood obesity in the US. Runners participated in a marathon each day and visited elementary schools along the route. Four support crew who accompanied the runners manned drop-bag and water stations, drove the runners, ran errands, and helped with daily data collection. Also, a research team took measurements or solicited fecal/urine samples at various points throughout the race."
    "My research team—Caitlin Thurber and Herman Pontzer from Hunter College, Lara Dugas from Loyola University—and I examined energy expenditure and the number of calories spent each day by the runners. We measured basal metabolic rate, body composition, and total daily energy expenditure of the runners at the beginning, middle, and end of the race with hopes of detecting possible metabolic adaptations to such extreme levels of physical activity. "
    "Researchers examining running biomechanics, how gut microbiome changed during the race, and the physiological impact on the heart were also part of this massive research effort. So, not only were the RaceAcrossUSA participants running over 3,080 miles in 140 days, they also had to sleep in tents most nights, wear uncomfortable heart rate monitors, and, yes, collect their own feces to be FedExed to research labs across the country. Crew members helped with daily data collection and took charge of specimen shipment. But, to their credit and vast patience, the runners and crew took all of this in stride and kept a good humor and attitude throughout the race. The runners and crew not only faced grueling physical and research demands, but they did so with a group of strangers. Strangers they ran with, ate with, and shared living quarters with for 140 days. The mental effort of waking up each morning to the reality of another day, another marathon is taxing enough. However, navigating the wide variety of personalities under similar stress levels is equally if not more

daunting than the race itself. The mental and social component of this transcontinental trek was not something that I had considered when planning the data collection. However, when we met the runners for the first round of data collection before the race began, we all took notice. The nervousness among the runners was palpable, which I initially attributed to excitement and apprehension over the long, physically demanding journey ahead. As I met each of the runners and crew members, I wondered how individuals differing greatly in age (30-73), beliefs, and backgrounds would get along under these trying circumstances. How would the interactions at the beginning of the race change over time? Caitlin Thurber, describes best the early behavior she saw: 'Initially there was an atmosphere of excitement and activity among the runners as they adapted to their new routine of setting up and breaking down their tents, organizing their supplies, planning daily meals, and running errands. There was a lot of socializing. The general excitement of the task ahead and the need for group bonding resulted in playing games, taking walks or hikes together, and an active nightlife of going out to bars and restaurants." (Well, a few nights. But not for me, NB)

"Though the early excitement and frenetic activity eventually waned, and everyone fell into a quiet and easy routine, the bonds formed within this small group at the beginning enabled the runners' success at the end. For example, one of the runners often suffered vertigo when crossing bridges. To help distract him, one of the crew members would come and run with him across the bridge." Cara Ocobock is an assistant professor of Anthropology at University at Albany, SUNY Thank you, Cara, for giving permission to use this!

What follows will be short snapshots. I can't possibly tell this tale in 5,000 words. Apologies to Transcon Icons David Warady, Jesse Daley Riley and B J Timoner who visited us, to runners and stories left out until a bigger version is written.

The moment to start has arrived … I yell, "Wait! Don't go! I need to find a plastic beach toy like teammate Patrick Sweeney finds." I don't know him yet. I've seen tons of beach toy pics he posts on FB. He found one moments ago after we waded barefoot into the Pacific Ocean. I trot swiftly down the beach away from the start line with voices yelling, "Newton, get over here! We're starting!" What's wrong with me? The biggest run of my life, and I'm doing this? Got to find one. Just a little further. Never be another opportunity. And there! Something orange. A plastic **turtle**! I already know I'll be slowest in the group. I've trained with a Turtle Plan: Slow! I only have to run a mile at a time. Maintain a long-term vision while keeping an intense daily focus. But I will get there! This turtle's a sign. And a birthday present. Today's my birthday! Patrick's, too. The group sings Happy Birthday to us. I announce, "I'm too old now to do this." Laughter and we're off. 140 days later, 3085 miles, I become the second oldest man at 73 to Transcon the USA.

We start on a well paved bike path, a white line dividing it. My I-phone has a map guiding me along what looks to be 100 intersection turns, but it is not operating correctly. I panic and speed up. 200 feet from the start, I'm running too fast, yet have rapidly fallen behind everyone. Got to keep somebody in sight to know where to go. Rounding a long bend, I catch sight of two women entered to run only four CA stages. I return to a sensible pace, my RAUSA teammates already far out of sight. My phone begins to ding relentlessly. It is Birthday wishes pouring in. I sink into the enjoyment of the run when, WOOSH! Yikes! Brushed from behind by a cyclist. Didn't hear him coming. A new way to be taken out of the race: spandex clad bikers roaring past. Half giving no warning. Stay on my own side of the white line and don't stagger! The white line forever!!

> Running down streets and on sidewalks in towns,
> Always on watch for the dogs and the hounds.
> The painted white line my guide to the East.
> Endless black asphalt chews on my feet,
> a gravelly, growling, shoe eating beast.
> In poor shape are some houses,
> next to some really quite rich.
> And along every roadside,
> there's trash in the ditch.
> Paper and pampers, plastic bottles and cans.
> Beer, wine, twine strapping, in the ditch it all lands.
> Hubcaps, license plates, car parts and more.
> Broken glass, money, it's a wide open store.
> Bolts, nuts and screws, clothing one could still wear.
> Whatever you might want, you're sure to find there.
> In California there's spandex, tiny bikinis.
> People ride past on high speeding bikes.
> Waves, tans and surfboards, everything sunshine likes.
> Hills in California lead to the Arizona State Line,
> where the road extends endlessly miles straight ahead.
> And the sense you make progress,
> plays games with your head.
> But a mile is a mile.
> You do them one at a time.
> Relentless pursuit of the roadside white line!

To school kids, we talk about who we are and why we are running. A question and answer session follows. Kids ask really insightful questions: "Where do you go to the bathroom?" And the teachers: "SHH! SHH!" We pose for photos with the students. At one of the early school visits, I was struck by the beauty of a couple hundred plus kids from kindergarten, middle school and high school. Mostly of Mexican-American, Native American descent. The dark eyes, silky black hair, bone structure in the smiling, curious faces filled with smiles. What fun we had with the kids. How interested and appreciative they were. Our country is filled with such a variety of cultures and ethnic groups, all so special! What a garden of beautiful flowers we are together. After stage finishes, we fend for ourselves when it comes to food, buying and cooking what we eat. At 54 campgrounds, I had to put up and take down my tent, for me a difficult task with some right shoulder and both hands arthritic, along with about 80% flexion in my left foot (broken ankle 2008) and left knee (dislocated, 6-hour operation 1963). Couple teammates remarked how funny it was watching me try to crawl in and out or get up off the ground. We also stayed on floors in churches and school gyms. A hotel was a treat upon reaching a State line. 12 runners started the race, 7 finished.

    Was running into Payson AZ and it's very hot. I'm very thirsty. Discover I'd forgotten cash. Coming around a corner, I catch up to Darren and borrow two dollars. I pass the church we'll be staying in again tonight and go into a Dairy Queen next door. Wanting a chocolate shake, I'm a dollar plus short. I explain what I'm doing and will be back tonight and will come over to pay the difference. The young girl across the counter isn't sure. She asks another girl mopping the floor what she thinks. She doesn't know. "I'll go ask the manager out back," says the first girl. I wait so long, I think about leaving. Finally, she comes back. "Sorry, he said no." I leave to search for where I can buy a small coke. One minute later, a car pulls up, the window rolls down. "Can I get you a drink or something?" It's Alexandra, an EMT from Canada, along to assist our team for awhile. I mention a chocolate shake and she says to meet her less than a mile up the road at a McD and she'll have one. It happens. Then, a mile beyond, I buy a cold coke with my two dollars. But wait, later that night, Jessica Hardy has a story about the same DQ. While my episode was happening, she hadn't yet arrived in Payson. After I'd left, she'd gone into the same DQ and asked about a shake. The manager invited her to come behind the counter and make her own. Gave it to her free and said another runner had been in!

    My first running struggle was to get up hills and not miss turns out of CA and into AZ. Run went well until in NM, I hit the beginning of what I call the 6 Days of Hell. Entering Socorro, NM yesterday, got sore muscle about 2 inches above right knee on inner thigh. Struck at mile 19. Felt bad. Hurt to run. Ice, duct tape, massage and walking fast worked. Soreness did not interfere with walking but did with running. Last night, used an electric circular sander to which Chris Knodel had attached some soft, padded stuff. Massaged the heck out of sore area. Today, felt great, but I walked about 90% and only ran some the last 6 miles to be cautious. We are rapidly coming down off 20 days of altitude from 8,000 ft. Headed to a middle school where we will stay 3 nights in the gym but have to pick our stuff up early every morning to store in closets because kids have school. Lights out every night at 9PM. And always: shop for food, shower, cook, eat a ton, prepare drop bags and clothes for tomorrow, social media, download stage map, attend 6pm team meeting, charge phone, rub on EPSOM_IT, sleep, get up, sunscreen, lip balm, TP, sunglasses, kleenex, run, find road surprises. Fill out daily medical research papers after getting weighed. Do it all over again. Yay!! 'Tis a Journey of a Thousand Moving Parts!

NM. Running out of Carrizozo Valley of Fire, I was happy 'til last 4 miles. Some 20 mph winds picked up to 35-40 mph in my face, nonstop, just as the forecast had promised. Blew me backwards. Sideways. Couldn't stand still and stay upright, was spinning around, exhausted. 500 feet to go, Andrea spotted me and ran out. Leaning on her, she dragged me to the car. I flopped across the hood until recovered. She is special!! She was my crew person, as well as doing job establishing finish/ start line. She recorded weights and finish times of all runners, picked up last finisher or two, (usually just me), drove me to buy food, carried baggage for me and helped put up my tent. On the hot days, toward the end, she always found a coffee shop for a delicious, cold Frappuccino! I ran 3,000 miles. She drove 12,000 with all the ferrying, plus a few airport trips for other people.

VERMONT MAN BITTEN ON REAR END BY DOG WHILE RUNNING -

But it didn't stop him!! Happened running out of Historic Lincoln, AZ where Jesse James used to ride and the Lincoln County War took place. Yes sir, big pit bull, head up to my waist, left his yard, followed across the road from me. A woman back in the dog's yard started yelling at him. He crossed the road, came up behind me and chomped onto my right butt. Could feel teeth, but they didn't break through. I yelled. Lady was still yelling. Max, crew for NM state runner Charles, came roaring up in his car. He had been alerted by runners ahead of me about a loose, aggressive dog. Great guy that he is, he came back to try to find it and watch over me. Had the attack continued, he'd have been there in seconds. Two miles later, a State Policeman pulled up and asked how things were going. I told him about the dog. He said he'd go back to look into it. Don't know what came of that, but Max is a smart guy. He had taken a picture of the house and the #. Said he'd forward that to the police. Picacho NM Feb 26th. Hardest marathon I've ever run. A driving, freezing rain first 13 miles covered me with about 2 pounds of ice. Rain stopped or don't know that I'd have finished. Wind in my face was brutal. Couldn't see, so took off glasses as they were plastered in ice. Then, glasses off, I couldn't see. With no rain second half, got rolling again. Feb 27 near Roswell New Mexico, *marathon stopped at 18 miles because road closed – ice*. Won't start tomorrow 'til road is reopened. Estimated start time around 12:45 pm. But got off to a troubling start. Director's car was broken into. Tools, our school speaker and some running shoes were stolen. A sheriff checked it out. The window was covered with plastic to be repaired later. Because of the recent weather and road closings, we adjust our plans to keep on schedule. Today we'll run 30 miles, and another 30 plus tomorrow, to make up for mileage lost during road shutdown.

Stage #1 Texas March 4th-Brutal day. Very cold, drizzling rain that turned into freezing rain, then sleet, then snow and for 20 miles, steady, gusting winds to 20 mph. First 13 miles very difficult. Can't take gloves off to do Gels or check watch time. Map not working and Texas had no mileage signs. Never knew how I was doing for time or what my distance was. I had to trust my walk/run pattern. Five people stopped to ask if I were ok or wanted a ride. One lady drove up from behind and pulled in straight across my lane, blocking oncoming traffic and me. She rolled down her window and held out $40. "Get off the road and get yourself something to eat," she said sternly. A bit confused, I asked, "Are you making a donation? I'll give it to the Kids 100 Mile Club." She admonished me again in a motherly tone: "You buy yourself a warm meal!" Two State police cars pulled up as she began backing up to turn and go in the opposite direction from me. They turned their police lights on as she maneuvered, and I thought we were both going to be arrested. She drove off. Police asked if I were ok, smiled, waved, and left. A mile down the road another pickup truck pulled over. A little old man said there was a DQ a mile ahead and I should get in. He'd drive me there to get warm and buy me a hot chocolate. I thanked him saying no. He said I should stop in when I got there anyway. I did. I used the bathroom, answered a lot of questions from two young, male workers, found a penny in the driveway, keeping my coin found in every state streak alive, and headed down the road into the wind and sleet. Run from Tolio TX toward Brownfield produced a spectacular surprise and enduring memory tying me to Vermont. I hear loud honks of geese. Looking up, I see wave after wave of giant V's: geese flying from my right to left. They appear as far as I can see. And they just keep coming. I count groups of 70 plus. There have to have been thousands. Must be going North. In Vermont, I see small groups, 12 to 25, small flocks headed South in the fall. I laugh and call to them, "See you this fall!" I'm trying to get pictures without getting dizzy looking up, circling and falling down. A whiskery guy in a pickup stops, rolls down his window and yells, "Y'all be careful there. Keep doin' wha-cher doin, yer likely ta git sumpen in yer eye!" He laughs, waves. Then he, the geese and I are off.

Louisiana- April Fools was a rest day. Alex, a master with computer graphics, hatched a plan with me to post a FB picture with his dreadlocks cut off and my beard shaved clean. A great picture, most people couldn't or wouldn't believe it. But some did. Next day, we posted ourselves back to normal. I remember a big sign we passed somewhere that said, "Here Normal is just a setting on the Dryer."

In Arkansas passed a field with, what a man told me were, 350 roosters with another 200 breeding in the barn. Each rooster sells for between $500 and $1,500. Most are sold in Mexico for Cock fights. He said the owner makes hundreds of thousands of dollars.

MS- We all talked about getting to the huge bridge and crossing the mighty Mississippi River. Once across, we'd truly be on the East side of the USA where rivers flowed a different direction. I was thinking I should leave a memento in the river, maybe toss my hat. No, hat was too precious and littering wouldn't be good. As I mounted the bridge, I peered carefully over the side. Vertigo did not bother as there was a big shelf extending out from the side barrier. Suddenly, a huge barge poked out from under the bridge. I made a nice video. Looking up, I see Andrea racing across the bridge toward me. She is flying with a strong wind pushing from behind. I turn to greet her just as a huge 18-wheeler comes whooshing past. From the truck pass and the wind, my precious, beloved, roadrunner visor I'd purchased and worn since Parker AZ, flew off my head, over the side rail and into the Mississippi River.

Itta Bena MS - April 12th, we celebrate Alex' 30th Birthday with him giving us presents. His mom came to visit and brought Runners High Tye Dye t-shirts Alex had made. He inked his feet and stamped them on each of our shirts. Mine included little Hubcap circles.

Running out of Columbus MS, a car pulls over in front of me. A young woman jumps out and yells, "Mr Baker! Is that you?" For a second, my brain debated the answer. Admitting who I was, I asked, "Who are you?" It was Lindsey Lorinovich Carlton, from my hometown and a former MHS basketball star and student in the fifth grade where I taught. She was taking a son to a doctor's appointment on a route she didn't often take, saw me and something registered. I had a full beard she'd never seen. She said she'd heard something about me doing a run but wasn't sure when or where. She pulled her car over and looked me up on FB. About 20 minutes before, I had found a MS car tag and posted myself holding it on FB to tease my teammates: "Got another one!" I learned this day the importance of behaving myself even far from home!

AL Talladega- After each of us signed papers, we got permission and a top security escort to drive onto the Talladega Race Track and park in Breakdown Lane. We were allowed to run around the 2.6 mile track. It was overwhelming and awesome. We were all giddy. The top lane on corners looked almost vertical. Our guide said it was close to 4 stories high. Our pictures couldn't begin to show it. People who got to the top could hardly get down. The guide said many people had fallen and broken collar bones. You have to see this to believe it. Now I can't wait to watch a NASCAR race here. I have great, new respect for drivers. Speed record here is 200 MPH. Seating capacity of 175,000! I had found a little, toy, red race car alongside the road in Mississippi. I brought it to the Talladega Race Track to get a picture of it on the track. I'll give picture and car to Ken Squire as a souvenir for taking my calls live from the road to his radio station. He was the voice of NASCAR ON TV. He owns and broadcasts on WDEV 550 am and 96.1 FM in Waterbury, Vermont, hometown to both of us growing up. Ken was recently inducted into the NASCAR SPORTS HALL OF FAME!

AL- Saw a Shilo Baptist Church sign: "Where will you spend Eternity?" I thought, "It will not be in this event, though there are moments it seems like it." Had a lengthy chat with a man who said he wouldn't look good in a picture, "and besides, I got a couple gold teeth and I don't want anybody to see them and come after me!"

First stage of the Silver Bullet Bike Path in Georgia was memorable. Alex often dallied at the start, then would soon catch me. This day, he came up from behind without a word and I picked up my pace to match his. We ran in sync. He said nothing, nor did I. I wondered how long I could keep the pace, knowing I shouldn't. But we were on a roll. Neither of us said one word for 6 miles. Didn't need to. It was an awesome, magical moment. To this point, we'd run over 2,000 miles, and here we were, in sync, sun peeking through the tunnel canopy of tall green trees. Bushes closing in on the sides, birds chirping, a light breeze, cool temperature, Alex bare feet silently padding along, my running shoes tapping out a steady, light beat. We glided quietly forward side by side, down straight-a-ways and swept around gentle curves - doing what we came to do- running- together. I slowed and he ran on. Later, I mentioned it to Andrea. She said,"Whaat? Six miles? And you didn't talk?"

Somewhere in GA, 4 kids were 200 feet off the road on a trampoline. As soon as they saw me approaching, they jumped down and ran toward me. I knew they must have talked to a runner ahead of me when they asked: "You got a card?" "You running to Washington?"

I gave the two biggest kids one of my cards, but with only one left, handed it to the littlest and said, "Can you share with him?" She pinched her lips together, shook her head "NO" and started to walk away. "Come back and be in a picture," I said. She scrunched her face up. "NO!" Bigger sister said, "I'll share mine. You can keep that one." The littlest came back and happily posed for a picture!

Stage 6 Heading out of Athens Georgia, I meet a dad out walking his very young son and a newborn bundled in a blanket. The conversation started when the little boy, 3, asked, "Why you run?" As he kept repeating that, I'd say, "It is fun." I told him we started at the ocean, touched the water, and we would run to another ocean. He wanted to know if I was going to jump in. Then it was back to "Why you run? Wanna see my shoes?" His dad and I visited. He unwrapped the blanket around the baby for a picture. I said goodbye to Ben, little Crawford, and new baby, Maryann. After meeting Ben's family, the run was a bit of a struggle, just the way some days go. Suddenly, at mile 22, the magic began, as only it can on the road: you least expect it, and little things lead to bigger. Ed Sims spotted me looking at his very interesting yard full of car parts and repairs. He walked toward me and said," You decided to walk to Washington?" "You've been talking to my fellow runners." "Yup, a young fellow up ahead of you." We visited about the run and our families. I mentioned collecting road treasures and not finding a Georgia plate. He said he didn't have one, but he had a North Carolina motorcycle plate if I wanted it. Indeed, and he came back with a nice NC car plate as well. Thank you, ED SIMS!

I got to mile 23 and decided to stop for a another, cold, chocolate milk at a gas/grocery store. While paying, I set down the NC license plates and the lady asked the key question. And the stories began. She loudly urged me on with many questions. I gave her my card, and a man waiting behind heard the conversation and said, "Come up the road a bit to my place at CarQuest. I've got a Georgia tag for you," and soon after, waved to me as he drove past. I found his place and he was cleaning a Georgia plate.. We told stories, chatting ten minutes about his dog, escaping drug addiction, losing a job, then took pictures. Thank you, SID. I headed up the road and stopped to check my location. I was at mile 26, a mile to go. I glanced down. BOOM! A license plate ... And from Georgia!!

South Carolina- The kind of traffic and roads being travelled now are not conducive to finding car tags. What to do? I decide to look elsewhere. In a place they might be. Automotive repair shops! I spotted a nice looking shop and thought, "This is the one." Immediately met a very nice gentleman who said indeed, he had one out back and would be glad to contribute it to me. We visited. He used to repair VW's, now repairs forklifts, used to race motorbikes, then asked if I were "of the faith?" Said he is a pastor in a church about a half mile down the road. I ran 3 minutes off course down a side road and got a picture of his church! Thank you, Dale Cross!! Another unexpected surprise from the road revealing some kind people across the country!!

Met new friend Peter Ross at mile 22. He, recognizing the gait of a distance runner with a two-bottle pack in 88-degree heat, pulled over to see if I needed a lift or a drink or "anything else I can help you with?" We exchanged running stories. He is one of the top area distance runners. Little wonder he had the insight and concern to pick me out and offer support. I got some cold, lime Gatorade from him. Thank you, Peter, your well-behaved dog, and little guy in the back seat. Another gift from the road!!

SC Stage 4 Spartanburg- Always a great moment when I get to run a bit with Alex. At mile 13, I catch up to him and take his picture on his 100th ROAD MARATHON in his running career. CONGRATULATIONS "DANCING FEATHER!" Finished today in 90-degree heat. When I get home, I'm going to paint a white line on my treadmill belt, pull up a chair, turn on the machine and watch the white line go by. WHITE LINE: most enduring vision on run!

Stage1 NC 82 degrees. Very humid! Two visits: 1. "Hey, where y'all running from?" I crossed the street to talk to 4 men in hard hats, leaning on shovels. They'd seen my fellow racers go by. A small steam shovel was digging a ditch a few feet away. "Don't worry. He won't hit us." I kept moving away as the machine would swing around. They leaned on their shovels and asked a lot of good questions like school kids do. Ten minutes later, I asked about taking a picture to post on FB. "Better not," one said laughing. " We don't want to be seen not working". They each wanted one of my cards, and off I went.

2. In a poor section of town, two African American ladies sitting on their front porch yelled, "Bless you boy! Keep it up!" They were so much fun, laughing and trying to get the dog to stop barking. I yelled from the roadside to avoid the dog. We had a fun chat for 5 minutes in between cars going by and the dog yapping. As I left, I mentioned my age. One hollered back, laughing and waving, "I'm gonna work on livin' as long as you, but do it sittin' right here on this porch!" There are all kinds of good people everywhere! I ran on, all smiles.

NC Big road surprise! I make a right-hand turn at an intersection. Down ahead, I see some people hustle out of a car and cross street while peering up road at me. They face me holding up very colorful signs. What is this? I get closer and see it is Linda Baker and family. Linda was a teacher colleague in Montpelier School System with me. She's visiting her daughter Jessica, a NC runner and RD. They drove an hour to intercept and surprise me. Jessica Baker-Brundige jumped in and ran 9 miles with me. Next day in Albemarle NC, another generous surprise from the road: The owner of a vacuum cleaner/sports store (VAC'N DASH) treated us to dinner and a free shirt of our choice from his store. An enthusiastic supporter of our event, he sent a newspaper reporter to interview us. We got a tour of his store. He showed us his machinery in operation, printing out shirts.

NC Stage 6 to Sanford. Early start with 90-degree heat. We plan to visit 3 schools today and will be guests at a health fair in the evening. Finished Stage with a 97-degree index.

Met more friends today. First, Ina came out to see what was going on at our halfway aid station. She wondered if it were a car wreck and came out to check. Said that's about all that ever happened out there. Told her, "I'm probably the only wreck you'll see today." We had a good laugh, talked about the race, then off I went, she with her cane. At the finish line, surprise! Running friend Jimmie Barnes, returning to Alabama from his 48 hour race in New Jersey, met me with two ice cold cokes!

May 24-Today's stage dedicated to my son, Silas Baker, (19) who will be running his 1st marathon tomorrow, wearing my retired Hall of Fame #84 in the 27th running of the VERMONT CITY MARATHON. It's the 1st one I will miss! Bring it home, Silas! Good luck. Love you, DAD. And he finished in 5:30.

On our rest day, we spoke to the entire student body at Townville SC Elementary School. First, we ran laps around the school yard with these little guys, then played with them before going in to address 275 students. A 100 Mile Running Club school, a map was posted with our pictures and a short biography pinned to the state we are from.

May 19th-This one for you mom and dad, as it's the 100th Marathon in our RaceAcrossUSA. Ten years ago you both sat in

wheelchairs, May 2005, at the finish line as guests of the VERMONT CITY MARATHON and saw me run my 100th marathon, the ONLY one you ever saw. Within a year and a half, you both died. And Dad, after my very 1st marathon you said, "Isn't it nice your first and last marathon went so well?" "What do you mean last marathon?" "Well, at your age, (then 39) you're not doing that again, are you?" Today was my 100th marathon in 4 months in the RaceAcrossUSA and 315th lifetime. I'm sure you would have enjoyed it as much as I did. REST IN PEACE. Finished 27.10 miles in 5:13.

Samantha, Garrett, and Andrea: our crew and car drivers. We've praised them many times, deservedly! They have been dedicated, on time, even tempered and helped beyond the call of their job. They have interacted at schools, with people they meet, are learning about other cultures, ethnicities, and geography across their country. They do all this with a sense of humor, intelligence and do some running with us. Can you imagine how this will look on their applications to grad school or employment? Their candidacy should rise to the top. I hope their parents, relatives and friends appreciate what they are doing. They are the heartbeat driving the race on the road!! Co-Race Director Sandy VanSoye drove the 4th vehicle and oversaw everything else, a next to impossible job! Last stage to DC. What do I find?

I'm nearing the end of a bike path on the outskirts of DC. An approaching cyclist tells me to be careful of a **turtle** in the path around the corner. And there it is: a giant turtle resting dead center on the path, eyes slowly blinking. My turtle plan worked! The final sign. But not the last surprise! Finished what should have been 27-plus miles by messing up a turn at mile 15 and heading over a Bridge to Maryland. Cost me about 45 minutes. But, approaching the DC finish, a fair-sized crowd blocked the way.

Had to ask people to move. An 8th grade field trip of 40 middle school kids from my hometown in Vermont happened to visit a nearby museum. They heard about the run and waited. Had I arrived on time, they'd have missed me. They cheered, presented me with a Vt flag purchased in the museum and posed for pictures. A final glorious road surprise!

My greatest vision throughout the run was the end. The REAL END. I would come roaring home on the train, the engine's one eye blazing yellow, bell clanging, whistle shrill: "clear the way!" My family waiting, maybe a few friends. I'd step off the train, sigh and a big smile!! But, I had NOT envisioned 60 plus people, a reporter and the tears and laughter that did greet me. For several minutes, we all shared a joyous, magical moment. And then, HOME!

Chapter 17

Henrik Aarup Svendsen, Denmark
First Dane to run across USA
13th of January 2016 to 8th of May 2016
Santa Monica Pier, CA to Central Park, Manhattan, NY

The reason for running across the USA was founded in my youth where I read a book about the first continental foot race across the USA back in 1928. This book stayed in the back of my mind for several decades… until I was 49 years and started on my dream… it was never a race to me, my dream was to fulfill the distance. I took the decision of my run about 1 ½ month before my departure and with hartly no planning and only knowing the route fix points of LA-Chicago-NY, we planned the distance running day by day, using "maps" on Iphone, here's the shortened story, the holy story can be found on:
https://www.facebook.com/Running-Across-USA-for-a-good-cause-483139878525542/?ref=settings

Day # 1-10 Tough start due to cold and jet lag, however it's really great to start the run. My knees are complaining a little and my right ankle and shin started to hurt a lot and I feared not being able to continue, so I slow down the pace and took necessary breaks. My motivation is still 100% and if only I will avoid injuries - I firmly believe in fulfilling the total distance from LA to NY.

Day #18 Born in '66, Today I ran 66 km on Route 66 Oh, and I also completed the "DEVASTATOR TACO CHALLENGE", eat a 6,6lbs taco in less than one hour. Only one guy has done it - now there's two! The record to beat is now 48 minutes.

#11 By coincidence I met the organizers of the famous Mojave Death Race! David, Vivian, Gary, Peter, Gustav and me (https://www.facebook.com/MojaveDeathRace/)

#24 During laundry, I received good news, the next 350 miles will be "downhill" We have entered the big Navajo reservation which overlaps into several States. On our way, we will meet few towns and the distance between is far. Nature is very beautiful and on the nights, the Stars seems very close.

The Mojave Desert is 3 times as big as the size of Denmark, so it will take me days to pass it. No Internet service out here.

Yesterday I met a family who belong to the tribe: Diné (formerly known as The Navajos). We were lucky to be invited into their home for grilled salmon, Navajo Tea and cozy stories. We saw some of their petrified wood, which they fabricate and sell as Native American jewelry. It was interesting to experience how their lifestyle is nowadays, and experienced a blessing ceremony.

#31 I'm happy to get away from the frost and snow. Although it is cold in the morning 24-44 deg. F, I have started to run in shorts and T-shirt by mid-day. Yesterday, I bought a pair of sunglasses they are good against the morning sun, which always is directly in my eyes as I usually run towards east. More important, the sunglasses are a good protection against dust, gravel and stones coming towards me from the cars and big trucks. By midday the sun is always at my right side and today I managed to get really sunburned... like in RED legs and arms... but only on my right side. I suppose that I can buy sunscreen in the next city in 2-3 days.

Prior to my run across U.S.A I had the opportunity to meet the American Ambassador in Copenhagen Mr. Rufus Gifford to tell him all about my run.

#33 This day started unexpectedly with a fast introduction to poison rattlesnakes (I fear snakes!) lizards and big Tarantula spiders. They all like to be on the roadside due to the warm asphalt...which is just where I'm running. The railroad (1862-1869) which goes through the USA from East to West is due to its reliable water supply, the basis for the road system. In the early 1900s the National Old Trails Road was built, later in 1926 it was paved and became highway 66. Later Route 66 was in 1973 bypassed by Interstate 40. They are all 3 linked closely together and never far apart. It means, we are sleeping with the Railroad on one side and the Highway 40 on the other. They are both equally making the same level of NOISE! Good night and sleep tight.

#36 Suddenly after nearly 900 miles and running uphill, I felt a need to take off my shoes and socks. Running barefooted was a great experience. Automatically you take shorter and more steps. Our RV needed another repair and this time it was the side entrance door. I was running too far without anything to drink. My luck came when I passed a Mexican lady selling fresh fruit from the trunk of her Toyota. Without her speaking English and I Spanish, she could clearly see that I needed a fresh orange. I managed to explain that I didn't have any money with me, but it didn't matter. I become very happy and emotional when people show themselves from their best side. It was a great little moment, thanks! Today I crossed the famous river Rio Grande (1.906 miles) shortly after crossing the river, I saw a place with quite a few policemen, so I decided to have a small talk. Sheriff Manuel Gonzales III from Bernalillo County Sheriff's Department New Mexico gave permission to take a group photo before we all had to continue our work and run. Another day has passed with good meetings between positive and nice people!

#39 I am running 80 miles on Highway during Saturday, Sunday and Monday. It has been really freezing cold today and there has been a headwind during all 38 miles. By now I am getting to know quite a few of the truck brands. I believe Kenworth is one of the most popular around here. The distance of the run is decided by the next exit of the highway. Today's distance was longer than other days and I found a new definition of hunger: when your brain unconscious starts to focus on all the roadside litter, in order to guess the name of the coming fast food chain, then you are hungry!!

#44 After crossing New Mexico in 14 days, I have now entered Texas. Time zones are a bit funny, on the West side of the sign, the time was 10 AM, one step forward in East direction the clock was 11 AM. Now I am 7 hours behind Denmark and it gets easier to talk with the family at home. Arizona and New Mexico has been relatively hard to run through due to mountains, cold temperatures, snow and the altitude with less air. Our logistics has also been tested to the fullest, as we went through desert and reservation with long distance between people and towns/villages. Here we needed to think ahead on our supply of food, beverage, necessities, petrol, propane (heater), water (kitchen, shower and toilet) along with the absence of phone and data connection. As and add on, we have had no planning of the route from back home, the route has been decided from day to day. We are staying in the small village Andrian, Texas. The village is PRECISELY the midpoint between Chicago and Los Angeles.

#45 We met Fran Houser, Midpoint Cafe, Home Of Ugly Crust Pie, Adrian, Tx. She is the reason why the city Adrian has been acknowledged as the Midpoint between Chicago and Los Angeles, after 23 years of hard work. The Midpoint Cafe was used by the animation company Pixar, as inspiration in the movie "Cars 2006" Fran is also known as the character "Flo" which runs the "Flo's V8 Cafe" If you want to meet "Flo" in real life, then do stop in Adrian and say hello to Fran and her lovely dog

Brodie. Many of the small villages along the Route 66 is placed with a distance of 13-14 miles; examples of this are the villages which we are now passing by Adrian, Vega and Wildorado. The funny coincidence has a good explanation. It is the distance a horse could bring a wagon without getting new water! When the horse wagon was replaced by the trains, the trains stopped the same places, as the locomotive also needed water for the coal fired steam engine. Water is and will be important, then as well as now.

#50 Change of supporter makes it not possible to run today. Later today and just before midnight my wife Lotte will arrive and in 2 weeks, my youngest son Magnus on 18 will arrive too. I'll spend the day with the last cleaning of the RV and washing some clothes. At 10 AM I was at the TV-Station. I was interviewed by Hector Flores. After the interview, there was time to see the studio where I met Chris Martin, he broadcast the weather forecast every 15. Minute. In between he gave me my personal weather forecast for my running route - and Chris I hold you up on your promise of being out of the tornado and hurricane season! Later, I'm going back to see how to mix and cut the interview. It will be shown on channel 4 KAMR Local at 4,5,6 and 10 PM plus FOX KCIT at 9 PM. The TV-Station will link to my Facebook later this evening.

My wife Lotte and me, finally united. The day we spent hiking in Palo Duro Canyon, TX.

#52 It is 2000 kilometers since I left Santa Monica, LA in January! "Two up three more to go" I have taken the miles as they come together with the weather, wind, sun, frost, snow, mountains and the landscapes.

#57 - Distance (ZERO km / 0 miles) It has been a very difficult day. I have been forced to take the decision not to run. Unfortunately, I have not been in doubt about not running, because it hurts a lot just lifting my leg or walking, so I didn't even try to run. My leg above the ankle has swollen and is very sore. I have no other option, than hoping for the best for tomorrow morning. I must admit that mentally it is hard not to know when I can run again!? In order to keep up the good momentum, we have decided to do some practical things and not least... some luxury! For the first time since I departed from Denmark I stay in a hotel. This means a good nice shower with lots of water and even at the temperature you like!! Perhaps it sounds like an everyday thing, but it reminds me about all the things which we just take for granted. We have used the day washing all the running clothes, normal clothes, towels, sheets and bed linens. All beverage and food supply has been purchased along with some nice chocolate. I have been to the hairdresser at Adam's Edge in Clinton - many thanks to Austin Hayes for a good job and for donating an amount to Youth For Understanding organization. It is afternoon and I am in the hotel swimming pool to recharge my batteries. I hope tomorrow will be a good day on the road again!

#58 14.59 km 9.11 miles
My leg has become a little better, but unfortunately not a lot. I did a small test run at the parking lot and decided to change into my running clothes. My first goal was to run the 4 miles to the first truck stop. I barely made it and it was turtle speed. After a long break, I ran some more, pause, and then some more. On one side, this morning I would be very happy for being able to run 8-9 miles. On the other hand, it is not a lot and especially not when I had to fight for it. Just to be on the safe side, I bought a new pair of running shoes, also I am using some sports gel. My hope is that a good night's rest will help

#63 Was it a coincidence? - I doubt it! Due to my running injury, I consulted the clinic OSSO - an orthopedic sports clinic. This clinic is treating and working with some American National teams. Doctor Thomas C. Coniglione is the specialist on running injuries for many years. He is also the Medical Director for OKC Memorial Marathon and has also been running many marathons himself. We parked our RV for the night only 1/2 a mile away from their address and they were our closest Internet search next morning. The fact that I have come in contact with some of the finest doctors on running injuries in the USA... cannot be just a big coincidence!?!

I am deeply thankful for the very professional treatment and the fantastic helpfulness which I received at the OSSO clinic. Also, a big thanks to James Click and all the rest helping and meeting me during my visit. I have had this injury for 2 weeks and my leg is swollen to an almost firm and tight kind of ball. The muscle is due to over stressing squeezed in between two bones and it is decreasing the blood circulation. The good news is that the X-Ray didn't show any fractures. The not so good news is that my problem will not go away in a foreseeable time. With the help from Thomas, we will do some different things to change my running and after today's run, I feel in good hands and also positive towards a solution. After tomorrow's run, I have another appointment with Thomas. After the visit at the OSSO clinic, I had a recording interview with Oklahoma TV Station Channel 4 KFOR. It meant that I didn't start my run before 3 PM. When I stopped running, the Sun had gone down and now it is time for a good night's sleep and recovery.

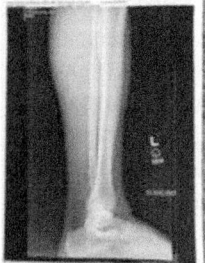

Doctor Thomas C. Coniglione

#65 I got hit by a car Yesterday, but I was very very lucky. It all happened so fast that I didn't even had time to jump to the side. By instinct, I was throwing my shoulder as much as I could away from the roadside and I hear a loud noise from the side mirror and shoulder hitting each other. I'm standing at the roadside and cannot understand why it doesn't hurt more!? Apparently, I managed to turn my shoulder so much that the side mirror impacted almost on the back side of both my shoulder and arm. I have woken up to some marks and a sore shoulder. Really lucky!

#68 It has been a great day to me with lots of positive energy! I have met the person who has been an inspiration to my across USA run. Even though it was only in shape of a statue, it moved me a lot. In his home city of Foyil outside Claremore there is a bronze statue of Andrew Hartley Payne (1907-1977). He participated and won the 1928 "Great

Transcontinental Footrace" from Los Angeles over Chicago to New York - THE SAME RUN WHERE I AM NOW MIDWAY. My intention was that this update should only be about "Andy Payne" but I will also like to mention the "Davis Arms & Historical Museum" in Claremore. Besides the 20.000 firearms, you will find 1.200 German beer steins, a large collection of boot jack, various cattle horns, posters from WWI. Definitely a visit worth! The managing director Wayne McCombs is a great ambassador for the museum. He tried to set up a meeting with the relatives of Andy Payne. Unfortunately, without luck. It would have been a great experience. A memorable day for me!

#72 Just as I was about to finish the day's run... I got an unpleasant surprise... a big and black snake was just in front of me!! It is 5-6 feet long and I am terrified- this is what I have feared. It is not moving and I get the impression that it is dead, but the skin is very shiny and I can't see any damages. It is dead. Wow... I got scared. Later. It was a "Western rat snake" (Black Snake) it can become 6 feet long, is very fast and aggressive, but you will not die from it. Missouri has 47 different snakes and 88% of them are not poisoning, the rest are! Picture from the restaurant; *John Wayne: Courage is being scared to death – but saddling up anyway...*

Andrew Hartley Payne bronze statue outside his hometown Foyil

#74 In the outskirts of Springfield, I ran by a small sign saying: "Springfield Underground," which did not at all justify the enormous area underneath. Big refrigeration trucks and even railroads are going into the Rock. It showed to be one of the world's biggest limestone caves and it gets bigger by day, still mining. The limestone is used for building houses and roads, e.g. the highway 44 which I am running along. The all year constant temperature of approx. 60 deg. F is excellent - the nature's own sustainable fridge. The biggest multinational companies are using this giant "freezer" as it is a logistic center for a big part of the USA. Manufacturing and storage of many different kinds of products such as dairy and meat, paper and electronic. The whole underground is closed to the public. The day ended in Marshfield (6.633 pop.) where famous Edwin Powell Hubble (1889-1953) was born, the person whom gave name to the HUBBLE Space Telescope. He discovered external galaxies and the expanding universe. You will find a good replica of the Hubble Space Telescope in the city, it is 1/4 size of the one out in Space.

#75 A very beautiful morning, birds singing, green meadows and forest. I have seen many different birds and eagles on my run. At the quintessence of a truly idyllically forest lake, I'm walking out on some low rocks to grasp it all. Suddenly a goose jumps up in front of me and it hisses very loudly. It continues and I'm stepping to the right whereas I can see the nest with 7 big eggs- this is the explanation.

After running from Marshfield to Lebanon, we are arriving at the legendary Route 66 motel: MUNGER MOSS MOTEL from 1946. The motel is neatly repaired along the years and not rebuilt/changed like so many other motels. The big neon sign beside the motel is from 1955 and made of porcelain. When it comes alive during the dark, you can watch the most beautiful neon sign between Los Angeles and Chicago! By the check-in, we meet just as legendary Ramona, she and her husband Bob Lehman has run the motel during... 45 years! Bob comes out to say hello and I just love listening. The conversation and storytelling cannot be re-told, you need to experience it yourself. You will not find a lot of people with this much Route 66 life experience as Ramona and Bob - but some are still along the old highway. These storytelling "lighthouses" are the glue along the world's most famous road. If you embark on Route 66, then Munger Moss Motel is a must!

3000 kilometers

#80 The Bunion Derby / Flanagan's Trans-USA-Run. I started to read the book about the Footrace Across USA back in 1928. It is still a thrill to read it again here more than 30 years later! But there is a difference. I am right now running the same race distance. It is very motivating, to read about the same cities, deserts, mountains, valleys and even the same roads, e.g Route 66. The stress and hardships which the runners faced at that time, has not changed much; snow, rain, cold, heat, wind and sandstorms are still the same. The

nature invites you to dance -and you are not leading. I have been running and thinking about what it takes to become a long-distance runner? I am still in the learning process, but already now I know a lot more. It is a fantastic run which I have begun and I feel very happy!

#81 Distance 70.70 km 44.18miles Today I reached a new milestone: 2.000 miles! Arrived in Saint Louis which lays at the Mississippi River. The city is from the settler time known as the gateway to the West. In a newer time (1963-1965) "The Gateway Arch" was built and is today the symbol of Saint Louis. The Gateway is 630 feet tall. Saint Louis will also be the last of my run through the State of Missouri (approx. 313 miles) as we early in the morning, will be crossing the Mississippi River. The river is also the State Line between Missouri and Illinois. My driver Jens is from Spentrup, Dk and not mentioning his age, I decided to run 70 kilometers that day.

#89 I have been smiling a lot while running... imagine... I ran 2.300 miles from Los Angeles to Chicago! It is big for me. I have been in shower now, and it tickles my stomach, it feels like the evening before Christmas when I was a boy! I am full of energy and knowing that the city is only about 30 miles away, makes me want to put on my running shoes now! The today's run was rain and rain, but after 5 miles I met Elvis and The Blues Brothers... It makes you happy, right! The mood was already high from the morning, as we were invited for a stop at Nelly's on Route 66 in Wilmington. A very nice place, Tina and the staff are wonderful, and I will recommend those of you traveling out of Chicago on Route 66, to make your first stop at Nelly's after approx. 50 miles. Please say hello to Tina from me and Jens. The next 29 miles was one long shower, but no wind...how lucky! Now I'm really close to Chicago and my wonderful journey on Route 66 will end.

#90 so far 2.316 Miles 3.707 Km
I made it to Chicago! YES! It is fantastic and of course a big milestone! First time I saw Chicago's Skyline was 16 miles outside Downtown. It was very enjoyable to see the skyline coming closer and closer. Well, this was also the end of Route 66, the road I have followed for almost 3 months. We have been walking and sightseeing in the Chicago downtown area, and we find it both beautiful and interesting! Celebrating (Prime Rib) the arrival at the famous bar and restaurant: Miller's Pub was a very good idea! The most difficult task of today: finding a parking lot for our RV - not easy!

#91 A farewell to both Chicago and the state of Illinois (approx. 322 miles), as I ran into Indiana. I started down by Lake Michigan in beautiful sunshine and 42 deg. F. So many nice activities are located by the lake. Also, you will find a very nice cycling and running trail, it is a part of Chicago 1/2 and full marathon. I ran by 4 other runners(!) and I was so lucky to run about 3 miles with Christopher Kempt - thanks for good company and fast pace! He was the first male runner that I ran together with - but also the first male runner I saw since I started from Santa Monica... after more than 2.300 miles! Later it became rather industrial, refineries, steel mills and related companies. We also had enough drama! A man drove across the street full speed and directly into a house - Jens and our RV was only 50 feet from the cars lane. A policeman and myself tried to make contact with the driver to bring him out, but for some reason he kept keeping the speeder down causing so much smoke that we couldn't see anything. We were also afraid that the building would collapse or that he would back the car out hitting us. About 3-4 police cars and firefighters got him out (almost) unharmed. After another 3-4 miles of running, I ran into a demonstration outside the town hall of the city Gary - so Indiana gave us a hectic start.

Muhammed Ali: **IMPOSSIBLE** *is* **NOTHING**

#99 The day started with a radio interview with Danish Radio P4 in order to create awareness for the good cause which I am running for. The first city which I ran through was Perrysburg -and along with Washington DC these 2 cities are the only ones planned and built by the American Congress. In the afternoon, we met with Jamie Withem from YFU. Later we had a mutual evening dinner with a lot of students from 5 continents! Earlier I had an interview with the local newspaper The News-Messenger. We have enjoyed a fantastic day with an American Family, which at the same time is a host- Family for young students. Yet another experience with a lot of hospitality!

#102 The advantage by having NO knowledge about the daily running route, is that every day is like opening a nice gift which is beautifully wrapped! I ran through Valley City which is no less than the Frog Jump Capital of Ohio! This special event which in 2016 will take place for the 55. time. If you want to attend on the day of championship (+600 frogs) and you didn't bring your own frog, you can rent a frog by the hour!

#103 The landscape has again been very beautiful, nice roads, hills, forests, very well-kept houses and particular new cut lawns all over. Miles have been flying by so easily almost without noticing them. A lot of motorcycles, probably because of the nice weather? ...no it was St. Michael's annual BoB (Blessing of Bikes). The annual blessing for a safe motorcycle season! The priest sprinkles holy water on each motorcycle, today more

than 200 bikes. It is a free service, but a man with a donation bucket is following the priest! This BoB is the 10th season to bless motorcycles in Windham, Ohio and the number of bikes increases year after year. After the service ended, I had the pleasure of the bikes passing by waving hello, Harley's, 95% of them.

#107 In the morning and on my way out of the city Brookville, I got frightened as usual, when 4-5 dogs came barking towards me. I yelled out loud, but the front dog continued. Out of instinct I hit the dog hard with my fist and then it ran back. After lunch it got cold, windy and the rain continued. We are now in 2080 feet, 500 feet higher than yesterday and the clouds are in the same height. All my clothes are wet, I'm trying to dry gloves, hat and reflective vest for tomorrow.

#111 A very nice start through Reeds Gap State Park and even on new asphalt. It is peaceful to run in the forest listening to birds singing. Later, in about 90 minutes of running - I stand almost in front of a BEAR! It is terrifying!! Especially when you come from Denmark where we have no

dangerous animals at all - and now I'm watching a bear without a cage! It must have been smelling food from our RV. When I was about 50 yards away, both the bear and me saw each other, but luckily it heads towards the forest and runs away. When I run further, I look at the forest, in another way, but continue my way towards New York. Cool cities still exist in the USA.

Satisfied arriving to New York. The world is open for new adventures... Later November same year 2016, I returned to the USA and used by good shape to win the Icarus 144h (6 days) race, my first competition as a newborn Ultra Runner. Covered 10.000 Km during 2016.

#117 LAST DAY

(days of running 111) Accumulated 3.155 Miles – 5.049 I made it !!!

I ran from Los Angeles and all the way to New York. I have now lived my dream... and I can without any doubt state that it has been the Run of my life.

A dream which was a lot more vivid that I could ever imagine from my kitchen table beginning of January... To run the very last leg of my run to New York City was really fantastic and definitively special -and I have been so fortunate, that after 10 days of rain, the sun began to shine just only 5 minutes before my very last run towards my goal. The Run to Manhattan was truly a pleasure and one of them was to run a few miles with Tony, a little later I was suddenly in the middle of a carnival of the Mexican "Cinco de Mayo" – that is how New Jersey/New York is! A green hilly terrain leads me up to George Washington Bridge and I feel the pleasure of

overtaking all the cars driving slowly up the steep road. At this time, I have only about 6 miles to Central Park and a very fine view to Manhattan from the tall bridge.

In the entrance of the park, I meet Lotte and Ronny -they have made a great banner and we are running towards the HCA Statue. We receive a lot of positive "thumbs-up", good wishes and applause, this is naturally making me happy and suddenly... I feel joy and real acknowledgement, running in the park, which for one day feels like mine. Hans Christian Andersen, is sitting and waiting for me in the most beautiful sunshine... and when I am hugging him, my tears are running from my eyes... now I am here... A choked-up feeling is mixing with the joy present...

From our home, Lotte has brought our flag "Dannebrog" (world's oldest flag) along and everything feels so right and beautiful -and we all feel happy! It only gets more joyful by the Danes already there, wishing well and congratulations.

One of my concerns and therefore now one of my biggest joys, will be that my body stood the distance and I am arriving in New York with super much energy and lots of power both mentally and in my body.

I am very thankful for all the Facebook support and wishing well, it has been really motivating for me. Thanks!

Without Gustav, Peter, Kenneth, Lotte, Magnus, Jens, Steen and Ronny -the trip would be a lot more difficult -I owe you some special thanks, not only have you been wonderful company, you have also been individually a very important part of fulfilling my dream.

I feel that the most interesting part of my journey and run, is not about me, but more on the fact that we humans can do whatever we aim to do. Therefore, momentarily my last words shall be about a lovely encouragement to you all, to strive towards your dreams - and also supporting, helping others in making their dreams

Greatest support Team running across USA (Kenneth unfortunately absent)

come true... this is where you will feel your life in the present.

Chapter 18

Pete Kostelnick
A Tale of Two Transcons
September 12 to October 24, 2016
San Francisco, CA to New York City
July 31 to November 5, 2018
Kenai, Alaska to Key West, Florida

To me, besides the passage of time, the purest part of our time spent on earth is the physical passage from point A to point B. Growing up, my parents, four older siblings, and I drove everywhere for vacation in our 1987 Dodge Ram van. I had been to 47 states, including Alaska, before I had ever set foot in an airplane. To this day, I cherish the chance to move from point A to point B on ground and seeing all there is to see between.

Meanwhile, in 2011, I "moved on" from the predictability of road marathons to ultramarathons, a sport with the widest breadth of possibility (and uncertainty) as any. As luck would have it, I ran into a man named Marshall Ulrich at the 2011 Pikes Peak Marathon, whose book about running across America I went on to read several times. Over several years I became good friends with Marshall and a man named Charlie Engle, who had run across the Sahara among other endurance feats. Charlie became the ignition switch that made my eventual run across America possible in many ways.

I'm often asked how long I had trained before running across America in 2016 to attempt to raise the bar on Frank Giannino's sterling 46 day, 8 hour, 36 minute record (67 mile per day average), set in 1980. Well, it never occurred to me that I might be able to break his record until the summer of 2015, when I started to win several road ultramarathon races. I credit my slow build-up of mileage, starting in 2009, as the reason why the record attempt was possible. Training over 150 miles a week is not easily done without serious injury unless you build up to it very gradually over years and years of building durability.

With some luck of meeting the right people at the right time, I put together a four-person all-star team to join me for my entire run across America in 2016. There were Chuck and Dean, who would leapfrog in a van over 1,500 times across America a couple miles at a time to attend to my nutritional and physical needs. There was Cinder, my running mom, who would drive the RV, cook, and provide professional massages and stretching every day. There was Trasie, who would take care of all other logistics and documentation of the run to make sure we could operate smoothly. Not to be forgotten, there was also my sister Ann back in Iowa as our route guru. For the first and last week of the run, we also had my friend Zandy on board to take photos as a superb photojournalist.

On my 29th birthday at 8 am local time on September 12, 2016, I took my first step from San Francisco City Hall towards New York City Hall, perched 3,070 miles away. It took me nearly 40 miles of running with new and old friends before I even made it across the San Francisco Bay. Still on day one, I found myself running on Niles Canyon Road at rush hour outside Fremont wondering how many times I would get the feeling on this run that I would surely get hit by a car. Shortly thereafter, I tripped hard and also wondered how many times I would trip on this run. Luckily, not again until Paterson, New Jersey on the final day.

Growing up, my family and I were never big fans of Yosemite due to all the traffic. We preferred National Parks harder to get to with no crowds in sight.

On day 3, I ran right through Yosemite, and now dislike the park for a different reason—the elevation gain one gains there when traveling in from the west. By the end of day 3, already through two 80-mile days, my tibialis anterior was completely cooked by over 73 miles of mostly Yosemite rollercoaster running. It took three more days of stubbornness, but by the time I reached the long, empty stretch of Highway 6 between Tonopah and Ely, Nevada, I knew the pain had me circling the drain. Along with severe fever and chills, I decided there would be absolutely no running or walking on day seven.

With limited service in the middle of the desert, negative thoughts of what the talk would be ran through my head on that Sunday of rest. "Pete can do all the training in the world, but a run like this takes guts and experience, neither of which he has." I remained optimistic, even attempting to send funny "selfie" photos of myself in a Clown Motel shirt to my family that ultimately didn't go through.

Very cautiously, I set out on day eight with something to prove. On that day, I met a man named Charlie who flew and drove out to the middle of nowhere just to run a marathon with me. I'm forever grateful that he suffered with me in the extremely dry Nevada afternoon heat.

Next up on my horizon was making it to Fairview, Utah. Fairview, Utah was where Chuck, Dean, and I broke down in my parent's borrowed Jeep while driving out to San Francisco before the run began. In what felt like a team unwinding moment brought me closer to Chuck and Dean thanks to us meeting Kimberly at the museum in town while we waited for the Jeep to get worked on. Kimberly cheered us up and gave me a necklace she was wearing at the time that had a rock shaped like a shoe on it. I wore it the entire way (and still do from time to time) from San Francisco to New York as good luck.

By day 14, I noticed my pace naturally start to creep back into the low 9-minute per mile pace, after it had been stuck in the 10-minute range for quite a while. That was the day I knew in my heart that with all the aches and pains, I was going to break this record I wanted so badly. My body was broken in and I was ready for whatever the road threw at me up ahead.

Colorado brought more and more friends out to share miles with, hardened ultrarunners like my friends Jon and David, who survived entire days with me. To this point, most of the miles had been quiet solitude. By the time I reached Ft. Collins on a Friday morning, it felt like a party. Friends of old, friends of new, all coming out to do a shift with Re-Pete Kostelnick. By the time I reached the Nebraska border, the state I had lived in for five years up until the start of this run, I think I was actually enjoying myself as the great folks of Grant welcomed me through. Unfortunately, the Nebraska winds caught wind of my wife and me intending to move to Missouri, and made the next day feel like running the wrong way through a wind tunnel. To be fair, there were a couple days where the tailwind made it feel like I only needed to pick my legs up to make it to my destination.

The true "Forrest Gump" part of the story comes in the Midwest. Running through Lincoln, Nebraska, I was able to run by the house that my wife and I had just sold. Our realtor literally put up a sold sign in the yard as I had lunch there with friends in a surreal moment also involving severe storms blowing through. Several days later, I ran by my parent's house in Boone, Iowa, and then a duplex I had lived in during college in Ames. A week later, I ran down state highway 303 through Brunswick, Ohio. Two moves later, I am happy to report, I can look outside my window at the same highway 303 here in Brunswick.

As I headed towards Pennsylvania, I began to see places I had never seen before. I was familiar with the West, and certainly the Midwest portions of the route. But here I was, passing through small, historic villages in Pennsylvania that were foreign to me. While passing through eastern Ohio and Pennsylvania, I made three new friendships that mean a lot to me to this day. There was Brooks, who ran a marathon with me in Ohio and surprised me on the last day to run over 50 miles with me to the finish, and now lives nearby here in Ohio. There was Adam, who ran with me over the Ohio-Pennsylvania border on a lonely day, and who has joined me on many other adventures since. And there was Tony, who joined me for over a marathon in eastern Pennsylvania and has taken on some big mileage races with me since. Even though Pennsylvania, with all of its hills and windy roads, was my least favorite state, I joke that it at least gave me good friends.

Dating back to Valparaiso, Indiana, I had done the math with my friend Brad to predict that I would finish the run on October 24, in 42 days and change. I knew that the last day would mean running roughly 80 miles across New Jersey, plus several more into New York City to reach City Hall. Given the extra 15-20 miles over a "normal" 70-75-mile day, I decided to start the final day at midnight on the PA/NJ border to hopefully finish in New York City before dark later that same day.

The right guy to start that day off with running was Todd, a professor from the US Military Academy in West Point. However, on and off throughout the day, I was scared that I was going to have to walk the remainder into City Hall and finish well into the night. I was spent, I had nothing left to give except a mediocre final performance on short rest.

You're about four days ahead of record pace, so just be happy that you made it Pete. Not good enough.

Somehow, it never ends that way. I had Brooks. I had Charlie Engle fly in to join me. I had new friends on and off. I had Larry to block traffic. After I tripped in front of probably over a thousand following Charlie's live Facebook feed, I found the last piece of adrenaline I could in this run and ran with a bloody knee all the way to Times Square, where I saw my lifelong friend Dylan waiting for me. I was so shocked to see him that I almost forgot to run. With a crowd of friends and strangers, I found a gear that I hadn't had since day one and arrived at New York City Hall at 5:30 pm on October 24, 2016. There to greet me was my wife, who I hadn't seen in over 50 days, and Frank Giannino with a baton in his hand. The new record for running across America was now 42 days, 6 hours, 30 minutes.

To end the story there with a fantasy ending would, however, not tell the whole story. For days, months, and quite frankly, over a year, I struggled with what running across America in record fashion meant to me. The national media attention in the day or two to follow was overwhelming. I loved it, but I also hated that I knew others accomplishing similar feats that would never get covered in the same way just due to how quickly and easily it is to say "hey, this guy just ran across America!" I loved all the congratulations from friends and family, but all I wanted to do was do something more impressive. For months, my body wouldn't let me. I began to drink too much and avoided socializing with others in a new residence of Hannibal, Missouri. If I wasn't about to do something incredible, I would rather just spend time alone so I wouldn't have to live in the past.

Fast-forward about a year to late 2017 when I began to think "rationally" beyond the 2016 run across America. To me, the only solution to running across America for a record that brought a lot of pain (in addition to pride) was to do it again, but for fun. Being the competitive person that I am, I needed to find a way to make it challenging in some way. While running one day, a road trip I had taken in 1999 with my family to Alaska came to mind. On that trip, we met several people motorcycling from Alaska to Florida. I wondered if anyone had ever run from Alaska to Florida? And how about self-supported with a stroller full of gear (which is what most people do on transcontinental runs)? That was it! I was going to be the first person to run from Alaska to Florida, do it self-supported, and do it in under 100 days. And to make it even more fun, I would start in Kenai and end in Key West: "Ke2Key, Unlocking My Wildest Dream."

The plan was to start on August 1st from the town of Kenai in Alaska, flying straight there from the Badwater 135 race in Death Valley. Unfortunately, I was unable to complete the race after severe cramps brought a run to a walk, and a walk to a standstill. Very upset after pulling myself from the race, I decided it would be best to hang up ultrarunning for awhile and go back to our new home in Ohio instead of Alaska. I tried to cancel my flight and first few nights of reservations in Alaska, but it was too late. I told Nikki, my wife, that I would just fly up to Alaska and run the first few days. After all, I also had my stroller and equipment waiting for me up there. After a few days, I could quit in Anchorage and fly home after "deciding" that it was just too dangerous to continue.

With good advice from a friend of Frank Giannino's, I decided to start a day early on July 31, 2018 at Anchor Point on the Kenai peninsula. Anchor Point is the furthest west you can travel on continuous US highways. If I was able to make it to Key West, I could say I did the furthest west to furthest south road trip you can do in America on foot. At 3 am at my motel in Kenai, a lady named Summer picked me and my stroller, the Amelia Dawson, up and drove us an hour south to Anchor Point so I could begin the run by 5 am. I'll never forget her asking me to look for moose and bears on my side of the truck as I remained cool. At Anchor Point, we met Mike, a fisherman either putting his boat in or taking it out. The two of them wished me well as I set forth for Key West, a destination further away than Beijing, China. Good luck, kid.

By day three in Anchorage, I had a choice to make on whether to continue. Running all day in beautiful scenery with trout streams and ocean bays can make you forget a lot—I reported back to Nikki that I was having the time of my life. Onward.

As I thankfully split off busy Alaska highway 1 towards 1 heading east to Palmer, I immediately heard the peaceful silence that I would enjoy for the next month. I still had a fear of animals of the wild, but by this point I had at least become comfortable with the uncomfortable. If they wanted to eat me, they would have by now. At roughly 55 miles of running per day, I was quickly into remote Alaska, with town names on a map typically just indicating an air strip, lodge, or river. What Alaska lacks in concentration it makes up for in great people. I met many travelers and residents who all

seemed to be genuinely interested in the guy in a blue singlet and black hat running down the highway with a stroller.

All nights spent in Alaska were unique. From motels to lodges to cabins to camping, I saw it all, and would continue to be dazzled at the places one can lay their head each night until I reached Key West. Perhaps the most fascinating overnight was near the Alaska-Yukon border, camping behind a gas station next to two abandoned buses that served as your "last chance in a long, long time to get gas or snacks." I lived on a calorie-dense trail mix for many days and filled up my water bladders any chance I got.

Crossing in and out of Canada was a breeze, because I came prepared with my passport and a good attitude—something most in line ahead of me lacked. I spent over 40 days running through Canada in the Yukon, British Columbia, Alberta, and Saskatchewan. I ran alone for over 30 days between Alaska and the first half of Canada, but met many new friends along the way, including black bears, grizzly bears, herds of bison, moose, coyotes, eagles, and of course porcupines. I got stuck in Watson Lake, Yukon for a day due to forest fires closing the Alaska highway. In order to stay on schedule, I ran a double day of over 90 miles to catch back up to my lodging reservations. As I neared the finish of that sleep deprived double day, I thought I saw my friends Neal and Mike from Iowa waiting for me along the road up ahead. Wait, I did! Neal and Mike drove over 30 hours straight from Iowa to spend a couple days with me, putting together an incredibly professional five-minute video that can be found on YouTube.

The two primary rules I set out from the beginning of "Ke2Key" to the end were simple. One, never get in a car (although I had to for about a mile in the forest fire section) and run everywhere you go. And two, find everything you need along the route (except have new shoes and tires shipped to motels). I had to turn down several free meals and nights at generous people's houses due to this. I stayed with others if it was close enough to the route to run to, and I allowed others to buy or cook me a meal if I was otherwise in a place where I could find or buy it myself. This was my great human migration!

Crossing back into the US at Portal, North Dakota brought a number of tears splashing the medium-width paved shoulders. For the better part of that long 68-mile day to Kenmare, I ran on pure emotion rather than Clif bars and crackers. North Dakota turned out to be one of my favorite states with straight, low traffic roads, and plenty of new and old friends.

There really were no bad states, provinces, or territories on the never-ending fall-like weather "tour de harvest". Illinois brought the greatest number of police officers (two) checking to see what I was up to. Alabama brought the "RSO" (rumble strip only) shoulders that made for some very intense moments with traffic and a creaky stroller full of 40-50 pounds of water, food, and gear. Cedar Falls was the highlight of Iowa with an overnight at my sister Ann (still my route guru) and brother-in-law Ben's

house. I'm amazed that I was able to run the following day after all the beers and treats that were had that evening with family.

Not every second of the Ke2Key run was terrific, but by the time I reached the southernmost point in Key West at mile 5,384 on the 98th day, I think I had found what I was looking for. Instead of counting down the miles like in 2016, I was always counting up. I saw each day ahead as an opportunity instead of an obstacle. I took photos, I wrote, I solved problems, I laughed more than I cried, and I felt like a true pioneer. It wasn't the destination; it was the journey.

Chapter 19

Jan Walker
March 1 to October 8, 2016
Oceanside, CA to Ocean City, MD

I'm going to go about writing my story in a little different way than most here. I want to give you a little background about the lead up to the point of me even being able to start a solo transcontinental run at the age of 57.

I had briefly toyed with the transcon idea as far back as 2012, going so far as to sign up for "The Last Annual Vol State Road Race". The "Vol State", as it's affectionately called, is a 314-mile footrace across Tennessee in the middle of July. Somehow, while researching long distance running, I had gotten connected with John Price. John had done several Vol State's and at least 1 transcon at that time. (he has since done a 2nd transcon). John told me I should try Vol State first because it was sort of like a mini-transcon. This Race has a 10-day limit, so you have to do at least 50K (31.2mi) per day to keep up with the cut off time.

At the time I was talking to John about all this, I had never run an ultra in my life. (an "Ultra Distance" Race is considered any Race farther than 26.2 miles) The longest distance I'd done was a marathon, and that was way back in 1996. I was WAY heavier and a whole lot older now. It's not like those of our ilk are known for making really wise decisions. So I did what any crazy transcon planner would do, and promptly signed up for the Vol State Race as John suggested. I signed up in Dec of 2012. The Race was July 2013. Six months to train to run a minimum of 31.2 miles a day for 10 days straight. Surely nothing could go wrong with that scenario, right?.

I got to training in earnest and signed up to do my first 50K Race in Feb 2013, "The Palm 100". I hadn't a clue what I was doing. I just went out and ran A LOT. Not much rhyme or reason, just LOTS of running.

Now when I say I run, that's pretty much how I look at it in my head. In reality, it's more like a VERY slow shuffle. A 15-minute mile is a sprint for me. Add to that, I definitely do not "look" like a runner. At the time I'm starting to train for this, I am over 50, quite a bit overweight, and slow as a herd of turtles stampeding through peanut butter!

You can imagine the puzzled looks I got when I told people what my plans were.

The Palm 100 came and went. I blistered my feet up pretty bad at that Race, and around mile 27, I was sure I was on the verge of certain death. But I waddled on and finished. My first ever ultra Race was in the bag. It's still my PR for a 50K race. (10hrs:35min)

I signed up for 3 more 50K's that year, diligently working my way toward the Vol State Race in July. At each one I got slower and slower. But I finished them all.

The day to start the Vol State finally arrives. I look around at the other competitors and immediately figure out I am WAY out of my league here. But hey, I'm here, I planned, I sort of trained, might as well give it a go, right?

Because I was so slow, I was way in the back of the pack. Now all races have "back of the packer's", but the Vol State has a few iconic ones (unbeknownst to me at the time). In this case, I was in the back with Diane Taylor. Diane is famously known for being the last (or nearly last) in every Vol State she has ever attempted. At the time I met her, she had completed 2 and dropped out of 1. And it is important to mention that Diane does not run. Ever. She walks, but her walking pace is as fast as most people's slow running pace. She is a walking machine. In my case, I had to nearly sprint to keep up with her!

Diane and I had stopped to rest around 5 miles into the Race. I looked over to her and said, "If I EVER tell you I'm planning to do ANY Race other than a 5K (3.1 miles), hit me on the head with a hammer and knock some sense into me!!!

I did finish the Vol State that year. It took me 9 days, 10 hours, 11 minutes, 42 seconds, and I actually finished before Diane. But Oh. My. Gosh., it was sheer agony!

Along the way, she and I had some very deep conversations. Those conversations and her wisdom helped me get my head straight and eek out a successful finish, even though at times I could barely walk. However, as John Price had told me, it was a great introduction to multi-day, long distance running, or "journey running" as it's sometimes referred to in the Ultra World. You have to push yourself beyond what you think your limits are, then just keep going. You sleep out wherever you can find a place. You live in dirty, smelly clothes for days on end. You find food, water, and resting spots in places you'd never frequent in the "real world". So, Yeah buddy. It's a little mini-transcon for sure!

The human brain has an innate survival mechanism. It conveniently forgets the agony of painful situations after some time has passed. Thus we humans continue to plod along, sometimes trying the same stupid things over and over again because our brains tell us, "Hey, it really wasn't that bad. Let's try it again and see if we can do better!"

Finishing Vol State gave me the confidence to set my goal Race for 2014 to be Ironman Florida Triathlon. I was still swearing off a transcon, but hey, a bunch of my buddies were doing Ironman, surely I could do one too!

So I signed up, then thankfully had half a brain's smarts to hire a coach this time. Ironman Races are super expensive. There's the exorbitant entry fee to start with. But there's also the cost of a bike, travel, pool memberships, and the list goes on and on. With this much money on the line, I couldn't go out there and just run a lot. I would have to train in earnest, in 3 different disciplines (swim, bike, run). The only way to do structured training, and have a better than average chance of success, was to hire a coach.

I started coached training 8 months before Ironman race day. It was hard, slow, and VERY tedious work. And I mean it's WORK to train for an Ironman. You have to have tunnel vision for months leading up to Race day. It consumes every part of your life, and I was just training to finish, standing upright, before the midnight cutoff!

Did I mention it was WORK?!?!?!?

Race day arrived. I'll shorten that story for you and tell you, yes, I finished before the cut off. It wasn't pretty and I nearly froze to death (the worst cold front the Race had EVER experienced came barreling in the night before, with 30-40 degree temps, 25-30mph headwinds and windchill down in the teens!). But I finished, and was now an Ironman!

Hmmmm, that Ironman was pretty hard. If I can do that, maybe I can do something a little more intense(?)

After I completed Ironman Florida in November of 2014, I began to think I could revisit my planning for a transcontinental run. Endorphin overload will do that to you I guess.

Oh, there's that brain survival thing popping up again. Bad, bad, brain!

Secretly, I started planning and saving the funds I thought I'd need to get a transcon started. But just 4 months after Ironman, I had a VERY BAD bicycle accident and broke my left shoulder in 4 places, completely pulling the ball out of the shoulder socket, splitting said ball into 3 pieces, breaking the whole thing off the main arm bone, and damaging every major nerve from my shoulder blade to my fingers. Basically, there was nothing keeping my arm from falling off but skin. Oh, and I was also right in the middle of training for a 170 mile, 7 day multi-day stage race in Utah only 6 months from when I had the accident. (the 2015 goal race I had scheduled for myself) With the break as bad as it was (multiple screws and plates to fix it and near catastrophic damage to the nerves), I would not be able to train for at least 8 weeks of that 6 months. Putting me WAY behind on getting ready for the Race, and putting a major kink in my transcon plans.

What to do?

It was past the refund cut off date, and the Race entry fee was too expensive to just pull out. Plus there was expensive, specialized equipment I had to buy just for this Race that wasn't returnable. So I made the decision to go ahead and do the best I could, hoping I could get enough training in to at least be able to power walk the course. Up to this point, even though I was always slower than nearly everyone else, I had never not finished a Race, nor had I been pulled from a Race for not making a cut off.

The first day of the Utah Race, I failed to make the 3rd checkpoint cut off time and was pulled from the Race. Talk about dejected!

I asked to stay on in camp and volunteer for the rest of the Race. The Race organizers allowed me to stay and assigned me to help Lisa Reader, who was the Official Finish Line Timer. Lisa really didn't need much help. She had her system down pretty well. So, I ended up doing a lot of sitting around doing nothing.

Photo by Michael Hutchison.

What does all this have to do with my run across the US you might say?

About a month into the transcon Run, I got VERY sick while traversing through the middle of New Mexico. I was out in the desert at least 5 days running distance from the next town with no way to get anywhere to be seen by medical personnel (at the time I just thought I had a bad cold). I kept getting sicker and sicker by the hour. I could barely breathe and toward the end of those 5 days my right ear drum burst from the inside out. I was finally able to get to a small clinic in the little crossroads town of Carrizozo, NM thanks to a road angel named Andrea. The physicians at the clinic gave me a couple of shots, and a prescription for antibiotics and an inhaler. But the closest pharmacy was 56 miles away, in the opposite direction I was going. (the clinic didn't have a supply of meds to fill the prescription there) It didn't matter anyhow. I had no way to get to a pharmacy, or anywhere else for that matter, except on foot. (no taxi's, buses, Uber's out in the desert ya know). By the time I got to the clinic though, the infection had progressed to the point of severe bronchitis just short of pneumonia and I couldn't hear out of my right ear. The doctors there told me I had to stop and let the antibiotics work and my ear to get better, or I risked an even more severe case of pneumonia and an ear infection that could spread to my brain.

Here I was, miles from nowhere. I hadn't the funds to pay for an extended stay, nor did I have any way to get the medication I needed. I didn't even have a way to get to an airport or bus station to go home. I was quite literally stuck. I was so dejected. I didn't want to quit, but the infection was getting worse and I had no real way to fix it.

While I was pondering what to do, I got a text from Lisa Reader, the lady I had been assigned to help back at the Utah Race. She had picked up my Run travels on my Facebook page and had been following me. She texted me and told me she would come down and get me, take me to her house, and I could recover there. Now, it was a 4 hr drive, one way, to get me. That meant she had to take a WHOLE DAY to come get me and take me back to her house.

Photo by Michael Hutchison.

At first, I objected, telling her it was too far for her to come. She said, nonsense. She would come get me, take me to get the medicine I needed, and I could stay at her house till I got better.

I thought I would be there maybe a week. Two rounds of antibiotics and finally my ear drum growing back, I ended up having to stay 25 days!

I had only known Lisa for about 3 hours before this. We were nothing more than passing acquaintances really. I had met her husband Garth at the Utah Race too but only because he was the trail sweeper behind me when I failed to make the checkpoint time cut off. But, when I needed it most, they took me to their house, never let me pay for a thing, and even had a friend of hers, who is a physician's assistant, come to the house to see me for medical care so I wouldn't have to go out in the cold windy air.

If Lisa and Garth hadn't taken me in, at best, I'm sure I would've had to end my transcon run, and I don't know if I would have been able to ever start again. At worst, it was a very real possibility I would have succumbed to pneumonia and an ear infection, in the middle of the desert, days away from being able to get somewhere for help.

Lisa and her family single handedly saved my whole trip. And they really didn't even know me!

There would be countless other "road angel's" crossing my path as I made my way from CA to MD. This short story has just a few snippets. John, Diane, Andrea, Lisa and Garth made up only a small fraction of the providence I received over the several years of planning and training, to the execution, to the final success of my adventure when I walked into the Atlantic Ocean on October 8, 2016 having run 3154 miles across the entire continental United States. I would need a whole book full of pages to tell about the many road angel's and how their small (and large) acts of kindness, to a total stranger, helped me succeed with my Run. (I am indeed in the process of writing a book about my whole experience with all my interactions with those beloved road angel's)

When I needed Guardian Angels all along, starting as far back as the initial planning stage of this adventure, they seemed to just appear out of nowhere. No rhyme or reason for them to even be where I was, but yet there they were. Most of them, perfect strangers, or people I barely knew, having no knowledge of who I was, or what I was doing. They just wanted to help someone in obvious need, without asking anything in return.

Needless to say, my interactions and experience during my transcontinental Run, fully restored my faith in the American Spirit and what we stand for as a country. Here I am, a 57-year-old female, running solo (by myself), pulling everything I need for the trip behind me in a cart attached to my hips. I looked very much like a homeless person. The majority of my route was also out in the middle of nowhere. Some nights I hadn't a clue where I was even going to sleep at the end of the day. It could be a run-down roadside motel, or more commonly, it was a dirty ditch, hopefully behind a bush to shield me from being seen by passersby. Yet I was always looked after by a variety of random characters who always showed up when I needed them most.

We tend to be very jaded in this day and age. What we see and read on social media and in the news tends to make us very suspicious of giving or taking help from strangers. Nowadays, because of my experiences along the road on my adventure, if I see someone walking along the road who looks hot and tired, I stop and at least offer them a cold bottle of water and ask them their story. When people took time to do even that small gesture for me, it meant more than all the gold in the world. I am determined to pay that forward as many times as the opportunities allow.

There will always be bad people in the world and you definitely have to be vigilant. But, the vast majority of people are basically good and want to help. They want nothing in return. They are just good, decent people, living their lives just like you. They have big hearts and are drawn to helping those they feel might be less fortunate than them.

Embrace the good in humanity. Be the good in humanity yourself. Your life will be MUCH more enjoyable as a result!

Chapter 20

Lindsay Monroe
November 13, 2016 to August 16, 2017
Myrtle Beach South Carolina to Lincoln City, Oregon

Some walkers may start off by giving you some stats, or about what kind of charities or causes they are doing this for. For me it was never about how many miles I walked a day or the total mileage in general, it wasn't about anything bigger than myself. It was about me wanting to push myself to accomplish this feat and the experiences that led me from start to finish.

I was living a life that I wasn't excited about; working 70 hours a week, never taking time to be with my loved ones or to truly focus on what makes me happy. I was tired, uninspired, and just chasing my tail in circles, but I needed something more.

While flying over the country from Massachusetts to Colorado for the first vacation I had taken in 5 years, I looked out the window at the vast landscape and empty spaces below me. I wondered who lived in these places, how far away was the next town or a grocery store. I said out loud to my family "I want to bike across America" my mother and boyfriend responded with "you have not ridden a bike since you were a child", they were not wrong, so I responded with "fine then I will walk across America."

Before walking 3,200 from Myrtle Beach, South Carolina to Lincoln City, Oregon in all directions of planned and unplanned states and roadways, I had never spent a night in a tent or really even gone hiking. My idea of camping was friends on a trip in a pretty place where we would enjoy being on the water, drinking too much beer by a toasty fire, and passing out in our tents. Bear Grylls eat your heart out. Extensive research and preparations would be made, but in no way was I truly prepared for what was to come. Having been a bartender for 15 years and a college athlete, I wasn't afraid of being on my feet all day or of a physical challenge and pain. That was the easy stuff.. I was afraid of the mental aspect of this journey. Who or what would I find being alone with myself?

On November 13, 2017 I took my first steps on Myrtle Beach, I was naive, green, out of shape and unaware of what the hell I was getting myself into, but I said I was going to walk across America, so you better believe it, I was going to walk across America

Everyone told me I was crazy, I mean they weren't necessarily wrong, I think everyone who tries to do something like this has some form of crazy that pushes them to accomplish these things. There were plenty of times on the road when I realized what I was doing was insane, like the time a maniac chased me down the Silver Comet Trail, he 100% wanted to use my intestines as a necklace and have my head on a spike, I was about to be the next primetime episode of Dateline. Luckily, I outran the man and called the police and was safely escorted to my motel that night.

Why did you walk across America? Why, why, why, it was the number one question on everyone's mind, and I would give them whatever answer I felt like at the time: "I lost a bet" "Because someone told me I couldn't", "because life was getting me down so I wanted change"," I needed an adventure" ,"I am riddled with wanderlust", "to see the absolute best in complete strangers and have my faith in humanity restored", " I am a photographer and I want to see this country through my camera lens and from a point of view that very few people ever have", "to have the adventure of a lifetime" ," because I want to be truly free."

Every single one of those answers were factual (not the losing a bet one, that was just fun to say to get a reaction out of people). I thought freedom was walking 20 miles a day with the sun on my face and shoulders, I thought I was free because I didn't have a job, I didn't have to worry about deadlines or clients, or a boss breathing down my neck, I thought that was freedom. But I was walking looking at my fitbit mile by mile checking to see how far I had gone and how many more grueling miles I had left until I hit the next town or until I had gone around 20 miles for the day. I was always on google maps mapping and plotting every step I was going to take. So how free was I?

Then one day at the top of a winding dirt road in Altus Arkansas everything changed. We all have a story to tell, every person, every tree, every bug, every dog. We all have things that change us, that shape us and make us who we are.

This story is about how meeting a wild stray puppy in the middle of nowhere, changed my entire journey across America, this story is about how a 7 month old dog taught me what the true meaning of freedom is, and showed me what I was searching for on this insane journey.

I was walking up a dirt road called something like "0098945" according to google maps, so not a road any normal human would use, unless you are one of the 3 people within the three mile road that lives on that "road", I even got laughed at by some men on the dirt mountain road with their cows in tow asking how I ended up on that "road", I told them google maps is an asshole and asked how to get to Chateau Aux Arc, they chuckled and said "keep climbing up this massive hill, eventually you will hit pavement in like 2 more miles, take a right and you will see it on your left in about another mile or two."

I thanked them as they laughed their way down the dirt mountain road. As I reached the top of the mountain I stopped I turned around, and I saw the entire state in my rear view, all those blank endless days of rice fields and dry counties and cold ass days, they all seemed so beautiful when

I got to the top of this "road/mountain/foothill of the ozarks" whatever the f**k you want to call it, it was all behind me and it was beautiful, I took a couple of photos and as I saw the flat dirt road ahead of me, I decided for the first time in my whole walk to put my headphones on and listen to some music.

I plugged into my phone and I hit a song that my dad played for me as a child and taught me how to whistle. "Blackbird" by the Beatles. I started down the flat dirt path with a skip in my step and a whistle on my lips, the sun on my face, a winery to head to and sleep at for the night, already set up in advance.

As I whistled, I saw a shadow once or twice, I thought it was just my jacket that was tied to my cart, so I blissfully whistled and sang along down the path. Suddenly I was attacked from the back, my whole body fell forward, my heart fell into my stomach and my stomach fell through my asshole and I screamed out loud, but there wasn't a house in sight so there was no help anywhere.

I looked down and all of a sudden, I see a black and tan 7-month old hound/doberman looking dog staring at me. Now this wasn't the first time a stray dog had started following me, and I realized the shadow I had previously been seeing was actually this pup. I kept walking and she kept following but keeping her distance and examining me. I came across a house about 1/2 a mile down the road and I asked if it was there pup, "that stray, I'm pretty sure it has killed a couple of our chickens."

I realized at this point that this dog was a wild stray and mother nature is what she called home. I immediately kept walking, and the pup followed, we came across a truck on the dirt road and again I asked, and they said "that f**king stray….." I kept walking, I assumed that by the time I reached the main road the dog would stop following me and stay on the 3 miles of dirt road that she was accustomed to.

I could never have been more wrong and more blessed. 1.5 miles down and the winery in sight. I had a color filled sunset on the horizon and a wild pup at my feet. We were greeted by the vineyard owner as she pointed to a flat, grassy area by a pond to set up my tent. After setting up camp and making the nightly cup of noodles for dinner, I kicked the dust off my boots and slowly crawled into my tent exhausted from the 20 mile day.

A 35-degree breeze pierced my tent flap as I began to pull the zipper shut. I peeked out one last time as the pup looked at me as if she wanted to come inside. Then suddenly we heard the screeching sound of coyotes in the near distance and the pup took off like a warrior into battle. I could hear her bark getting further and further away as she ran towards the coyotes, letting them know this was her space. After her bark faded, I dozed off to sleep and was actually a little sad that I had lost my new companion. As the dawn began to break, the orange rays of the sun softly kissed the rows of zinfandel vines and reflected warmly on my tent. I immediately began to unzip the flap to photograph the sunrise. To my surprise, there was the adorable pup sitting right in front of me with one of my boots in her mouth.

Thina, the morning after we met

The third night at the vineyard, the temperatures fell below freezing, right around 22 degrees, I was shivering in my tent and I felt the pup shaking against my tent, we were two animals in need of warmth. I let the possibly flea, tick and worm-infested stray xinto the tent. This wild stray that has never been touched by a human curled right up and let me spoon her like I had known her my whole life. Her tail settled down, we both stopped shivering and out of nowhere this cold tent felt like the sun was shining down on us.

I still had no intentions of keeping this pup, I had not even named her yet, I was hoping that someone would see my posts online and offer to adopt her, or for some family that took me in to adopt her down the road, Audrey the vineyard owner offered to take her in if she packed up with her 6 other dogs, she did not, the only pack this dog had was me, she had imprinted on me, she also killed a chicken on the vineyard so that did not help her cause.

I was trying to keep myself alive on this journey, I was in no position to try to keep a wild stray who had never been in a house, a car, worn a collar, or ever been on pavement and surrounded by tractor trailer trucks, cars, cities filled with humans and bustling. I also would have had to start carrying water and food for the both of us. Why would I ever take on the headache of trying to keep another creature alive.

I had so many good reasons for not taking this dog with me on my journey. There was just one problem, she wouldn't let me go anywhere without her. We spent 2 weeks on the vineyard and the dog never got further than 5 feet away from me, if I left the vineyard to go to dinner or head into town for supplies, she would sit next to my tent until I got back. I finally gave her a name, other than "Girl". Cynthiana was the name I chose, Cynthiana is the

Arkansas state grape, and the vineyard we stayed at happened to be the largest producer in the world of that grape, it was also my favorite grape in Arkansas. I decided to call her Thina for short because the letters were in Cynthiana but also because it sounds like Athena who was the goddess of wisdom and war. I figured this pup must be wise and quite the warrior to have survived all that time on her own in the wilderness, I kind of considered myself kind of a warrior of the road at this time too.

As I was preparing to leave the vineyard and get on with my journey to the west coast, I realized Thina wasn't going to let me go anywhere without her, and at this point I didn't want to go anywhere without her.

Chateux Aux Arc, the view from my tent at night

Once we got out of the rural part of Arkansas and closer to Fort Smith and the Oklahoma border, traffic got heavier, and Thina got increasingly uncomfortable. She would not wear a collar and leash so she would just follow me sometimes stepping into the road too far for my comfort level, I would plead with her to wear a leash and every time I put it on her she would lay on her back and refuse to walk. I cried and cried, I was ready to call Audrey the vineyard owner to come and take her and find her a home, because the last thing I wanted was for any harm to come to this dog that I had started to fall in love with. She was afraid of going under and over every bridge and underpass that we came across, I had to pick her up and carry her 40lbs and push all my stuff. I was suffering and struggling, but I had realized that we were a team now and I would not give up on her.

I remembered what it was like the first two weeks I was walking, I was scared of every car that was going over 30MPH, if a shoulder was narrow I would push my cart over people's lawns and through farmland and mud to avoid being on the road a little bit. But by the time I got a state or two in I was so used to walking on the side of the road that I had no fear and would take the space I needed and face off with a car that didn't want to go around me. Thina just needed to get more comfortable, this was all new to her, I was basically watching her go through what I had been through, once I realized that, I was able to be as patient as she needed me to be.

As days and miles went by Thina became more comfortable with all these new things, she had never been in a house or a car. She got really used to laying on people's couches right away though. For the first time in 7-8 months this wild stray had a roof over her head every night, whether it was the roof of a tent or a stranger who took us in. Thina no longer had to scavenge for her next meal, her belly was always full.

One day about 200 miles west of the vineyard, Thina and I were walking down the road when a much larger dog ran across the street to investigate us (Thina was still not wearing a collar or leash). At first the two were getting along ok, but this dog was much larger and started getting a little bit more aggressive. Suddenly the large dog jumped in the air and lunged at me with its fangs ready to take a chunk out of my arm. Thina my much smaller, 8-month-old pup leaped into the air grabbed the dog twice her size by the scruff of its neck and threw the dog a good 5 feet, then the other owner finally made it across the street and retrieved her defeated dog. Thina then sat down and looked up at the collar and leash that I had in plain view attached to the cart and I looked puzzled at first, then she nodded at it and I grabbed the collar and put it around her neck. She stood up and started marching right alongside me.

Lindsay and Thina in Oklahoma

It was in that moment that I realized we were in this together, we had each other's full trust and loyalty, we would do anything to protect one another. She was officially a dog walking across America, on a mission and journey of a lifetime.

It wasn't until I was halfway across the country, just outside of Oklahoma City, that I finally realized what that freedom that I was searching for was. I chose to go down a much more rural dirt farm road parallel to rte 66. I would often choose these roads so I could take Thina off leash. As we headed down the road there was winter wheat about as tall as Thina, filled with field mice. Thina climbed under the barbed wire fence next to the sign that said "no trespassing" and she began prancing through the winter wheat popping up and down in the winter wheat, playing with and trying to catch a mouse. She played for the whole half a mile of wheat

Thina and I headed over Mt. Hood in Oregon

on this farm, she didn't know what that sign said, that fence didn't mean stay out to her, it meant "I have to go under this." To Thina, the whole planet, the whole rock that we live on was hers, every horse and cow was for her to chase and bark at, every chicken was a potential meal, every wheat field was the perfect place to nap. Every cow pond was the perfect place to grab a drink and cool off on a hot day. As I walked beside her playing the whole way I was smiling from ear to ear watching her excitement and pure joy. For the first time I stopped looking at google maps and how far I had gone and how far I had to go, I was finally living in the moment, enjoying the sun on my face, I was paying more attention to my surroundings, and playing with the cows and petting every horse. I even climbed under and over some fences that said no trespassing on them! I was finally free, just living in the moment and loving every second of it. I loved being sore in the morning because it meant I worked my ass off the previous day, I loved the smell of my hard earned sweat, I started taking more roads less traveled and playing instead of looking at my watch and trying to get from point A to point B as quick and efficiently as possible. Efficiency is for people with jobs, I was out for an adventure, and I was finally truly free. It just took an 8-month-old puppy to teach me how to be free.

On August 16th 2017, after 91 nights in a tent, 30 or so nights in a motel and 156 nights in strangers homes, Thina and I jumped into the Pacific ocean on Lincoln City Beach in Oregon, finishing my 3,200 mile walk and her 2,200 mile walk.

I never intended on falling in love on the walk, but I did, over and over again. I fell in love with living in my tent, I fell in love with so many people and families that took me in. I fell in love with sleeping on the side of the road, with never knowing where I might actually lay my head down to rest for the night, where I was going to eat, what I was going to eat, or who I was going to be eating with. I definitely never expected to fall in love with a dog, but most of all I never expected to have that dog teach me how to love all of those other things, but also she taught me how to love myself and this entire crazy journey.

The finish line in Lincoln City, Oregon

I had said that I was walking across America for "the adventure of a lifetime" but instead it ended up being the adventure of 100 lifetimes.

Chapter 21

Noah (11 years old) & Robert Barnes (Noah's Father)
January 1, 2017 to December 9, 2017
Key West, FL to Blaine, WA - 4240 Miles

When eleven-year-old Noah touched the saltwater in Blaine, WA (1/4 mile from the Canadian Border) on December 9, 2017, he set a world record for being the youngest person to cross America on foot. The 4,240-mile march began in Key West, Florida on January 1, 2017 when he was just ten years old.

If you had told me in 2015 that I would march across America on foot, I would have said you were crazy. Approximately 400 people have documented crossing America on foot since they started keeping records in 1909. Some of those people, and potentially even more that we never heard about, chose not to tell anyone what they were doing. Noah is completely different, he wanted everyone to know he was marching across America and why he was doing it. How a crazy idea develops into a yearlong family adventure is tough to pinpoint, but it began in 2007 when 16-month-old baby Noah was diagnosed with Type 1 diabetes. Like most parents, we had no idea what was wrong with him. He acted like he had a cold, but no fever. He was very thirsty and urinating frequently, something just felt wrong. We took him to his doctor 3 times over a 10-day period. The doctor told us it was just a cold. The second time, he told us it was a pretty stubborn cold. The third time, he said it was the flu and it could take 2 to 3 weeks for Noah to get it through his system. We took him home from the doctor's office that Friday and agreed that if he hadn't improved by Sunday, we would take him to the ER. Monday afternoon, I left work early and we walked into a pretty full ER admitting area. The head nurse knew exactly what was wrong and rushed us right in. Noah was so dehydrated, they had a tough time getting an IV in him, finally locating a vein on the top of his head. Suddenly, I find myself trying to comfort my infant son, as wires and tubes are being attached to him. I'm frozen still as I watch 3 nurses and a doctor trying to do what they can to get Noah hydrated.

Noah was experiencing Diabetic Ketoacidosis (DKA) where your blood sugar level rises from that lack of insulin in the body. Over simplified: when your body doesn't produce enough insulin, it will burn fat for energy. Burning fat for energy creates acids called ketones. This process throws off the chemical balance in your system. If not treated, your blood sugar level will continue to rise and your body starts shutting down. You will slip into a coma and never wake up. Over 100 people a year in America die from undiagnosed diabetes.

Back at the ER, my wife, Joanne, was going through a wave of different emotions. Frustrated at the situation, upset at how this could happen and crying, trying to comprehend how he got diabetes. Noah didn't smoke, he wasn't overweight, he didn't have a bad diet, he was only 16 months old. We spent the next 3 days in the ICU and they got Noah stable. We spent another 2 days in the hospital getting educated on how to test his blood by poking him with a needle, drawing blood and placing a drop on a test stripe, this would be done 6-10 times a day. Then depending on what he eats, we get to inject him with a needle of insulin 4 to 8 times a day for the rest of his life. Over the next few months, Noah the happy and bouncy boy, stopped progressing, he refused to walk or even laugh, he stopped smiling. It was like he was dealing with depression. Joanne was an emotional wreck, having to deal with managing his glucose levels, watching our precious baby slip backward in development. Eventually he started smiling again and started the long road of living with type 1 diabetes.

In 2015, after about 9 years of life with this horrible disease, Noah decided he wanted to quit being a diabetic. Hitting an emotional "wall" is common for people that live with type 1 diabetes. In most families there is the caregiver, the parent that manages the levels for the child to ensure proper management of the sugar levels. It is a 24 hour a day 365 days a year task. Normally it's the mom and the mental toughness required to manage a life threatening disease is overwhelming at times. Any little thing can throw the entire balance off. Ambient temperature, humidity, altitude and a variety of other environmental conditions impact how the body reacts to insulin. For example, if the ambient temperature is above 80F, Noah's insulin works twice as fast, meaning that if we would normally give him 3 units of insulin, but he is going to go outside for a walk, he would only get 1 or 1.5 units. If you give him the 3 units and he goes outside and walks, the insulin will cause his body to have a "low" where your sugar levels fall below 80.

It's similar to being drunk, you lose reaction time, you don't think clearly, your speech is slurred and you can make poor decisions. If your sugar levels fall below 50, you can pass out. The other issue is at extreme sugar lows you can lose your balance and fall, where you hurt yourself complicating an already dangerous situation. That constant stress spills over into the marriage and creates another dynamic to an already complicated situation.

Simply managing the sugar levels is extremely complicated. Assuming you manage to keep your child's levels above 80 and under 220 (somewhere between 220-240 is when ketoacidosis starts) that is still not enough. It is common for diabetics to lose their eyesight or a limb because they don't manage their levels. The fear that not managing your child's sugar levels correctly will give them long term organ damage and take their ability to have a normal life as an adult can't be expressed into words. Many caregivers feel under-appreciated and it's a frustration point. There is a never-ending pressure of checking your blood levels almost hourly, counting carbs, and dosing insulin through needles or a pump. The constant management is emotionally and physiologically exhausting, thus Noah announced that he was through with being a diabetic. As a father, your heart breaks that your son has to live with this and you are helpless to do anything about it. I tried to comfort him and explain that he wasn't the only one, but he was feeling pretty low and defeated. Joanne recently had to pull him out of public school because of ongoing issues with managing his sugar levels. Managing type 1 diabetes is complicated and you have to make adjustments on how much insulin to use verses how much and what kind of food Noah is eating. After 6 weeks of conflict with the School Nurse my wife, Joanne, went down to the school and withdrew both of our boys. She called me up and announced we were now homeschooling. Now, I never liked the idea of homeschooling and most of the homeschooled adults that I had met seemed awkward. Joanne is very artistic, and extremely talented in many things, but academics and especially math and science are not her strongest subjects. Being supportive, I wanted to help with our new homeschool program. I asked Noah to turn his frustration about diabetes into research and find out who is actually working on a cure and what types of things are they working on.

A few weeks later, Noah came to me with the iPad to show me "walk for a cure." He asked me, "What is this walk for a cure and can we walk there and be cured?" My heart tore in half, he did exactly what I asked him to do and as a 10-year-old he thought he had found hope. I struggled to explain to him what they were doing is fundraising for researchers and no one had a cure yet. After facing his disappointment, he understood "fundraising." He asked me "If I come up with a fundraiser, will you help me?" "Of course," was my reply.

A short time after that Noah watched the film documentary "Into the Wind" about Terry Fox and the Marathon of Hope. In 1980, Terry Fox, a 20 year old Canadian who had lost a leg to cancer, started running across Canada. The film explains how in his first province no one really seemed to care. His second Province of Quebec, he didn't raise any money at all. In Terry's diary he mentions that maybe no one in Quebec gets cancer. By his third Province, he had tons of media coverage resulting in much money being raised.

Right then, Noah discovered his mission and my ten-year-old son decided that was something that he could do. When he came to me the next day, he seemed to have put a lot of thought into it. He told me that he wanted to cross America starting from our home in Jupiter, FL and go to his cousin's home in Olympia, WA. He even took out a map of the United States and showed me a rough outline of a route. He continued with "Terry Fox only had one leg, I have 2 legs and I have America, I got this!" I laughed out loud and told him that he was a very funny kid, but NO that is crazy, come up with something else. He wasn't dissuaded at all, he simply walked away and came back to me later that day asking how we can do this? This went on for about a week and I kept telling him no. Finally getting frustrated with me, he looked me right in the eye and said, "Why won't you help me, don't you want me to be cured?" It felt like he had kicked me in my chest and took the wind out of me. How do you reply to a question like that?

Noah really challenged me to dig deep into my life. What had I done that was so great? What was the purpose of my life and was I living it? The concept to cross America on foot is absolutely crazy but considering how to walk away from everything I had worked for and trek across America was frightening. I really struggled with how to transition from the stability of a high paying corporate job to a crosser with all the unknown struggles ahead. I knew the journey would be tough and crossing with my family of five just adds to the already challenging journey. I was at war with myself, nothing made any logical sense, but I knew with all my heart we had to do it.

Before we got ahead of ourselves, I wanted to make sure that Noah could physically do the journey. We would need to average about 15 miles a day to cross within a year. We would be crossing Missouri and Kansas in the heat of the summer where 96F temperatures with 60% humidity would make for some tough days. We were living in South Florida so in the mornings, I started taking Noah out for 2-hour walks. My thought process was not focused on mileage, but more about time, how many hours could he physically handle. After the first week, I started really pushing him. I wanted to make sure this wasn't some kid idea that he would get bored with after a few weeks and want to quit. After the first hour of walking in the sand, with temperatures around 90F I asked him "does that hurt?" He replied, "yes." I asked him, "Do you want to quit?" Immediately, "No." I pressed on, "Are you sure?" He shot back, "Yes, I'm sure." I continued like this for about a week. We were going out longer and pressing more miles, getting harder and harder on him just to see how far I could push him. Finally, we were walking on the sand and we were about 3 hours into the walk, I started asking him the series of questions. His frustration with me mounted to the point and he snapped "Dad, I don't know why you keep asking me these silly questions, yes it's hot, yes this is going to be hard, yes it hurts, but I got this. I have to do my part for a cure." I stood there stunned, like another kick to the chest. Just baffled that a child comprehends that if you want something to happen, that you have to do something about it.

Up until this point I had chatted with Joanne about crossing America and she thought it was charming but didn't take it seriously. That night I had a serious conversation with her about how we were going to support our child on a mission to follow his heart. Of course, she started asking all the rational questions. How is he going to do it? How are we going to pay for it? Where are we going to stay? She really worked herself up and then broke down and started to cry. I tried to comfort her with the idea that it is a leap of faith and things will just work themselves out. She wasn't drinking the Kool-Aid yet. I just asked her point blank. "Look back over your life, all the decisions you made and all the choices, tell me one, just one, that made a massive impact?" She just looked at me with that blank stare, but with those piercing eyes. I pleaded with her "Our son is doing something for not only himself, but the entire diabetes community. This will have an impact on millions of people's lives." She gained her composure and asked, "What if no one cares?" Which is a fair question, I deal with people all day and many are focused only on themselves and their needs. I had to be completely honest with myself and let's just assume no one did care. What if nothing happened, no media, no sponsors, no donations. We get out there and we are completely on our own. I just looked my wife in the eyes and said "Well, we will have one heck of a family adventure." Which she then looked at me with those glaring eyes and stated, "I don't like you right now, in fact, I really just want to punch you in the face." She stood up and started walking toward the kitchen. She looked back over her shoulder, "I'm going to need wine, lots of wine."

Noah, Joanne and I were all set to start doing the actual planning for a trip. We looked at our route and decided that our house was a boring starting point, Noah suggested Key West, FL. We looked at the map and that looked great to us. We then looked at Olympia and that isn't a cool place to end. We looked at the 2 points the northwestern point and the western-northern point of America in Washington state and Noah decided on the Peace Arch, the northernmost western point of Continental America on the US Canadian border. We had a starting point and ending point, now to pick a starting date. Beginning of the year, fresh start and a new adventure, January 1 at sunrise in Key West, FL just sounded really nice.

We quickly got a website up and started getting all the social channels up and running in the hopes of getting a sponsor. I sent a ton of emails, filled out a ton of grant and sponsor applications and had not a single person even replied. I finally got someone on the phone at a shoe company and they told me Noah would never finish. He went on to say he wouldn't make it out of the state of Florida. That was a little hard for me to swallow. I had to take a serious look at what we were thinking. I asked a couple of people who had gotten corporate sponsors and they explained it's all about having an audience. Unfortunately, we didn't have one, and they let me know it was going to be an uphill battle getting any support. I then reached out to the diabetes groups and was completely shocked when they told me they wouldn't do a thing to help Noah. I explained that if they could help us with food and places to stay we would fundraise for them. They really liked the idea of us fundraising for them but told me we were on our own for any support. I asked about media support and they started getting annoyed with me for even asking for anything. I was in complete shock. How can a group that says, they are working for a cure sit back and not lift a finger for a kid who wants to help promote funding for a cure? I was beyond baffled. My initial response was rage. I was so frustrated and started feeling helpless. I had this idea that we would be out here and people would rally to support us. What a shocker it was that 60 days before we had told the world we were doing this we didn't have a single dollar raised to help us and not a single sponsor. We started selling off everything and embracing the minimalist lifestyle. We held on to a few things, the boys Legos, their bunkbeds, Joanne's china and crystal, and photos. Everything we owned could fit into a 10x10 room. We cashed in our 401k and depleted all of our savings. We thought we had enough money from savings and the items we sold that would last us for most of the journey. The reality was closing in that we had nowhere near enough money. When I did some quick math, we had enough money to get us about 25% of the way. Then I got the phone call. My previous boss called me up on the phone and offered me a job. Healthy 6-figure income, an awesome schedule and the perfect environment that I truly dreamed of working in. I told him I needed to chat with my wife and I would call him back. I went and found Joanne in the living room and asked her to sit down. I told her that I had a really important decision to make. We have to choose between what is in our head and following our heart. One gives us all the safety and security we need and the other has the cliff with all the uncertainty and unknown on a daily basis. She didn't even hesitate, "We have to do this. I know I will cry as soon as you get off the phone, but we know it's what we have to do." I called my former boss back, told him no and just like clockwork as soon as I got off the phone I could hear her crying in the other room. There are not many wives that could have made that decision. Women in general like to have a home. Joanne likes to call it her "nest." I knew right then, this journey was going to be the hardest on her. The next morning Joanne woke me up by pouring hot coffee on my chest. She claims it was an accident, it was dark in the room and she thought she placed the cup on the end table. After I gained my composure, I gave her the benefit of the doubt of the coffee accident. She wanted to talk. I could tell she was really stressed out and on the verge of tears. "Are you sure we are doing the right thing, can you absolutely guarantee that everything is going to work out?" I just looked her in the eyes "I have no clue how this is going to work, but I know in my heart if we don't go, we will regret it for the rest of our lives." Joanne took a moment then replied "I know we have to do this, I don't like not knowing how. Do you want more coffee, in a cup this time?" As she stood up and walked out. We were both scared about facing the unknown, but we agreed we had to do it together.

We started all the planning, google maps, city research, food research, stretches and trying to be proactive. We reached out to other crossers for advice. The first one who replied is Ron Zaleski who went across in 2010 barefoot. His girlfriend ran support from an RV. He gave us great advice, unfortunately none of it we could apply to us. Then we chatted with Milton Miller who had crossed twice. He gave us a ton of great practical application advice for the actual daily walking. As great as the info was, there was a ton of unknowns for us. We are a family of 5 and we didn't have an RV. We couldn't find a single family that had done anything like this. Of course, this really freaked out Joanne. Most people that cross with families leave them behind. That wasn't an option for us. We were going as a family or we were not going at all. We have a saying "I go, we go!"

The final few days before we left was intense, like something exciting was about to happen, but the stress of having little money was starting to set in. Joanne was very tense all through the holidays. Her father had been living up the street from us would come over and added to her stress. He thought this was the stupidest thing anyone could do. He didn't believe a child could actually cross the country and he thought we should have a million-dollar sponsor before even leaving the front door. The rest of Joanne's family thought we were crazy and gave us little support. My family thought it was a little nuts, but they were not in a position to give us any real financial support. We were on our own.

Our first week we had lined up a friend with an RV to help us so we could make it the 93 miles through the Keys of Florida. The Keys during New Years is a really fabulous vacation spot, but extremely strict rules on where you can park, camp and park an RV. There is no overnight Walmart parking, they will tow you with you sleeping in the RV. Joanne made arrangements with the local Home Depot which gave us a spot for the evening with no issues. We were excited and things were starting to look up. The plan was to meet down at Key West on New Year's Eve get some sleep and start at sunrise. The RV was running late getting down to the Keys and needed to stop for gas in Fort Lauderdale. We loaded up the car and started driving down when we got the phone call at 6pm, the RV was broken down. We had no place to stay down there for that night and the rest of the first week. We turned around and drove home. Went right to bed and got up at 2am New Year's morning. Loaded the kids in the car and started driving the 4 hours to Key West. We were a little concerned about drunk drivers, but there was almost no traffic. We pulled into Key West about 6:50 and Sunrise was 7:15. We got to the Southeastern Most Point Buoy and started getting ready to take some photos. We had heard people were going to join us, but no one was there. It was 88F very humid, free range chickens, 6 toed cats, the smell of booze and urine filled air. Then it began to rain. I was thinking "Great, what else can go wrong?" We set up a live stream and about 3 minutes in realized we were not actually live streaming. Had to do it again. Then we had Noah get set up to touch the water. We had to crawl over a concrete pony wall to the rocks where the gentle waves were coming in. Noah crawled down there, and it was a little slippery and he tried timing a wave to put his shoe toe in the water. Except a bigger wave rolled in and soaked his socks and shoes. Noah began his March Across America in flip flops as we allowed his shoes to dry. When people started seeing the initial posts on social media about what we were doing, they saw Noah in flip flops and freaked out with our parenting skills thinking Noah is crossing America in flip flops.

At the end of our very first day, we had done 17 miles, but we didn't have a place to land, rest, and recover. Joanne thought we had given it the all-American-try and we would just head home to figure the rest of it. I just felt we had started, now we were going to finish. We had a backpack with some clothes, a tent, Noah's medical kit with supplies and $100. I just knew it would all work out. Joanne asked Noah if this is what he wanted to do. Noah felt pretty confident that he was going to be just fine, he had me, we had some gear, and that the two of us would be ok. Joanne started to make some calls, pulling favors. The first person she called was our new crossers friend, Ron Zelleski. Of course, it was New Year's Day, and pretty much everyone was not answering their phones. Ron happened to be living in Key Largo at the time, except he was out of town for the holidays and at a family funeral.

Eventually Joanne did speak with Ron and he had a few friends that he reached out to in order to help us out. New Year's Day in the Florida Keys, all hotels were either fully booked or charging their maximum rate. Ron got us in touch with his friend in Grassy Key who agreed to host Noah and I for a few nights. By this time the sun was setting, we had been up since 2 am. We pulled up to Kirk's place and it was a few acres that were overgrown and had some construction materials all over the place. Joanne kissed us good-bye for the time being and left us, heading home with our two younger children. Noah and I were

truly on his march alone. Kirk had a little trailer that they were working on and let us camp out in there. We thought we would tent it, but it was supposed to rain, so we thought the trailer would be a better idea. It was about 90F and really humid, with a slight breeze. We just poured water over our heads and just allowed the water to evaporate off us to keep us cool. We went right to sleep. Day 1 was done. It was an emotional tornado just to get to this point and we had only just begun. Noah & I spent the rest of the week strolling through the Keys averaging about 17 miles a day. We

would stop at little gas stations and chat with people who mostly were on vacation. Conversation would go like this. Someone would ask, "Where are you from?" I would reply "Jupiter, FL but Noah and I are marching across America for diabetes." They would reply "When did you start?" which, the first time someone asked us was kind of funny, it was about noon of the day we started. My reply, "about 4 hours ago." This of course got them looking at us with confused, head tilted looks, thinking we were crazy.

We had many people offer us a ride, which is always a funny conversation. They would pull up and ask, "Where you going?" Noah would reply "Washington State." They would always pause for a moment to digest that, especially on the eastern part of the US. Then we would explain what we were doing. Day 5 we had 3 white cargo vans offer us a ride, my initial thought was, even if we actually did need a ride, would I allow my son and I to get into a creepy van?

Running support is all the stress with no reward. Joanne was amazing throughout the 11 months running support. How do you feed, clothe, run media, do press releases and keep the family together for 11 months? Very few people could have done this and kept their sanity. It truly is the hardest part of the journey. Many crossers lose their support people along the way.

On our website we answer a lot of questions about details of the journey. Things like how to plan your route, how to get a sponsor, how to get free stuff, how to write a press release and hundreds of other things to consider. We also point out a bunch of crossers to use as examples. When you decide you are going to cross, the first decision you have to make is why are you doing it. Are you an Advocate, Athlete or An Adventurer?

Decisions become easier to make when you keep it simple. Just focus on your journey and be honest with yourself, everything else seems to work out.

More about Noah's March & diabetes advocacy please visit us: www.BackToTheBarnes.com

Chapter 22

Nick Ashill
May 14, 2017 to August 2, 2017
And May 30, 2022 to June 19, 2022
LA to NY

I am honored to be asked to write this chapter. My story is quite a bit different from the other runners. When this book was first published, I had not completed my run from Los Angeles to New York. I started my adventure on 14 May 2017 at the end of Santa Monica Pier in Los Angeles. Nearly three months later, on 2 August 2017, I was hit by a pickup truck at 50-60 mph (about 100 kmh) on US highway 40 near Columbus, Ohio. Sadly, I was thrown into a ditch that was not visible from the road and was left with life threatening injuries. More on this later. What follows is not just about my 3942 km of running and the wonderful people I met; it is also about the love and support I received from so many incredible people during my 4 months in hospital. The heroes are my wife who saved my life, the surgeons at Ohio State University hospital who repaired my broken body (and saved my life), and the physical therapists who taught me to walk again. I hoped that one day I could run again and finish the remaining 1000 km. Now I will share my full story for the first time.

    I am 53 years old and for the past 11 years, I have lived and worked in the United Arab Emirates (UAE) as a Professor of Marketing. The decision to run over 5000 km across America was taken in 2015. I had run Marathon des Sables in the Sahara Desert in 2014 and was looking for the next big challenge. Crossing the United States had always intrigued me, and I had a fascination with historic Route 66. So much of America has traveled on, been built along, or exists because of Route 66. I wanted to experience this long history and the iconic landmarks of America's most favorite road. It was certainly not the quickest route across America but one filled with nostalgia and intrigue.

    Two years earlier, in 2015, I lost my mother to a horrible disease of the lungs, known as pulmonary fibrosis. British Lung Foundation research suggests about 6,000 people in the UK are diagnosed with idiopathic pulmonary fibrosis (IPF) every year and there are approximately 32,000 people living with the disease. In America, around 200,000 people live with pulmonary fibrosis. Globally the disease affects 5 million people and a staggering 50% of all sufferers die within 3 years of diagnosis. There is no cure. My family received so much love and support during the last few years and months of my mum's life and I wanted to use the run to give back. In late 2015, I linked up with a charity in the United Kingdom called the Pulmonary Fibrosis Trust (http://www.pulmonaryfibrosistrust.org/) which provides practical, emotional, and financial support to those affected by the disease. After speaking with another crosser in late 2015 (Adam Kimble) and reading a wonderful book by Nicholas Baldock called "Running Across America: A 132-day run across America to raise money for the Josie Russell Trust Fund" (a truly inspirational story), I set a target date of May 2017 to commence the run. The starting point would be Los Angeles and the finishing point Central Park in New York. The run would be over the summer months. I have always loved running in hot climates. Welsh by birth, I moved to Sharjah (near Dubai) in the United Arab Emirates in 2008 after living in New Zealand for 20 years. All of my training over the past decade has been in heat and I welcomed the challenge of a US summer. By mid-2015 with the help of my wife Sarah (more about this wonderful woman later), the project had gathered significant momentum with logistics, organizing a support crew, fundraising and training. My eldest daughter (Emily), father-in-law (Pete), Jeff (work colleague and dear friend) and Kieren (friend of Emily's) agreed to support me. Emily and Kieren lived in Australia, Pete in New Zealand and Jeff lived in Sharjah in the UAE. Emily and Pete would start with me in May, Jeff agreed to do a 10-day stint in June/July and Kieren and Emily would provide support over the final months of July and August. Throughout 2016, we generated funds to finance an RV for the run. Friends and family were keen to donate toward support costs associated with logistics and several company CEOs in Dubai made personal donations. We were able to negotiate a good deal with RV Share (a website recommended by ultramarathon runner Adam Kimble). In May 2016, I met with Peter Bryce in the UK, who heads the Pulmonary Fibrosis Trust to discuss ways in which the Trust could help to promote the run. During the same month, I also spent time at the School of Sport, Exercise and Health Sciences at Loughborough University. Professor Laura-Anne Furlong agreed to study my biomechanics over the 5000 km run using sensors on my running shoes. I was extremely excited about being part of a major research project at one of the UK's leading universities.

    Training over the next 11 months focused on endurance (50-60 km runs in the desert, 4 times/week), time on the mountain bike and time in the gym. I left Dubai on 11 May 2017 feeling well prepared physically but with so much fear about the unknown. It was hard saying goodbye to Sarah and our two youngest daughters, but I was excited about seeing them again 100 days later in New York. Sarah had put together a fantastic webpage and numerous social media accounts (Facebook and Instagram - www.facebook.com/nickrunsamerica/). In planning the route, I bought the Route 66 Map Series for all US states. This proved to be a great investment with each map providing detailed information about the route and historical places of interest along the way. Today, Route 66 is a discontinuous collection of original road bed, interstate frontage roads and state and local highways.

My flight to LA took 15 hours and I met Pete outside the arrivals gate. We made our way to a local motel (Emily would fly in from San Francisco the next day) and we were both in bed by 8.30pm! At 9am the following morning, I met 57-year-old grandmother Valeria Hatcher, at McDonalds near our motel. Valeria is an ambassador for the Pulmonary Fibrosis Foundation in Los Angeles and has been living with pulmonary fibrosis for 7 years. We discussed the number of people living with PF in the US and how the Foundation provides support to those in need. She was a truly inspirational individual who has such a zest for life. Later that day we picked up Emily from the airport and made our way to Fontana in a hired a car to pick up the RV and shop for linen and groceries. It was our first night in the RV. The next morning (13 May), we made our way back to Los Angeles and stayed in a Walmart carpark about 25 minutes from Santa Monica Pier. Walmart carparks were to become our common home over the next few months. After discussing the running plan for the next day, we were all in bed by 9pm.

Emily, Pete and I, Los Angeles Airport, California, 12 May 2017.

The following morning, we were up early, and we arrived at Santa Monica Pier by 6.30am. After a few pictures at the end of the pier, hugs to Pete and Emily and a conversation with my Mum, I was off. We agreed to meet up for breakfast at around 20 km with the objective of reaching Walmart in Duarte by the end of the day (a distance of 63.3 km). This first day was probably the worst in terms of fatigue. I totally misjudged my water consumption and experienced dehydration due to high temperature (a high of 35 degrees centigrade / 95 F). Emily's curry that first night was truly memorable and certainly made up for the disappointment of the first day. The higher-than-normal temperature remained for the next two days but by Day 4 everything had changed. Approaching Cajun Junction, I experienced snow, sleet and driving cold winds as well as 900-meter climb. Fortunately, I had brought wet weather gear with me. By the end of Day 4 we had made it to Victorville and our first RV camp stop to take on water and fresh food supplies. The vast Mojave Desert lay before me.

On the morning of 20 May (Day 7) after running 29 km, I met up with Pete and Emily at the famous Bagdad café landmark, near Newberry Springs. This stop was a particular highlight of Route 66 in California. Two women (who worked in the café) and one young man greeted me at the front entrance of the café with a bottle of vodka! For the next 30 minutes, we discussed the dangers of running in the desert and the types of snakes to avoid. Emily, Pete, and I then ventured inside the café to explore the memorabilia on the walls. The next 26 km were hard. 36 degrees was the average temperature that day and I developed my first blister on the heel of my left foot. As we closed in on Needles, the temperature climbed. By Day 9 (22 May) it had reached 39 degrees (102F). It's a good thing I liked running in the heat because there was a lot of it out here. Fortunately, the blister problem had not become worse, and I was beginning to experience some real rhythm with my running. I also found that sinking my feet into a bucket of ice at the end of each day greatly helped with swelling. By this time, food preparation had become routine. To avoid waking the support crew in the morning, I would make a protein shake with my bullet blender (an awesome machine) the night before and prepare food for the first stage of the morning run (typically sausage, cheese, avocado and egg).

At the end of Santa Monic Pier, Los Angles, California, 14 May 2017.

Across the Mojave Desert, many town names shown in my map were merely railway place names (section houses and sidings). There was so much isolation and tranquility. The sunsets were stunning. Interaction with rattlesnakes basking themselves in the late afternoon sun had become a daily occurrence. By 25 May, I had made it to Needles (after 11 days). It was a psychological boost because the next day I would enter Arizona. I had run 547 km. That night we stayed at a KOA campground and watched two episodes of Breaking Bad! Pete had never watched it before and soon became hooked. Our plan was to stop at RV campgrounds every 4-5 days to take on water and empty the tanks. Some of these grounds had swimming pools so I welcomed the opportunity to cool down my body at the end of a run. The cool blue water melted the heat and long miles of the day's events. On 26 May, I entered into Arizona while crossing the Colorado River. It was a spectacular sight and a boost to my confidence. I had actually run the entire width of California! The first stop that day was the town of Oatman (a run of 39 km and a climb of 1000 meters). Oatman is a tourist boomtown that presents the romanticized image of a frontier-era mining community. There are wild donkeys roaming the streets, which are descendants of the donkeys that were used as mining animals back in the early 1900's. On the outskirts of Oatman, I was greeted with a 4-egg omelet by Emily (her 4-egg omelets are world-famous in my books) and we spent the next hour looking through the souvenir shops and museums in the town. At the top of the climb, I met with a lovely woman named Jo. She had stopped at the top of the mountain to take some photos of the breathtaking scenery and had seen the Pulmonary Fibrosis banner in the back window of the RV. She decided to approach Emily and Pete to find out more. When I had reached the top of the climb, we exchanged stories about the family members we had lost to the disease. It was very emotional. Jo lost her husband to the disease in 2016.

By the end of May 27, we had reached Kingman and we visited our first Route 66 traditional diner – Mr D'z. I devoured a plate of pork spare ribs, and regretted this on the run the next day! Emily sank root beer and ice-cream and Pete had steak. For the next few days, the runs were hot and sticky, and I consumed over 12 liters of water each day. On the morning of 29 May (Day 16), I passed through Peach Springs, the tribal headquarters for the Hualapai Indian Reservation. The Hualapai Lodge, a post office, and a grocery store are the only existing businesses in town. At the grocery store, I stopped for coffee and took on more water.

Jo and I, just outside Oatman, Arizona, 26 May 2017.

As I left the coffee shop, a local native Indian shouted "You be very careful out there." The words sent shivers down my spine. What did he mean? Was he the one I should be careful about? Two months later I would find out just how right he was. On 1 June, we reached the beautiful town of Williams and another rest day (I would typically rest every 8th or 9th day of running). Williams is the last bypassed community on Route 66, and the town is filled with treasures that reflect its colorful history and association with America's most famous highway. We treated ourselves to breakfast (pancakes) in the morning and traveled to the Grand Canyon for some sightseeing. The next few days saw lower temperatures as we approached Flagstaff and another KOA campground. Here, we met Dustin whose father had recently died of pulmonary fibrosis, and it was lovely to tell our respective stories of loved ones who had battled the disease.

Dustin and I, Flagstaff KOA Campground, Arizona, 2 June 2017.

The next few days were hard on my feet. Many states prohibit running on the shoulder of the interstate and I was forced to follow the fence line and run on dried mud. Avoiding snake holes became the norm. Small prickles were also a nuisance and I cursed having to stop to empty my shoes every few km. On 6 June, I finally left Arizona and entered New Mexico. Arizona had taken me 15 days to cross and I had now run 1183 km. New Mexico Route 66 is vast and varied, from the flatlands near Glenrio to the winding grades of Tijeras Canyon and the protracted climb up Albuquerque's Nine Mile Hill. I had more interaction with the police in New Mexico than any other state (except Ohio). Most days a passing police car would stop me to ask if I needed more water or a ride! An incident on 13 June seems funny now but not so at the time. After running 20 km, I decided to take some shade under a large advertising billboard on the Interstate about 180 km west of Albuquerque. It was also an opportunity to empty my shoes of sand and take on some more food. Within minutes of running again, two police cars approached from two different directions asking if I needed medical attention. Apparently, a passing motorist had seen me resting under the billboard and thought I was having a heart attack! The police officers (Kristian and Chris) agreed to a photo and after a brief discussion of how to stay safe, I was on my way! By 14 June, we had reached Albuquerque. I had run 1484 km. The next 3 days were designated rest days and an opportunity to stock up with more supplies, rest the body, say goodbye to Pete and Emily and welcome the new support crew member, Jeff. It was difficult saying goodbye to Pete after 6 weeks. He was so supportive throughout my run, and I found his encouraging words at the end of each day hugely uplifting. Some days my legs did not want to run!

The next few days were long, hot, and more fence line running. On 20 June, we reached Santa Rosa and by the 22 June, the Texas state line. New Mexico had taken 12 days to cross and I had now run 1833 km. It was at this time that I started to notice significant changes in scenery. We had lost the harshness and isolation of New Mexico. Cattle and green fields were now more common. Wind turbines too. We spent more time at truck stops during this period and experienced some incredible thunder and lightning storms. On 24 June, I stopped at Cadillac Ranch, which consists of 10 used Cadillac luxury cars, each purchased for less than $1000, buried to their windshields nose first in a wheat field. This modern art sculpture is truly bizarre.

Jeff and I, New Mexico-Texas state line, 22 June 2017.

On 27 June, I said goodbye to Jeff. The next three days were rest days and my body certainly needed it. Emily and Kieren flew into Oklahoma City on 29th June. I had reached Elk City when Jeff departed so after picking up Emily and Kieren on the 29th from Oklahoma City airport, we needed to drive back to where I had stopped running 2 days earlier. Kieren picked up driving duties. By 2 July, we had arrived back in Oklahoma City. The next day (3 July) would be my longest run so far (71.1 km). That night Emily and Kieren cooked an awesome burger meal. Because I had been on a Ketogenic diet for the previous 15 months, the burger came with no bun! On 4 July (Independence Day), we made our way to Bristow and parked by a beautiful lake (Lake Massena).

We bought some fireworks to celebrate and had so much fun. In contrast, the following day was memorable for the wrong reasons. Heading towards Tulsa, I befriended a pack of three dogs who decided to run with me. Despite many attempts to redirect them, they kept following. They were not strays and in excellent health. Sadly, a large passing truck hit one of the dogs. Overall, my experience with dogs during the run was not positive. In most states, I came across properties, particularly in rural areas, where gates were left open and dogs were allowed to roam freely. Many were extremely aggressive.

Oklahoma took me 11 days to cross. By the time we reached Quapaw on the Oklahoma-Kansas state line on 8th July, I had run over 2700 km. Time in Kansas was very short. I entered the state on 9 July and left the same day. Route 66 in Kansas totals 13.2 miles and nicks the state's southeast corner. It is the only US state where Route 66 is not interfered with by the Interstate. I certainly found running in Kansas very peaceful. On 10 July,

we entered the state of Missouri and headed towards Joplin. I had now run 2807 km. From Joplin to St Louis, Route 66 is rich in both scenery and vintage architecture. We finally reached St Louis on 18 July and enjoyed tasty St Louis bbq. Sadly, my time running Route 66 had ended. I had been running for 59 days at this point with 7 rest days. I started to believe that I could complete the run. Highway 40 would now be my focus and another 2000 km of running. Little did I know that the dream would be over in less than two weeks.

By 11 July, we had reached the famous 'Gay Parita' replica petrol station at Paris Springs Junction in Missouri. This stunning time capsule dominates the town. The owners, George and Barbara kindly allowed us to park up outside the garage.

George and I, Paris Springs Route 66 Garage
Paris Springs Junction, Missouri, 11 July 2017.

On 19 July, I celebrated my 53rd birthday with a run of 72.69 km. The day was long with a 36-degree c (97F) temperature and 80% humidity. Emily and Kieren surprised me with a birthday cake that night. We decided to spend the next 3 days sightseeing in Chicago. My body needed some rest, so we made our way to the Windy City on I-57. 150 km from Chicago we experienced a tyre blowout at 60mph and significant damage to several storage compartments underneath the vehicle.

By 24 July, I had hit the wall emotionally. Even though I felt refreshed from the three rest days, my mind was tired. I wanted the run to end. I was missing my family so much. I had put them through so much. I felt the same about my support crew. They had given up so much for me and I felt heavy with guilt. My spirits lifted after meeting Jim McCord just outside Vandalia (30 July). Jim drove an hour north from Cincinnati to meet me. I was honored to meet this 2002 US crosser and hear about his story. He is an inspirational man who has now become a dear friend. I did not know at this point that I would be meeting Jim again – in hospital!

The following day, one of my running friends from the UAE (Rhonda Strickland) joined me for a 16 km morning run. Rhonda is from Ohio and she is an ultra-runner. This was the first time in two and half months that I had run with someone else, and it felt magical. We talked continuously about the adventure, and I felt sad when our time together ended. That night Emily, Kieren, and I tucked into a plate of Mexican food at a local restaurant near Springfield. We parked up at the Twin Stars RV Resort. Tomorrow would be a rest day and a time to catch up with more running friends. 1000 km of my run remained, and I felt more positive about finishing. Little did I know that this would be my second to last night in the RV.

I was up early the next day to sort out laundry. Another awesome breakfast from Emily and Kieren. I was still in love with Emily's omelets and Kieren's dishes that involved cheese, even after 10 weeks on the road! We spent a few hours with a dear friend, Sydney and her two boys. Sydney and her husband Isaac had recently returned to West Virginia after living in the UAE for several years. They are both ultra-runners and we had become good friends. Sydney gifted me some of her homemade chocolate which I quickly packed for the morning run.

The next day (2 August), I left the RV around 6am. This would be my last morning of running and what I never imagined would be the end to my dream to run across America. I always ran facing traffic for safety reasons and the morning of 2 August was no exception. With two lanes in both directions and a wide shoulder, I felt safe. There was little traffic on the road. I checked in with my wife and daughters using skype at around 8am as I ran. We often connected while I ran. I would stash my phone in the front pocket of my hydration vest and chat with them while I gobbled up more miles. Meanwhile, they were on holiday in Cyprus. At approximately 8.20am, while still on the phone with my family, a dark colored pickup truck (1992-1998 Chevrolet or GM) came off the road and onto the hard shoulder driving at 50-60mph. I remember the truck moving from the inner to the outer lane. Nothing strange in this. It then moved onto the shoulder with increased speed. I made the split-second decision to throw myself over a small metal railing knowing that I would be hit. And I was. As I started to leap sideways, the truck smashed into my waist and legs. Broken, I landed in a ditch, which was not visible from the roadside. The force of the impact flung my phone from my hydration pack, but I could still hear Sarah's voice. Miraculously, the phone had survived, and even more so, our call was still connected. Sarah and my two youngest daughters, Bella and Abigail, heard my screams. Chaos followed. I laid at the bottom of the ditch with my right leg in pieces. I had no idea of the scale of my injuries, but I knew that my run was over. I started shouting for help hoping that the driver of the vehicle would be there to help. But it had not stopped. I started to experience shock and I was bleeding heavily from my

legs. Sarah's voice kept me awake as I started to drift in and out of consciousness. She immediately contacted the state police and my support crew, but at this point no one knew where I was, and I was not visible to other cars on US 40. Sarah asked how long I had been running and to provide a landmark so that she could inform the support crew and state police of my location. She established that I had not passed a local airstrip, so the state police were able to narrow their search. Her questioning saved my life. Approximately 30 minutes after being hit the phone battery died. This was a very lonely time. I made the decision to try and drag my broken body up the slope of the ditch, but I could not move due to a fractured pelvis. I kept shouting for help, but these cries soon diminished. I felt cold and just wanted to sleep. I kept thinking of Sarah and my girls.

Fifty-six minutes after being hit, state police and paramedics found me. I can vaguely recall their voices. The relief was immense. I was flown in a medical helicopter to Ohio State University hospital where trauma, orthopedics and plastics surgeons worked tirelessly to save my life.

I recall very little about the helicopter flight. I vaguely remember flashing lights inside the helicopter and everything around me seemed so dark. I also recall shouting at surgeons and nurses when I arrived at the hospital venting my frustration and anger at the person who had deliberately hit me.

When I came round after the first surgery, the feeling was a kind of weird exhilaration. I had survived. Even though I drifted in and out of consciousness, I did notice that Emily and Kieren were by my bedside when I first woke. I felt an immense sense of shame and guilt by putting them in a situation they did not choose. I so wanted to change my reality. My body had become a dead weight of 60kg and I felt so helpless. I so wished Sarah was with me at this point. She arrived from Cyprus after a 36-hour flight a few days later. Not surprisingly, she arrived hollow-faced with worry and loss of sleep. For the first week, she slept on a fold out bed in my hospital room, jumping up in alarm whenever I woke. Her love for me was unwavering. She had endured her own stress and drama enroute to Columbus. She recalls speaking with numerous surgeons along the route with no assurance whether I would be alive when she arrived.

For two months, I lay flat in bed, and I was not able to do anything on my own – I couldn't go to the toilet, wash my body, sit up, or move. I was oppressed with overwhelming fatigue during this time and sleeping for 18 hours each day became the norm. Sleep became my best friend. I quickly became depressed about my physical well-being and the sight of my broken body. The muscle wastage during this time was phenomenal. I hated myself for putting my family through this ordeal. I also hated the person who put me in hospital and ended my dream to run across America. Why did this happen? What did I do to deserve this? Why did this person drive directly at me? Why did they not stop? What kind of person would do this? I was terribly confused about what had happened. I replayed the incident in my head again and again. The time of day did not seem to matter. I knew that replaying the incident was mentally unhealthy, but I became convinced that by taking myself back there I could change the outcome. Over several weeks, I created different outcomes (running on the other side of the road that morning, leaving the RV 30 minutes later that morning, and not running at all that day) in an attempt to change my reality. "Why me?" constantly reverberated through my thoughts.

Over the weeks, time blurred. I also learned about solitude and isolation. The prevailing sense of helplessness was very difficult to come to terms with. I was dependent on Sarah and the nurses, and I hated not being able to do things for myself. By mid-August, the surgeons had performed 5 operations on my right leg and pelvis. Believing that I was out of danger, things took a turn for the worse. Unknown to the doctors, fragments of bone from my pelvis had pierced my bowel and I had developed a serious infection in my left leg and stomach. Emergency surgery was required. Prior to the surgery, the head surgeon informed Sarah that he might need to amputate the left leg because the infection had eaten away tissue. I learnt about this many months later. A decision was made to take the gracilis muscle from my left leg and use it to seal off the infection in my stomach. Fortunately, the surgery was successful, and I was able to fight the infection with a heavy dose of antibiotics over the next 6 weeks. Again, I have my wife to thank. She was the one who pushed medical staff at the hospital to undertake further scans knowing that things were not right.

During the third week of August, I was introduced to a physical therapy team (JD, Jenna, and Tony) who worked miracles. I developed a strong working relationship with this team and looked forward to their daily visit. I found JD was someone I could talk to about my emotional state, which was all over the place at this time. By the third week of September, the team was able to get me into a wheelchair and I was finally able to get around by myself. JD even gave me a haircut! Most mornings Sarah and Emily would push me over to the main hospital to have pancakes and coffee. The air was much cooler now and autumn had arrived. I loved getting out by myself. Propelling my body 200 meters in a wheelchair was a challenge during those early days but the sense of accomplishment was so rewarding. I was not able to walk yet but I was making progress. My 84-year-old father flew in from the UK on 13 September, six weeks after my accident. This was an incredibly emotional time. For the next 6 days, he pushed me around the hospital in my wheelchair. I also enjoyed spending time in the hospital grounds enjoying the fresh air and the autumn change. On 18 September, forty-six days after the accident, I was able to stand on my left leg for the first time (with JD and Jenna's help). It lasted about 3 seconds but was a start. I cried so much that day. I felt so incredibly grateful.

During my time in Ohio State University hospital, I had several visits from Jim McCord. Jim also brought another visitor – Paul Wheeler. Paul started his run across America a few weeks before my run. We kept in contact with each other throughout June and July and developed a close friendship on Messenger. Jim, Paul and I talked for hours about our running experiences, and I cried when they both left. Crying is something I did a lot of in hospital. Sometimes the tears were slow and weepy; sometimes they were uncontrollable and desperate. I would cry about the last few hours of my mum's life (I was by her side when she died) and the emotional stress I had put my family under because of the accident. For some reason everything in my world seemed unbearably precious. I had all the time in the world to reflect.

I left the Brain and Spine Unit at Ohio State University hospital at the end of September and entered Dodd Hall (a rehabilitation hospital). The next 4 weeks would see me become more functional. Therapy lasted three hours each day and I worked closely with two therapists – Allison and Kat. I would collapse into my bed at the end of each therapy session with exhaustion, but my body craved the progress. It was in Dodd Hall that I experienced my first shower (with the help of Sarah). This was a laborious and exhausting process but one where I was able to claim back some of my dignity. This was not the case when I was on my back for 2 months. By early October, my health had begun to stabilize (fewer scans, tests, and surgeries) and I got used to routine. There was an inexorable rhythm to each day – medication followed by breakfast followed by getting dressed followed by physical therapy followed by lunch and more medication followed by more physical therapy. During this time, I became acutely aware of what I had lost. My body was littered with scars, and I was so embarrassed to look in the mirror at my muscle loss. I was not able to stand upright in the shower so was wheeled in by Sarah using a specially designed shower wheelchair. I hated looking at my broken body. I longed to put on my Hoka running shoes again and start running. I told myself that if I could start jogging by the time I left rehabilitation, then things would not seem so bad. Looking back, I had a complete false sense of reality.

I entered Dodd Hall not being able to bear weight on the right leg but by mid-October, I was given a green light. I could now stand on both legs, which was a wonderful feeling. On 16 October, I left Dodd Hall. Sarah had rented a house in Upper Arlington, which was about a 10-minute drive from the hospital. The idea of leaving hospital scared me. The more I got better, the greater my frustration. I so wanted everything to be normal again, but I still needed help with so many things. Sarah was frightened too because of the uncertainty that lay ahead. She was now seeing me at my weakest and most exposed and I hated this. The first weeks at home were hard for both of us, and it demanded constant readjustment. After a few days home, I started outpatient physical therapy and met Cobey, a physical therapist at one of OSU's satellite medical centers. Meeting Cobey was a turning point in my recovery. He had expertise in working with athletes and was highly skilled in dealing with trauma patients. For the next 10 weeks, Cobey pushed me hard and I loved him for this. After a month of intense work, I was unable to break through 90-degree rotation on my right leg. He would use a belt and hold my leg in the air until it dropped. The objective was to break up the scar tissue that had developed after 10 weeks on my back. I do recall that my language was very colorful when Cobey used the belt for the first time, but we made good progress over the weeks. At my last session with Cobey on 4 January 2018, I was able to achieve 125 degrees rotation in the right knee. No pain no gain!

That fall and winter my whole family had settled into a new normal. My wife and daughters moved to Ohio. The kids started at a local school and made new friends. They quickly fell in love with their new American environment. Then, five months later, we left Columbus and Ohio on 5 January 2018 and returned home to the United Arab Emirates to start the next phase of my recovery. It was hard to leave a community that had given us so much love and support. Our youngest daughter did not want to leave her new school and friends. Returning home was a challenge to my now-accustomed hospital lifestyle. I had become great buddies with slowness and tiredness. The positive is that my mobility had much improved. I had a pair of crutches and a cane, and it felt great to be upright. I was back in the gym with physical therapy but I felt that I had lost my sense of identity by not being able to run. Perhaps with time and hard work I would be able to prove the surgeons wrong and run again. I am so grateful to my wife, and the medical team and nursing staff at Ohio State University hospital. My dream to run across America was still very much alive. One day I vowed to return to where I was hit and finish the remaining 1000 km. In the medical community there were few who believed my dream was still alive but that fire inside would not extinguish.

An update – 22 August 2022
After 16 surgeries and 4 years of physiotherapy, I returned to the United States in May 2022 to finish my run. So many people said it wasn't possible and I was ready to prove them wrong. Those long four years didn't come easily. I continued my physiotherapy. I continued to make slow progress.

Now that my immediate danger was over and my health had stabilized I was able to finally regain focus on other parts of my life. This was when Sarah and I were finally able to focus on our relationship again. The "all hands on deck" of a smashed body commanded center attention of all parties and once that noise finally subsided we found that in the intervening years we had grown apart. We parted amicably but I still love her and will forever thank her for getting me through that hardest time in my life. She helped me get my life back and with it, I intended to use it.

On May 30 2022, I started running from the exact spot I was hit in 2017. I needed a crew now more than ever and I was elated that both Jim McCord and Paul Wheeler - each veteran crossers themselves and dear friends - offered to serve as my support crew. What an emotional first day! I was joined by over 20 runners and bikers including surgeons from nearby Columbus who put me back together, physiotherapists who got me on my feet, members of the local running community and so many dear friends. We even received a police escort, thank you Lieutenant Thompson! On this first day, we ran 50 km to Ohio State University hospital where I was able to say thank you to nurses, surgeons, physiotherapists and old friends. I did not want to leave. Seven days later, I finally left Ohio and entered West Virginia. The next day I entered Pennsylvania, and it was time for some big elevation. Eleven days later I passed into New Jersey. The miles and states of the conclusion of this run were flying by me as if I were back in that hospital bed, deep in yet another virtual reality dream while my broken body refused to function. Only this time it wasn't a dream. I was doing it, and my healed body was giving me the joy of motion and movement as I made 65,000 flowing strides per day. After 19 days of running, Jim, Paul, and I finally made it to Coney Island in New York. My feet welcomed the cold of the Atlantic Ocean. Soon, we were greeted with several Nathan's hot dogs! Nathan's had its first hot dog stand on Coney Island just over 100 years ago and this was the first time I had sampled the beef in a bun iconic treat.

Thank you, Jim and Paul, for believing in me and having my back. You kept me safe. We will forever be brothers in arms. My daughters Bella and Abigail, thank you for your love and relentless support. My former wife, Sarah, thank you for saving my life. Emily, Peter, Kieren and Jeff, thank you for being by my side in 2017. The last four years have been a rollercoaster of emotions – sadness, depression, grief, guilt, laughter, hope, and joy. There was always flight and self-belief. I couldn't change what happened, but I was able to change the ending.

Jim, Nick, and Paul. May 30, 2022.
www.facebook.com/nickrunsamerica/

Chapter 23

Amanda Standley (Dancing with the Dirt)
January 10, 2017 to September 21, 2017
Delaware to California

If I had known what I was getting into, I never would have taken that first step. Thank god, I was naïve.

Tears of Happiness - Grasonville, Maryland
Why? Why would anyone want to walk across the United States? I honestly don't think I ever had a "good" reason. The idea came to me in a dream in the dark, wee hours of the morning. I was in a time of transition and the idea caught my curiosity but I never thought I'd actually do it. Then I mentioned the idea to a vibrant soul: a student of mine in wilderness therapy. He looked me dead in the eyes and said, "Do it." That one moment flipped a switch inside of me; it was no longer a choice. It was something I was compelled to do. I was going to walk across the United States!

I knew this journey was going to be transformative, but I needed a fundamental foundation. I needed a mission statement. I decided the journey would be dedicated to the dreamers, the non-traditional way of living, and liberating oneself from the constrictions of fear. I wanted to feel with my emotions, create human connection, and live life in all of its entirety. However, that still wasn't enough. I needed to make it larger than myself. I needed a cause and that cause would also hold me to my word. I turned to my roots in Dallas, TX, and discovered a non-profit, Youth World. I would raise money to help relieve economic burden and inspire hope and connection in the lives of children in South Dallas.

A man working in his front yard asked me where I was headed and where I started. I shared with him why I was walking and told him about being partnered with Youth World. After having a conversation for less than five minutes, he pulled out his wallet and handed me $20. I was baffled. I couldn't believe his willingness to give. I asked him his name and he told me his friends called him "Alias." I couldn't help but note the irony of his name. An angel named Alias; maybe he had a rough past or maybe he just didn't want people to know who he was. Either way, I walked away emotional and began to tear up. I kept walking and before long, I was sobbing. For the first time in my life, I was crying from happiness. Someone else believed in my cause! They believed in me!

Walking for Vitality - C&O Canal, Maryland
The choice to start walking in the wintertime was an attempt to find the lesser of two evils. Winter was not an if, but when. If I started in

the winter on the east coast, I'd have more people and more resources available to me if I got into life threatening situations. The alternative would have been to venture into the isolated Rocky Mountains and face blizzards.

There was no motivation to begin the day. I had a restless night filled with tossing and turning on a slope while random objects poked me in my side. Everything I wanted to keep from freezing was shoved inside my sleeping bag with me: water, stove fuel, phone, external battery, clothing layers, etc. It was one of the coldest mornings thus far and the dull, sunless landscape only furthered my disheartened state. I managed to convince myself to leave the warmth of my sleeping bag and race to pack up my gear. In order to save time, I refrained from heating up my strange, prepackaged Indian cuisine and immediately felt chills rolling down my back. I instantly regretted the decision. I was now twice as cold. My body had wasted energy internally warming the food instead of my appendages. I knew better but ignored my voice of reason. As I finally started walking, my hands and feet were numb. I was no longer walking on this grand cross-country adventure but simply for warmth, for vitality. The sun hid itself the majority of the day and snow perspired from the gloomy sky. Before I reached mile four of my fifteen-mile day, my feet screamed with immense grief. Everyone kept telling me to take care of my feet, but no one ever told me how. I knew I needed rest but between stubbornness and lack of resources, I didn't know how to help myself, at least until I got into town. I dismissed my pain and allowed my thoughts to engage in planning my evening. I needed to find a hotel. I day-dreamed about a massive pizza, just for me, delivered directly to my hotel room.

Somewhere around mile seven, I hit my breaking point. I plopped down in front of a big tree and had the sun briefly shining on my back. I felt defeated and stared down the trail as tears began rolling down my cheeks. I began to think of all the things I was grateful for and started sobbing. I thought about the support from my family, my friends, and from strangers that I've met and will meet. I then thought about how fragile the idea of the American Discovery Trail had been for me. Despite having lived on my own for the past few years, if my parents had put their foot down and told me, "No!" about doing this walk, I don't think I would've had it in me to continue without their support. Whether they realized that or not is a different story. I believe despite their fear for my safety they had a deeper understanding that I needed to do this walk and that in the end, it would be good for me. So, I sat there sobbing and hoped no one would stumble upon me on their morning run. I began to feel an unworthiness of the love and support behind me and my journey. I started to wonder why people believed in me but then a tiny whisper in my head stated, "Why not?" The twinge of hope was just enough to get me to start walking again but this time I felt numb. I was emotionally exhausted. I was now only concerned with the moment, with the day. I blocked out the uncertainty of tomorrow.

Eventually I made it into the town of Hancock. Music played from the local businesses, and people stared as I walked down the street. I didn't care. I felt more human among the brick buildings and my spirit began to lift. I made my way to the American Best Value Inn and was immediately greeted by a cat, a sure sign I was in the right place. As I checked in at the office, I awkwardly tried to socialize. I was pleased to find a personable atmosphere. The vintage patio furniture and a room to myself gave way to bits of excitement within me. I could heal for a couple of days.

Power of a Sandwich - Bridgeport, West Virginia

Heavy traffic, no shoulder, blind spots, and exhaust inhalation. There was no going around it. I had to go through it-- two miles exactly. I didn't have a huge issue with urban walking, but when there was no shoulder I had to develop coping mechanisms. To calm myself, I'd sing or narrate my actions. I couldn't allow myself to think about what I was doing. I had to do it regardless to move forward.

During these two miles, I'd seek refuge from the oncoming vehicles by slipping down into a ditch. "Oooh my, oooh my… I just stepped in something dead, didn't I?" I'd sing as I smelled a rotten carcass. Roadkill became a strange fascination. You could smell it far before you found it, but you couldn't always depict what the creature was. It was a disturbing way of gathering intel on the local wildlife. Different areas had different types of roadkill. Luckily, I soon spotted the decaying carcass of a deer and found comfort knowing I had not stepped in it.

The previous few days had been rough and I wanted to lift my spirits with good, wholesome food once I got into town. Upon arrival, I saw Domino's Pizza but decided to change things up-- pizza was my go-to food. Next, I walked by a hot dog-and-grill place but couldn't readily find the entrance. I didn't have the motivation to investigate further, so I kept walking until I came to a giant, "OPEN" flag outside the door of Della's Deli. The idea of a nice sandwich while sitting in the sun sounded lovely. I awkwardly squeezed through the doors and was met by Julie and Jeff. Their faces lit up in excitement and immediately inquired about what type of adventure I was on. I was asked what food I wanted but between me telling them about my journey and being indecisive, I never answered that question. I just wanted food! The build your own sandwich option was too overwhelming for me at the moment. So, I set my pack down and sat on the single stool while other customers were helped. There was an incredible amount of positive energy flowing and I became content sitting on the stool and talking to Jeff, Julie, and the other customers that walked in. Jeff eventually handed me warm soup and began making me a sandwich with simple either/or questions for what I wanted on it. Let me tell you, as soon as I took a bite of that sandwich, I literally savored every bite. I tried to distinguish each individual flavor and figure out what part of the sandwich it came from. There was sweetness from the honey mustard, but within the wheat bread there was another delicious flavor. I couldn't put a name on it! I took another bite and tried to hone in on the flavors. Next thing I knew, the sandwich was gone. After I hung out for awhile at the deli and talked to the regular customers, Jeff and Julie offered me a place to stay. I couldn't believe it. The night before I'd been thinking about getting a hotel room in one of the next towns, but instead I stumbled upon a wonderful family who wanted to house me.

That night, they took me to their favorite Italian restaurant where I got to meet one of their daughters and witness the small-town camaraderie that came after a victorious swim meet at the local high school. Julie let me borrow a pair of her slip-on, comfort fit shoes so I wouldn't have to lug around my winter boots. I felt light as a feather! I was moving my legs every which way, kicking and jumping. It was great. So, after I got that out of my system, we headed to the restaurant where I ordered a twelve-inch pizza to eat. I was willing to share, but everyone wanted to see if I could eat the whole thing. I managed five of the eight pieces and decided that if I wanted to be able to get out of the booth and walk out of the restaurant, I'd better stop.

I stayed with Julie and Jeff for two days and became immersed in their lives. I partook in a massive family breakfast, met their entire family, went to their son's high school basketball game, and was introduced to pepperoni rolls. When it was time to continue on my journey I almost tried to avoid the goodbye. I knew I had to go, but I really didn't want to. They didn't want me to go either, and it sparked an interesting thought. Walking was the very thing that attracted people to me. If I stopped walking, I would be taking away the serendipitous circumstances that allowed me to become part of their lives.

Why Do We Do The Things We Do? - Shaw's Orchard, Ohio

A woman, Krystal, walking on the outskirts of town started talking to me as I made my way to the local post office. The sky was grey and a soft rain fell from the sky. After sharing bits of my journey, she led me to the post office to receive my spring gear. She pointed to her house off in the distance and invited me to breakfast. The stormy weather conditions were forecasted to continue and even worsen so I accepted her offer and later, when she asked if I'd like to stay, I agreed.

It was wonderful learning about the Mennonite culture and their beliefs surrounding God. It gave me insight and further questions to ask myself to better understand my own religious beliefs. I joined the family on their errand runs and met an Amish family that sold eggs. They were excited to hear my stories and contributed home-made cookies to my journey. I had many questions swirling through my head. The Amish family had different structures and traditions they lived by but were incredibly eager to help me. I wondered if they would have been as supportive if one of their own daughters embarked on a cross-country journey. People's willingness to help me across the board contradicts what I've been taught in my life. Even if people don't approve of what I'm doing they still help in small ways- a meal, a donation, a lawn to camp in. The generosity people have shown me is beautiful.

The weather continued to be dreary and wet but I declined when Krystal offered another day for me to stay. I felt the urge to make progress, despite the weather. I had to keep going. It almost became an obsessive tendency. The only thing I knew how to do was to keep going and if I couldn't, my world would begin to fall apart.

I said my goodbyes and took off in the soft rain, hoping to gain mileage before more storms moved in. I felt confident in my ability to manage the rain. I knew I would stay warm as long as I kept moving. What I didn't plan for was getting lost. I'd missed a turn and upon trying to use my phone to revisit the map I discovered it had become saturated in my rain jacket. My phone screen was no longer working and had become useless when I needed it most. I sat on the side of the road and pulled out my American Discovery Trail turn-by-turn directions. I attempted to gain insight, yet the paper was also quickly deteriorating from the rain. I knew what street I needed to turn on but had no map to know where I was. Should I backtrack? Should I gamble and keep going? Should I wait for a car and hitchhike to the nearest town? I was now operating blindly so in an effort to resuscitate my phone and find shelter, I backtracked to the nearest house, which happened to have a cabin to rent out. I rented the cabin for the night and panicked when I realized the severe consequences of my phone being out of commission. Should I get a ride into town? Where was the nearest cell phone repair store? Do I backtrack or go forward? If my phone didn't revive itself, it was a game changer.

The cabin I rented was cozy and heated yet lacked electricity. I was grateful to have found shelter but questions and fear continued to tear at me. What compelled me to refuse shelter and adventure into the rain? Was it my ignorance towards the weather? I tried to find comfort in the mysterious ways God may be working but not much was found. Krystal's family had prayed for me that morning so that was worth something right?

As night fell and the thunderstorm began, I sat in the darkness wondering "Why?" I didn't understand. I didn't understand why I left a loving family and ventured into the rain. I didn't understand why my phone got damaged. I was afraid of losing communication with the outside world and I feared being alone. So, I sat in the darkness and asked, sobbing, "What am I supposed to do?" Suddenly, I had no direction.

I attempted to dry out my phone in front of the heater and eventually it revived itself. However, the weather had taken a turn for the worst. A massive storm had emerged through the night and there was thunder, lightning, pouring rain, gusty winds, and flooding without an end in sight. Needless to say, I stayed another night.

Through the hardship and uncertainty, I can only attempt to give meaning to my suffering. Maybe I was led to the cabin for shelter through the storms? There wasn't much shelter out there and my tent would have flooded through. Maybe I was being protected? Regardless, it was time to continue.

All the Love in the World - New Washington, Indiana

I spotted a white dog in the yard ahead of me roaming free without a chain and unbound by a fence, but he didn't seem to be aggressive. He let out a couple barks and neared me. It wasn't uncommon for dogs to be loose in the countryside; however, their reactions vary when they see someone walking. Cars don't bother them but people, not too many people roam the streets. Sometimes the dog would be lying down and simply poke its head up, other times it would come full sprint across a pasture, some would follow me, the more aggressive ones would circle behind me- herding me, then there were the ones that bark but won't bite, etc. You never know until you do, but regardless, I learned to show that I was an alpha.

This white dog was skittish, unsure of me. He let out a few barks and smelled me. He determined that I was alright and started wandering with me. I didn't try to instigate a connection. I didn't know how to take care of a dog much less figure it out while walking across the country. I figured he belonged to the house where I found him but he kept following me. He sprinted from house to house peeing on all the bushes. I caught a glimpse of mischievousness, grinning look on his face. He was having the time of his life, a completely different demeanor from when he first saw me.

I was worried though, he kept almost getting hit by cars. He'd just stand in the road. He followed me for at least three miles but I couldn't let him keep following me. I was nearing a highway and there he would definitely get hit. I tried several tactics. I sat down and rested, hoping that he would continue on without me. Instead, he'd come up to me and slobber on me before lying down at my feet. I started walking again and then sat down. Again, he'd stay near me. I called him and checked for a chip. He sat perfectly still and let me check his coat but I didn't find anything. He had beautiful blond eyelashes but something was wrong with his right eye. It was slightly red and closed more than the other one. In addition, you could see his ribs, he was malnourished. It disheartened me to believe this wonderful, well behaved dog was possibly abandoned. Why would anyone abandon such a lovable creature?

I couldn't allow him to keep following me so I tried to dissuade him and it broke my heart. I acted like I picked up a rock and made a throwing motion. He flinched from afar, confused. It temporarily worked and he distanced himself from me. I was disheartened and heaviness overtook my body. This dog had so much love to give and he started to trust me. I broke his trust. He flinched because he'd been abused. He'd had things thrown at him or been hit. He continued following me at a distance and I tried not to look back at him. He was still going house to house but it dawned on me, maybe he was looking for a home.

I rounded a curve at the top of a hill and looked back. He was standing in the middle of the road, unwilling to move, and both lanes quickly congested. From afar, I heard someone say what a stupid dog he was for not moving but he was smart. He demanded attention. One of the vehicles loaded him up in their van and I prayed that he was going to a loving home. He had all the love in the world to give and he wanted to give it to me but I couldn't take it. So I cried and prayed as I continued walking.

Something Wonderful - Marshal, Missouri

A gas station that no longer sold gas was the only business in town. Normally, I would've walked past without a second thought but I decided to take advantage of the flushable toilet, rehydrate, and enjoy the connection wifi brought me. The store was called Hardeman's and when I opened the door I was greeted with smiles and a hello. I moved straight towards the bathroom to avoid any staring that inevitably occurred. There on the bathroom wall was a sentence sent straight from heaven, "Always believe something wonderful is about to happen." My heart lifted. I left the bathroom and grabbed a gatorade, expecting a quick transaction at the cash register. The woman, Jackie, looked at me and asked if I was hungry. I softly replied, "I have tortillas and granola bars." She continued to look at me and instead asked, "What do you want? It is on me." Her kindness was unnecessary, but I was grateful. She brought out the special: fried chicken, mashed potatoes, corn, and coleslaw.

While munching away, a bicyclist, Richard, walked in and said to me, "You must be Amanda. I've been hearing all about you since Arrow Rock." I was confused for a moment but then remembered I'd stopped inside the Arrow Rock Visitor's Center and the park rangers took a picture of me and posted it on their social media. We exchanged stories while we both ate. Jackie soon came over and told me that she was a mom. She couldn't begin to imagine her daughters out in the world with nowhere to stay at night so she decided she would take me home. It would be an hour before she got off work so I kept walking. She could pick me up on her way home.

An hour went by but Jackie still hadn't arrived. I expected her to pull up next to me at any moment but time continued to pass. Did I miss her when she got off work? I felt baked by the sun but couldn't rest in the shade in fear Jackie wouldn't see me. I wanted to be easy to spot when she drove by. As I walked on the gravel covered shoulder I began to feel discomfort in my right ankle and wondered if I had somehow slightly sprained it. I didn't allow myself to worry about it and chalked it up to my leg muscles being too tight. Eventually, I did find a perfect resting spot and then Jackie appeared! She drove me to her home where I met her two daughters and husband and then she told me part of her story. She had grown up in the South Dallas area where I was helping raise money for a non-profit to help kids. She told me that if her parents hadn't been wise enough to move the family out of that area she could have been one of the troubled youth. After that, we both knew we had been placed in each other's life for a reason. Her family was a hoot and it felt right to be there. She told me too that it felt good to have my trust in her and that was a perspective I never considered.

The Push - Canton, Kansas
"Sunrises over sunsets because you get to watch the world be born again." – Chris S.
The light from the streetlamps gave way to a fog layering the horizon. Although beautiful I knew that would mean an extremely humid morning. I maneuvered in the darkness to pack up my tent and gathered the less than ideal cloudy water from the spigot. By 8am I'd walked ten miles and by 10am I forced myself to stop walking. There was 87% humidity and I was drenched in sweat. My body was incapable of cooling itself as the temperature kept rising. This left me with one choice. I had to find a house or business along the highway that had enough trees that could sustain shade for the entire day. The heat of the day was unbearable so I would need to transition into night walking.

The first house would only be shady in the morning, so I continued to the next patch of trees, one mile away. It was perfect! There was a ditch in the shade, between the highway and the line of trees, in front of the house/business. I plopped down, laid out my sleeping pad, took off my shoes, and sprawled out for a nap. It wasn't long before I was swarmed with gnats, flies, and mosquitoes. I covered my face with my hat and buff, trying to escape. The gnats were merciless. They would crawl under the brim of my hat, also seeking shade, and on my sunglasses' lens.

I laid there, in a perceivably relaxed position, with my legs outstretched and crossed, but I knew someone would eventually discover me. It took two hours but I was finally spotted by a post-woman driving by. I gave her a friendly wave, yet she still alerted the neighbors about a girl in the ditch. I had tried to lie in a peaceful, restful position so no one would be alarmed, but despite my efforts, I had an audience about 20 minutes later.

I heard a voice and lifted my hat off my face. A man and woman stood at the top of the ditch with a truck of three people to their right. I got up and said, "Hello! I'm okay, I'm just resting in the shade." The man walked toward me and I extended my hand and introduced myself. He told me they were debating on calling the police to make sure I was okay. I understood they were wary of me but I didn't understand why they didn't at least yell at me to see if I responded. Anyways, the police weren't involved and everyone went about their business.

As the sun maneuvered in the sky, a worker came and gave me cold water and the owner of the property, after getting his mail, stopped to talk to me. It felt good to have a stimulating conversation and to be able to share my story. His black lab came over and plopped on top of me trying to play. The dog was so happy and so loving! Next, an older woman came out of the house and gave me a bag of apples and granola bars. The gesture was so incredibly sweet! She told me I could keep shifting between the trees to stay in the shade, but I knew I'd have to get moving soon. I pulled up the hourly temperature forecast and saw that it wasn't going to get cooler as the evening grew nearer, so I started walking.

The humidity had decreased but the temperature was 93°F and I had twelve miles left to walk. Wherever there was a hint of shade, I was there resting and managing my body temperature. At this point, I was fighting my way to get into town before nightfall and without succumbing to heat exhaustion. I found a shrub, surrounded by thigh high grass, that produced sufficient shade as long as I hugged the base. I plopped my pack down and embraced the tiny bit of shade when I began to hear a motor. I assumed it was a passing vehicle and didn't think much of it. Without skipping a beat, a massive sprayer machine, the farm vehicle that looks like a monster truck with metal extensions on the side, zoomed past me. My life flashed before my eyes. The person driving was oblivious to my location and if any part of that machine (metal extensions) would've been off-centered from the road I could've easily been obliterated. The remainder of my walk into town was now focused on my perceived near-death experience. My mind was stressed and worn thin as I arrived in town. All I wanted was to quickly find a spot for my tent.

I knocked on the door at one of the first homes I saw, and the woman said I could set up at the church but the sheriff would probably talk to me. I wandered further into town and found a girl walking her dog. She informed me there was a park at the edge of town. I was exhausted, yet I wandered around scoping out a place for my tent. In reality, all I wanted was someone to see me and care. I found an abandoned elementary school and thought about that option, but I happened across a church and investigated the area. Between the inclined ramp to the entrance and the actual church building, I found a nook where I could set up. It was perfect but excitement evaded me. I entered the nook and sat there.

I had fought my way to get into town before dark despite nothing waiting for me. For the first time in my life I felt homeless. I was an invisible person and I felt like no one cared about me. I had nowhere to go and no one wanted me around. I quietly sobbed to myself until I no longer had the energy to do so. I set up my tent, escaping the bugs, and hid. I wish I could've hidden from my sorrow under the protection of my tent. It would be a short night. I needed to start walking at 4am. There was no place for me in this town.

What am I doing here? This vast expansiveness has filled me with emptiness. I feel like I'm on a never-ending death march. The towns I pass through are little oases for life yet when I reach them at the end of the day, loneliness is what fills me. I walk for shade. I walk for water. The Kansans are kind and helpful people but they are wary. Everyone is more than willing to help but I have to ask for it. Sometimes, I don't remember how.

Never Quit on a Rainy Day - Coolidge, Kansas

My breath quickened and my heart rate increased. Walking didn't seem right anymore. Two phrases filled my head. The first, "If you wake up enough days in a row and aren't happy with the situation, then something needs to change," and the second, "In the morning ask yourself if you want to walk or not and if the answer is no then don't walk." When I first read these words of wisdom, so long ago, they made sense but in practice they didn't seem practical. I needed to walk to make progress but I didn't want to anymore.

I found a shady spot next to the railroad and sat down. Several tears rolled down my cheeks, but I wasn't overly emotional. My thoughts circled around quitting. When I first began walking there was nothing else I had to do, no other choices. As I walked through my journey, I'd seen and experienced things I wanted for myself. I wanted a community of people surrounding me that I could have adventures with and rely on. I wanted some form of structure and stability. I wanted to learn about mental health and help people help themselves. All these things I wanted and none of them I could gain while I walked. I wasn't being present-minded and that initiated my downfall.

I was arguing with myself. What would be the consequences of quitting? What would they be if I kept walking? I had an impending urge to quit but I couldn't. I was between a railroad track and a state road somewhere in the plains of Kansas. I had to keep walking, at least for a few more miles. I pulled myself together and continued on. I knew one thing and that was I was determined to get to Holly (the first town I'd come to in Colorado). I was three miles from Coolidge and five from the Colorado state line.

For the hour walking to Coolidge, I rehearsed how I'd break the news to everyone. I had decided to quit. I thought about how I could word my failure into a success story. I was okay with that. It would've been an underdog story where lessons were learned but they still didn't manage to defeat the reigning team. I would've used this failure as a learning experience all while knowing if I quit I wouldn't return. I was okay with that too. Whilst all this was circling in my thoughts, I knew there was one thing I could do to salvage my journey.

I met a guy, Jonah aka DudeTrek, last summer and he'd walked across the country in 2013. When I'd talked to him about his experiences walking, he'd mentioned he had almost quit in Utah. That was what I was curious about. I wanted to know what changed his mind. The catch was, would this world traveler and adventurer (someone difficult to gain communication with) answer his phone? I had prayed for direction and I knew if he answered the phone it would be my sign to continue. I arrived in Coolidge and settled myself on a shady picnic table. I made the call to Jonah. It rang three times and went to a voicemail in Spanish. Disheartened, I decided to call a high school friend instead. She always radiated inspiration and wisdom. Yet, as I told her my thoughts on quitting I found myself hearing but not listening to what she had to say. "I won't let you quit," she voiced passionately. I knew though, the only person that could make me keep walking was me. At that moment, the majority of myself had decided to quit. My plan was to look to my grandparents in north eastern Colorado to rescue me from my sinking ship. Then, mid-phone call, Jonah called me back.

His voice was cheery as always. I tried to explain the situation while keeping my voice steady. He didn't tell me to quit or not to quit, rather he shared what was ahead of me and related to what I was feeling. I'd been feeling like I was floating in a third-dimension, separate from the world around me, yet somehow still interacting with it. He reaffirmed what I already knew about the beauty of the mountains and the awesome people I'd continue to meet. As for what had kept him from quitting in Utah, he'd made a phone call to the Delaware state coordinator and received advice himself, "Never quit on a rainy day," he was told. In other words, when you're at your lowest you should keep going because from that point onward, it can only get better. I asked Jonah how to fend off these sinking feelings because we both knew it would return. The more philosophical approach was to realize how strong one's mental fortitude would be after all was said and done. Mentally, I would be a rock and nothing would tear me down. The practical approach would be to list everything I was grateful for- especially at my low points. By saying the things I was grateful for, I could redirect my thoughts towards a positive outlook. Even with this advice, he kept it real. He confirmed my fears. It wouldn't get better in Colorado. In fact, it would get worse and more desert-like in the south eastern part of the state. With this knowledge, I decided to walk the two miles into Colorado knowing that I was willing to keep fighting.

Shocking Times - White River National Forest, Colorado

The name of the game had become navigating my route across the western United States via Google maps. After Denver, I decided to leave the American Discovery Trail completely and that introduced me to a new set of challenges. I was unable to think or plan for anything more than three days in advance. Anything more would be too overwhelming and cause me to freeze. This resulted in my inability to make decisions or forward movement. In addition, Google, so kindly, routed me on private land, roads that did not exist, and asbestos dump zones.

Due to my lack of information, I did not dare adventure on the beautiful wilderness trails of Colorado. Instead, I chose to follow roads that appeared to travel straight through the national forests. The positive, was that there was less of a chance I'd get lost and never be found again. The negative, was that I still had no idea what I was walking into.

I found myself in round two of my wilderness travels and this time, I unintentionally had another 11,000ft mountain to climb. I embarked on one of the steepest dirt roads thus far and it continued straight up for five hours. Logic told me it would soon be over. I should have known better. Through my exhaustion, I found entertainment. I began talking to myself as Forrest Gump would have and I motivated myself onwards and upwards.

After a time, I switched to Wookiee noises. However, I had to stop just about as quickly as I started. The attempt left me coughing so hard I almost threw up. In addition to my insanity, I spoke to anything and everything that was around me. A chipmunk would poke its head out and I'd say, "Hello." A beautiful limestone rock would come into my view and I would send forth compliments. I began talking to myself in third person and encouraged myself forward. I'd look up at the clouds and pray for them to be merciful. It was monsoon season.

   I continued gaining elevation until the terrain began to level out. I was at the peak! Except it wasn't a peak. Instead it was a giant meadow on top of the mountain and it felt like rolling hills. This was grand and beautiful until the afternoon thunderstorms rolled in. I quickly realized there was no escape. First rain and then pebble-sized pieces of hail fell from the sky. I embraced the dampness and the cold pieces of frozen water and told the sky, "Now, there won't be any rumbling, tumbling, or lightning while I'm exposed up here." I thought there was an agreement but it must've been one-sided because the clouds soon darkened and growled with thunder above me. I kept my cool and hastened my pace as I told the sky, "This is unacceptable." Immediately, the sky lit up with lightning above me and roared with instantaneous thunder. Adrenaline flooded my system before I could process the danger. I flung myself off the road and hurdled over bushes into the wild flowers, towards the blue sky. I was getting the hell away from the lightning. Never before had I felt such a sense of primal fear. My pack weighed me down, adding awkwardness to my stride, but when I reached another road, one I hoped I was supposed to be on, I paused and began hyperventilating. "I have nowhere to go!" I screamed at the sky. I was sobbing and struggled to control my breathing. I got further from the storm but still didn't feel safe. I needed shelter but the few available trees would have put me in more danger. They were the tallest objects around. I couldn't stop there. I only had myself to comfort me. With my labored breathing and tears rolling down my cheeks, I continued on my way all while praying I wasn't going to get struck by lightning.

Peace of Salt - Bonneville Salt Flats, Utah

   The terrain drastically changed to the salty wonderland known as the salt flats. It was an exciting day for me. I would see the "Tree of Life" (a giant metal tree sculpture along the interstate) and reach the Bonneville Salt Flats (where the land speed record was broken). The salt flats brought me unique challenges. One being, where was I supposed to pee? I was walking on the interstate and barbed wire fences prevented me from wandering too far off the road, not that there was much out there. My solution became the dispersed culverts. I could drop down into them or a ditch below the road but my main strategy became timing. I'd wait until there was a gap in the eastbound traffic (I walked against traffic) to quickly relieve myself.

However, I was at the mercy of anyone on the westbound side. I can only imagine the number of dash cameras that caught me peeing. Oh, well.

Shade and dehydration were also a challenge. My water would be so hot by noon that it became uncomfortable to consume. Instead, I'd splash it over my head to help with the evaporative cooling process. For shade (turned out to be more for giggles), I had a two-person umbrella. The idea was great until a semi-truck, speeding 80mph, on the interstate. six feet from me, about blew me away. I looked like Mary Poppins every time I caught a gust of wind. However, I'd still whip the umbrella out, tickled at the thoughts of what people must be thinking as they drove by.

I made my way to the Bonneville Rest Stop, and as I entered the parking lot a man stood by his car waiting for me. He greeted me with enthusiasm and told me he was an artist/photographer. Three hours prior, he had seen me as he traveled east. He shared his life stories with me and although I was excited to talk to him my body was weak with dehydration. I had to steady myself with my cart.

I walked towards the picnic tables and a woman popped her head from around the corner. "Are you walking? Do you want tea or water or both? Do you need money?" She handed me ice cold tea and water and scavenged a few dollars from her family in the car. The woman's teenage daughter donated a few dollars from her personal stash and that meant the world to me. It was one of the moments where I felt like I was able to empower and inspire a young woman to face the world and follow her dreams.

After that, my world became quiet and I observed. Families ran and bicycled along the salt flats and couples took pictures together. Individuals heading to Burning Man (artistic festival of self-expression in Nevada) danced in the salt. I admired their kindred spirits. I began to feel a slight longing to share the beautiful landscape with my loved ones yet despite this, there was bliss in the air. The salt flats held a familiarity to me but I wasn't sure if it was simply from a movie I'd seen or the stories my dad had shared with me. He'd traveled on his motorcycle through the areas I was now walking. Regardless, it felt right to be there and I knew one thing: I had to sleep on the salt.

As dusk approached I did exactly that, I stepped into the ocean of salt. "How far should I go?" I wondered to myself. I observed car tracks embedded into the salt and I began to fear a car running over me in the middle of the night. I walked for twenty minutes and deemed the spot no better or worse than the rest of the exposed terrain around me. For safety, I laid reflectors around my sleeping area. I hoped any roaming cars would avoid them. Even in this peaceful place I couldn't avoid deadly thoughts. After all, every night I discover something new that might kill me. I pushed those thoughts aside and stared at the Milky Way above me. "What is my place in the world? How have I made it this far in life?" The stars glittered the sky and the crescent moon maneuvered across the horizon as time passed. I let go of my worries while the sound of the interstate became white noise and peace fell over me.

The Best Friend They Didn't Know They Had - Elko County, Nevada

It is not the loneliness that gets me but the fear of being judged.

I felt lethargic but refused to let that get the best of me. I stopped looking at the time and didn't want to know the mileage; instead, I began to reflect on my life. The person that I have become is not who I was. I may look the same but my mind is far more inquisitive and free.

I snapped out of my reflection to see a state trooper pass by slowly. He later stopped and asked if I needed any help or if the car on the side of the road was mine. Before he headed back to his vehicle, I told him I was walking across the country. He didn't seem too interested but there was a hint of amusement on his face.

At the end of my walking day, right before I entered Wells, he popped up again and asked, "Still don't need any help?" I voiced my desire

for a place to set up my tent in town. He seemed to think the park was my best bet. I appreciated his help but was surprised to see him again. State troopers infrequently stopped to talk to me nonetheless stop again after they've already investigated me.

I woke up at 4:30am, exhausted. The sprinklers at the park had terrorized me all throughout the night. I had decided to sleep in the dugout and throughout the night the sprinklers popped on. I only had my umbrella to defend myself. I got back on the road at daybreak just in time to witness the fleet of state troopers driving to their assigned routes. One of the four vehicles beeped as they passed and I wondered if it was the officer from the day before. I was only starting my day and the fatigue in my body already had me questioning my ability to make it the thirty miles. The sky behind me glowed bright red behind a mountain, a beautiful sunrise, yet I worried it was caused by a wildfire. About mid-day, the same officer pulled over and asked if I'd seen someone else walking. Nope, I was definitely the only person out there. He told me there had been another call except the description was different, a woman wearing a white tank top. The description matched my white safety vest but I'd taken that off hours before.

Before he left, I took the opportunity to share that, if he really wanted to help, he could bring me pizza. He shook his head and laughed before saying, "That may be doable." He had to head back west at the end of the day so I shared with confidence that I'd be under the bridge at exit 321 about 4pm. It sounded like a plan and I was stoked. The whole situation was hilarious! The idea of pizza at the end of the day helped keep me going through the pain and I told myself that I had to get to the bridge or I wouldn't get pizza. Pizza and conversation were my motivation but a small part of me held doubt.

On my last mile, I began to see the state troopers heading home for the evening. One of the vehicles let out a beep, and I knew then that I wasn't getting pizza. When I got to the bridge it wasn't what I'd hoped for. There was loose dirt that created a steep ramp to the top and none of it was flat. I pushed my cart out of the road as best as possible and sat in the loose dirt. I didn't want to give up on the pizza idea. I told myself I'd wait thirty minutes out in the open and then retire to the shadows. I sat in the dirt and felt judgmental looks from the few cars that drove by. I began to battle with my thoughts about my self-worth. The people that drove past most likely weren't thinking negatively towards me, yet that's how I perceived it in my state of mind. The loose dirt kicked up a cloud of dust whenever I moved and I felt filthy. Rabbit holes were everywhere and occasionally I'd spot a few carcasses. In those moments, I felt exposed and impressionable and honestly, I didn't view myself as much. After thirty minutes, I scouted out a flat spot hidden from the road and away from the interstate. That's where I remained for the rest of the evening.

Finding my motivation for waking up at 4:30am every day, or at all, was increasingly difficult. My body hurt and my first thought of the day became, "I don't want to get up." I knew that wasn't an option though. I forced myself to have something to look forward to and for this day it was seeing the state trooper, a familiar face and friend in my highly erratic world. Like the day before, at daybreak the state troopers drove in mass to start their day but this time none of them beeped. Did the officer have the day off? I continued in my tired and worn state knowing that I needed to get into town, 20 miles away, and find my host family. It'd been about two weeks since I had a full rest day. I focused on the ground and mindlessly walked until a vehicle pulled over in front of me. I looked up and it was the state trooper! He got out of the vehicle with an enthusiastic "Good morning!" He could tell I was tired and gave me an encouraging, "One more state." He proceeded to tell me that I wouldn't see him again and that I would be leaving his jurisdiction soon. I don't think he knew how much I appreciated him telling me that. It was a goodbye, one that I knew was coming. He explained the pizza situation too. It turned out there wasn't a pizza place near the route he drove. I told him he should have made it up to me by bringing donuts this morning. It was light-hearted but he left me with a warning about an upcoming tunnel, the Carlin Tunnel. There was no road shoulder and "strange things" happened in it. Apparently, people like to close their eyes when they're driving through and others take their hands off the steering wheel. He told me there was a two-mile detour that I should take and told me to be safe before he left. I wanted to give him a hug goodbye but I didn't know what the boundaries were for a law enforcement officer. I watched him drive off and began to mentally kick myself because I never learned his name.

    I made slow progress as I kept walking due to my lack of consistency. I'd walk a mile and sit on my cart. Before I started again, I'd walk around the cart and inspect the tires. I'd start walking again and then decide I had to pee. It was this weird, twisted form of procrastination. I was tired of walking so instead I just wasted time which didn't help me at all!

    I took a rest day in Elko and met the most amazing locals at the family restaurant, Coffee Mug. While I was there eating lunch, four state troopers came in to eat (none of them were the one I knew). The host encouraged me to talk to them when I went up to pay (she knew what I was doing and I guess mentioned it to them) so for my own amusement I did. In the most awkward way possible, I approached the table of four and said, "Hi, I'm the one you've been getting all the calls about. Just wanted to put a face to the calls." While I said this, I was naturally in the way of everyone and had to keep maneuvering out of the way. All but one knew what I was talking about. They asked a few questions about why I was walking but at this point, I didn't know why. It was just what I was doing. I guess it had become more of a finish to what I started.

Good Morning
by Amanda Standley

She thanks God for surviving the night
While praying for the strength to finish the day
Doubt lingers in her mind
All while the officer goes, "Good morning."

She sits under a bridge in her dirt stained clothes
Debating the risk to be seen
To face judgmental eyes
While hoping for a giving heart
Leaving her worth on display
All while the officer goes, "Good morning."

She fights for peaceful sleep
Unknowing of the obstacles to come
Unruly sprinklers and roaring vehicles
She waits for better days
All while the officer goes, "Good morning."

The state troopers throughout the rest of Nevada had no idea but I was the best friend they didn't know they had. I'd wave and go out of my way to say hello. It became an exciting game for me. When would I see the next state trooper? Will they wave back? Just seeing their vehicle usually made me smile. After the state trooper in Elko County, my perspective on law enforcement shifted. They were willing to help me. They were my friends.

Burning Man - Lincoln, California

I arrived in town a couple hours before dusk and as I entered the city limit I couldn't help but notice all the shiny, new cars. I was on the wealthy side of town. I noticed a man in a suit and tie watering his lawn while talking business on the phone. I felt like I was on a different planet. However, as I reached the city park, I noticed that there was a heavy transient population despite all the children blissfully running around. I knew it wouldn't be a suitable place to sleep but I didn't really have anywhere else to go at that point. I sat down at a picnic table and a guy soon approached me. He just started talking and then came and sat across from me. I tolerated the conversation, trying to be polite, but it was strange. I continued to investigate the resources in the town while he talked and then he asked, "Do you mind if I take a bump?" I had no idea what he was talking about and after inquiring he made a snorting motion. "Ah, cocaine,"

I thought. I appreciated his thoughtfulness but told him it probably wasn't the best place with all the kids running around.

In hopes of finding a place to sleep, I called the police department and when I mentioned I was at the park he told me, "Be careful. There are lots of transients around." I thought humorously, "Yea, I know. There is one sitting across from me." He didn't seem dangerous so I remained polite and wished him well before I left to find a place to sleep. The officer told me there was a city ordinance against camping on public areas so I had to keep searching. I reached the outskirts of town and noticed two guys standing near their fence gate. It was always easier to approach people about camping on their lawn when they were already outside. So, I asked about camping on their property and he looked at me and gave me a hug before saying, "Did you know this was a Burning Man after party?" He welcomed me to his art studio and showed me the art car he and his friends had used in the Burning Man festival a few weeks before. As more people arrived at the gathering, my tired spirit was rejuvenated. I had amazing conversations about traveling around the world, mindfulness, and biking across the country. One of the women I met was Susie. She wanted to connect me with her friend in the town I'd be walking through the next day or so. She offered, "We'll just pick you up in the helicopter and drop you off at her place." "Wait, what?" I thought with a slight excitement rising in me.

Two days later I was on the phone with Susie, "We need an open space clear of wires and telephone poles." Her and her boyfriend, Dave, were prepping the helicopter and they needed to know their flight pattern and estimated landing zone before they took off. Susie gave me a quick rundown of how everything needed to be executed. "We're going to touch down and you need to stay back and wait for me to come get you."

I heard the helicopter before I saw it and I stood ready to go. I couldn't believe this was happening to me! I waved my arms in the air as they circled the elementary school soccer field. They spotted me and began their descent. They touched down and Susie jumped out and ran to me. After a quick hug, she instructed me to stay low, throw my backpack in the far seat, and sit. The noise from the helicopter was deafening but I managed to get the gist of what she wanted me to do. She buckled me in and put noise canceling headphones over my ears. As we took off and quickly gained elevation, I felt lightness in my stomach.

The land below was a cluster of gridded agricultural squares. Anything that sparked Dave's curiosity on the ground resulted in him leaning the helicopter to get a better view. Despite my excitement, I quickly learned that if I tried to investigate the ground for too long I'd become nauseous. I had to strategically find focal points ahead of me so when I explored the world below me for too long I could "ground myself." To help, Susie gave me ginger candies for my stomach. I wasn't going to let motion sickness stop me from enjoying my spontaneous helicopter ride! It was decided that we were flying to Bodega Bay! We were going to do a flyby of my end destination! We flew over a small range of mountains that took us into Napa Valley. The bird's eye view provided enormous detail to the geographical features and it reminded me how small humans are in the world. The mountains were lined with the parallel rows of grapes for the wineries and roads could be traced along the ridges. We continued west and we flew above the clouds. They looked solid enough to walk on yet we were traveling through them! Encompassed by white, we only knew we'd reached the ocean from the GPS coordinates. Dave directed the helicopter towards an open patch of clouds and we descended above the ocean. The white was quickly replaced by the depths of the blue ocean and I stuck my face into the window bewildered and amazed. I spotted my end point, the place I'd been almost a year before, Bodega Dunes Beach. We flew low above the ocean, parallel to the beach, and the surfers and beach goers looked at us confused but waved all the same.

On the ride back, I did my best to control my nausea but I was beginning to lose the battle with my stomach. Our next destination was Susie's friend that she wanted me to meet and stay with. We circled the home and looked for a landing zone. The best around was farmland but it was a risky landing. The remains of the crops were dry and there was a possibility of a fire starting. So, the second the helicopter landed Susie jumped out and scoped the area for any smolders. Everything was clear.

Beginnings - Bodega Bay, California

I knew it was my last walking day yet it didn't feel like anything significant was happening. I ate tuna for breakfast and wanted to start walking as soon as possible. I hoped for a decent shoulder to walk on for the last few miles but I didn't know what to expect. While walking, I had to allow myself to get into the groove of it all. Nine miles of walking was still three hours. I ended up taking a road off the highway and it was gorgeous! As I got closer the smell of sand and salt filled the air. The road winded through the trees and climbed steeply over the hills. I crested over one hill and the descent presented the ocean! What a magnificent sight! Two of my friends, Bob and Lia, were also going to meet me at the ocean but I was afraid I'd beat them there so I took my time. Rather, I took the time to appreciate the things in front of me. I examined the massive pine cones I found on the ground and took pictures with all the local signs. Then it was time to enter the last stretch into Bodega Dunes Beach. I knew exactly where I was. I'd made this turn almost a year before in my van while I was traveling on the West Coast. Right before I walked past the entrance booth, Bob and Lia drove slowly up to me and I greeted them with a weird facial expression before hugging them through the car window. They drove off towards the beach and then called saying they didn't see my parents. A spark of anxiety lit within me. "Where are my parents?" Before too much worry overcame me, they pulled up next to me in their vehicle and my dad jumped out. He was going to walk the last bit with me and distract me while my mom, Bob and Lia worked on a banner. When I got to the parking area, I sat at a picnic table and watched from afar as my loving family and friends created a banner for me. I felt no rush to get to the ocean. It wasn't going anywhere. After all, it is the journey and not the destination that matters. I waited and when they were done, we all walked onto the beach together and I waited again until they were camera ready and had the banner properly placed. That's when I jumped and did a slow-motion run (while throwing off all my gear) into the ocean!

There was uncertainty in me about jumping into the ocean. I imagined I would get caught in an undertow and be swept out into the ocean. It wouldn't have been the walking that got me but the ocean. Regardless, I did it anyways and took one last risk. The massive, powerful ocean was a foreign place for me but like the other obstacles, it wasn't going to stop me. After running into the ocean, I made a sand angel and grabbed a giant ocean root/seaweed to jump rope with. Then I went for a second sprint into the ocean. I was high on life and everything was beautiful. I did my best to absorb each moment and take mental snapshots but after it all I felt that this was not the end of a journey but a beginning.

I want to thank the countless beautiful souls that fed me, sheltered me, loved me, shared their lives with me, and supported me in any way. Unfortunately, I wasn't able to share all the amazing stories and transformative moments in this small snapshot of what my life was like for eight and a half months. I am eternally grateful and all of you will always be in my heart.

If you want to read a few more stories visit my website at dancingwiththedirt.com.

Chapter 24

Sandra Villines
Record-setting run: 54 days, 16 hours, 24 minutes.
September 11, 2017 to November 5, 2017
City hall steps of San Francisco, CA to City hall steps, NYC

"Come here there's something I want you to see," the sweet voice that had been so familiar to me over the last 7 weeks excitedly said. I was in a state of denial, or perhaps shock is a sharper way to describe it. Why was it now that it was "done" my bones hurt (like what I would imagine taking a bat to the bottom of your feet and beating them to death might feel like)? I slowly made my way over to "guardian of the mothership "as she is warmly known. I also call her "guardian of my sole." We were outside between the RV and the real shower I had just taken which also hurt. Mind you, I had grown quite accustomed to the shower in the RV that was home and had been for seven weeks. She was looking in the horizon and was pointing at the Statue of Liberty. "Can you believe we got here baby girl? Your Chevrolegs got us here." I stared and stared and still felt as though I had dreamed the whole thing. Did I really run all the way here? The dull skeletal ache reminded me that we did. Somehow the days all blended together between day 2 and 53 as some sort of fog. Every day had a story that someday I would have to sort through to bring some closure. Tears welled up in my eyes, it was all I had dreamed of for the last year, and now after all that we had endured to get here I was in a state of disbelief. Today was the first day after we had finished and I didn't have to get up to run, but I awoke several times by the sheer terror that I wasn't done and I was late now.

It may sound funny and I can sort of laugh a little about it now. It was a nightmare or night terror where my legs would start moving and I would wake up in a sweaty panic. How do I even explain this experience to anyone? It's been well over a year and it was like a taboo for me to speak about any of it. I rarely bring it up, for fear of the questions I would face. People are unknowing and sometimes the naivete of the questions ranged from, "How was the vacation?" to "How has your transition to eating real food been?" While this was something I wanted to do more than anything, it was by no means a vacation. For those that have ever endured such a feat, it's not realized just how much loneliness you have every day. Getting out of bed after the 3rd week had become a chore I no longer wanted anything to do with. The unknown awaiting me daily. Someone like me, so ordinary and not seeming like an individual who could ever complete such a run was scrutinized ad nauseam about the lack of credibility, skills and "non-champion" runs I had completed. I never once ever looked at any of the commentary or criticisms of those who made those comments. I focused on what I wanted and that was to run across America. For 54 days we lived in our bubble. Cinder, Jay and me. They did everything they could to protect me from any and all outside "noise" that could distract me from the only thing I was supposed to do, and that was to run. No contact or interactions with my family or friends, no social media or news. I had no idea what was going on in the world. Just the weather, every morning like clockwork I heard Jay asking, "Google, what's the weather today?" Jay and Cinder have become family to me, it was just the 3 of us for 95% of the run. We did have some visitors that were there for parts and I am forever grateful. It always seemed to be that people showed up when I needed it. It never mattered to me what people thought, so why these days am I struggling so hard with finding a way to be happy?

Running across America is a life changing experience that I will always have, the few that have shared it know what I mean when I say you will never be the same. To be one of the few that have done it and have a record is an unexplainable mixed bag of euphoric solitude. To say I did it still feels surreal to this day.

chapter 25

lazarus lake
may 8 to september 14, 2018
newport, rhode island to newport, oregon

when i was asked to contribute a chapter to this book on crossings
i was a little bit stumped.
how do you capture the magic of something so immense
in a single chapter?

if i had to describe the experience
i would describe it as an immersion in learning;
an educational experience so intense
that every day is a lifetime.

you are surrounded by wonders.
every day you see new things
at a pace where you can see so much more than you would if you lived in a place all your life.
history, geology, architecture, science...

and people.
the people are the most fascinating of all.

i think if every crosser's story shared a common thread
it would be that they could never have made it alone.
a crosser's story is really the story of many people;

road angels,
who always seem to show up just when you need them most.
each of them owns a little piece of the crossing.
and the crosser shares a little piece of the magic with them.

most of the east i was able to walk the days alone if need be.
but after i crossed the mississippi at dubuque
i was dependent on having someone to crew me.
i am too old and slow to bridge the ever greater distances between "something".
much of the way i was uncertain of what tomorrow would bring.
i had a crew today,
and it took all my energy to cover today,
with no strength left to worry about tomorrow...

if, eventually, some tomorrow there was no one to help me,
i had already decided that i would rest a few days where i was,
and then figure out how to get home.

somehow, there was always someone there when tomorrow became today.

and so it was that out in the middle of nebraska
a couple of guys from kansas city, missouri showed up to keep my transcon moving.
chad wooderson and george hager drove up in a big old RV to give a few days out of their lives
to keep the dream of an old hillbilly (who lives in the woods) alive.

after i got to iowa, the brutal summer heat had inspired me to a change of schedule.
each day i would start walking at 2200 hours (10 pm)
and i would walk until 1400 hours the next day (2pm)
during the hottest part of the day, i slept.

george was walking with me this night,
while chad slowly drove the RV up the road,
a mile or two at a time
a moving oasis with food and drink.

while we walked,
george told me his story.
everyone you meet during a crossing has a story.
until you make a journey like this,
you never realize how many fascinating people there are.

george had always lived in kansas city.
he had grown up in the rough part of town.
just another aimless kid with no future.
it takes two things for someone from places like george came from
to turn no future into a good life.
first, someone has to crack open the door for them to see that there are better things out there.
for george, one of those people was a coach,
who came up to him in the hall and said;
"you are going to be on my team."
it was not a question.
and george learned the lessons of life
that are taught on playing fields across america.

the second was a teacher,
who told him;
"it is better to ask a question and feel dumb for 5 minutes,
than to never ask the question and be dumb for life."

the other thing it takes,
is a person with vision and courage.
for george it meant deciding he wanted to do something with his life.
it meant walking away from the comfort and familiarity
of the people and things he grew up with.
as he told me,
the guys he grew up with were more than likely all either dead
or in prison.
after high school he knew he had to cut all ties with his former life
to walk away and never look back.

this is the kind of thing you learn out there on the road.
when george and chad drove up, i already knew chad was a special guy.
george just looked like anyone else.
walking and talking under the sky,
i found out what an amazing person he really was.

it didn't seem like i had anything to give in return
for all george had done for me.
but there was something....

after a long string of stormy nights,
this was the night walk i had been waiting for.
the sky was clear,
and there was no moon.
if you have never seen the night sky out west,
you have no concept of how many stars there really are.
no matter how great a night sky you have seen before,
having a bowl of unbelievable numbers of stars from horizon to horizon
is not like anything you have ever seen.

george had spent his entire life in the city.
he had never seen a real night sky.
he had never seen the milky way,
he had never seen the big dipper,
he had never seen a shooting star....

and not only were we out on the empty plains,
we were being treated to a meteor shower.

the sky was traced with shooting stars....

short streaks of light,
long rapiers that slashed across the sky,
thick tracers that ended in an explosion,
even tumbling balls of fire.
something amazing was happening every minute.

i showed george the milky way,
and explained that we were looking across the center of the disk,
to see only an arc of the far side,
and that what looked like a splash of spilled milk
was actually stars so numberless that we could not see them individually.

and then we talked about the other stars.
so many of them galaxies on their own,
so far away that all we saw was a single dot of light.
many of them with more stars than the milky way.
others were single stars, on our side of the milky way

there is nowhere on earth where you can really grasp our insignificance
like you can under the night sky out west.

and george who was not afraid to ask a question,
was equally unabashed to express his wonderment
at this unimagined spectacle surrounding us.

i showed him the big dipper,
and the north star.
we invented constellations of our own....

and every few hours,
we watched the international space station
as it dashed across the sky.
that one i owe to william dulitz,
another friend well met on the open road;
who had pointed it out to me in iowa.

as eagerly as i had anticipated this night,
experiencing it thru the eyes of someone who had never seen it,
who never dreamed it existed,
was so much more.

chad would drive ahead,

and then come back to walk with us.
and we three just walked along thru the greatest show on earth,
scanning the skies,
and calling out falling stars.
the miles passed without notice,
and i never wanted the night to end....

altho when it did,
it was with another magnificent nebraska sunrise.

there was one question that everyone i met seemed to want to ask;
"what has been the best day of your trip?"
and the answer was always the same;
"today!"

because i always knew that just over the next rise
just around the next bend
just a little ways up the road,
i was going to see something i had never seen,
or learn something i never knew.
the next adventure was always within walking distance.

laz

Chapter 26

**Thomas Curran
Feb 2 to Sep 21, 2019
Holden Beach, NC to Newport Beach, CA.**

On February 2, 2019, I began my 3,235-mile walk across America. The road can be a real a bitch. But she's the most beautiful bitch I've ever met. We fell in love but it took a while. Five days into our courting, she coiled up, struck fiercely and latched her gnarly fangs around my ankle. With pain so fierce I was brought to tears, she dropped me flat on my ass on the side of a lonely highway and begged me to surrender. I dried my eyes, swallowed the pain, locked my stare upon her unforgiving eyes and said, "No way. We were meant to be together." It took eight days to heal enough to restart and on Valentine's Day, she succumbed to my presence. Over time we learned to compromise, yield to each other's passions and respect our destiny together.

The road cradled me when I was lonely, fed me endless miles of adventure when my life had left me empty and relieved me of the burden that was awaiting me back home. Upon her, I shed my fears of social compliance and accepted the most fundamental job known to man – survival.

I started walking across America just two months after turning 50 and having lost most everything that I thought was important to me. I say most because, at the top of my list of incredibly awesome things in my life was my son, Holden, who ventured out on to the road with me on my first day leaving the Atlantic Ocean. Holden believed in me and my journey as much as I doubted myself and feared it. He was strong and ambitious and idealistic; he was everything I had once been. One mile in we stopped, hugged, cried and said goodbye. We both knew the journey was dangerous. We both knew that I was never the guy voted "Most Likely To Do Something So Stupid As To Walk Across A Damned Continent". I was not a hiker, camper, runner, work-out person or outdoor adventure seeker. The last time I had slept outside was about a hundred years earlier give or take a few days. But I was always the guy who did what he said he was going to do. I was always the friend with the fun, crazy job and stories of a somewhat wild and always adventurous career as a chef.

When I first told my friends and family that I was planning this journey, I was already dead set on going. It wasn't just a fantastical idea that I was having or a dream I was thinking of fulfilling, I was doing it and there was no room for them to talk me out of it. Luckily, nobody tried. Of course, they had their fears and worries about the physicality of such an attempt and the same for what could happen to me. They worried about people wanting to cause me harm, wild animals wanting to eat me for supper and the million or so cars that would fly by me at top speeds every day. But, I believe, their biggest worry was why I was doing it. Why would somebody abandon life and choose to subject themselves to a life similar to homelessness? Was there something wrong with me that I wasn't telling them? Was I terminally ill and checking a wild adventure off my bucket list? Was I having a mid-life crisis and couldn't afford a Ferrari? Or was I just on a new adventure and, if so, why not do the PCT or AT where at least there's a trail and known places to sleep? Besides not being terminally ill, my answer was a blend of all the other questions. I needed to stop…and I needed to go.

What they didn't know was that I was craving the challenge of loneliness and wanted to force myself to spend months on end in my head and contemplate decades of decisions that shaped the man I was now. I hadn't done bad things, I wasn't at rock bottom or ashamed of where I was. That wasn't it at all. I just wasn't happy with the "inside" me. I wasn't worried about my legacy or what others thought of me. I didn't need to change or find answers for anybody. I needed to change for me.

My inspiration to find those answers on the road came from Tyler Coulson's book By Men Or By The Earth. Whatever was going on in Tyler's heart when he wrote that book struck similar chords to how I was feeling in that moment of life. I know there are dozens of books written by trans-cons and I've read many and loved them all but something about BMOBTE hit home. Once I read it, I knew where to go to do my work.

I planned to leave Holden Beach on February 2 and head northwest towards Virginia, get over the Appalachians and head west as many crossers had done in the past. I planned for months despite being told by many great people like Kait and John Seyal, Brett Bramble, Jonathon Stalls, Tom Griffen, Eric Keeler, Chris West, Lindsay Monroe, and Tyler Coulson to not worry so much about the daily details. Of course, I now give the same advice about detail planning but, during the months leading up to my departure, I loved the time spent figuring out my every step from A-Z.

I got a dog. I was never a dog person. In fact, for most of my life, I've feared them. When I was a boy so young I can't even remember the story I'm about to tell, I was bitten several times on the face by my Grandma's German Shepherd named Brutus. I've been told I deserved every bite. My family says that I used to stand on the sofa and jump on his back when he'd pass by and, for some dumb kid reason, never learned my lesson. A few trips to the hospital for stitches apparently crept into my subconscience because, until I got Wink, I was fearful of any dog I couldn't possibly drop-kick across a room. Not that I would ever drop-kick a dog but if I had to I would want to be able to. I did have a little dog named Katie when I was in my late 20s but she was definitely a mutt I could manhandle. Anything bigger and I kept my distance. I went to a shelter in San Diego and met my new best friend and co-pilot, Wink. Wink is a rescued Mexico street dog. I think he's Beagle and German Shepard but who knows. I'm told the dogs rescued from Mexico have at least 10 breeds blended in. Whatever he is, he's my buddy and one hell of a road warrior.

I also added a charitable component to my journey. I raised $21,120 for the Pediatric Cancer Research Foundation which has been close to my heart for over three decades.

With a plan in place, gear in check and Wink in a kennel under the belly of a big plane, I flew to Charleston, SC to meet up with my son for a few days before starting my walk. On the way to Holden Beach, we met up with Jessie Grieb who was making her way south on her Canada to Key West walk. She just happened to be in South Carolina and I was happy to get to meet her in person. We became friends, messaged each other often, and lived a life on the road at the same time. I stayed a few days in Holden Beach with the help of Josh Holden whose family named the land back in the late 1800s. His whole family was there to greet us, feed us and get me ready.

On February 2, I woke up early and walked Wink down to the beach to have a look and watch the sunrise. Shortly after, Chris West showed up as did a few dozen other new friends and we made our way to the edge of the sand. I took my shoes and socks off, took Wink down to the water, scooped some up in a plastic jar, got my legs wet and said goodbye to the Atlantic. My toes wouldn't touch saltwater for another 231 days. Hard to imagine since I live about a half-mile from the ocean where I would finish my journey.

Five days into my journey, as I mentioned above, I had an ankle injury that stopped me for nearly two weeks. On doctor's orders, I had to re-route. There was no way I would be able to push my cart up and over the Appalachians. Remember all that day by day planning I did for months and months prior to walking? Gone. Out the window. I headed south and around the bottom of the mountains then west towards home. Every day was a twenty-mile search on Google Maps zooming in to find a place to sleep. That was life for 7 months. Just head west and eventually I would get to the Pacific Ocean where I call home.

I can't tell my entire story here but I can share some high and low points. I can only count on one hand the number of bad or ill-intended people on my walk and only two that could have caused me harm. On the flip side, I cannot possibly count the number of amazing human beings I was honored and lucky to meet. In every state, of every race and every religious and political ideology, I found compassion and awesomeness. I stayed with 58 different families in 12 states. These families, except for a few, were strangers to me. I was a guy with a dog and a cart and they allowed me and trusted me to be in their home where they raised their families. I sat at their dinner tables and slept in their beds. A few stepped way up and allowed me shelter for many, many days on end when I was injured or too sick to walk or when the weather was too dangerous to be in. I took shelter from tornados, was given bags of sandwiches, countless dollar bills, a few bibles, dozens of tabs paid for in restaurants and bars, and many, many hugs.

The bad – just a few. I had a follower one very late night when I was walking into Priceville, Alabama who stayed right on my tail for a few miles. Wink was barking and pulling on his leash to try to protect me the whole time but the guy didn't budge. He stayed right there with me all the way to my motel where he was arrested shortly after. Then, in Prague, Oklahoma, Lindsay Monroe, who had walked a few years earlier then rode her bike back across America and who is a bad-ass bartender in Massachusetts, flew out to walk with me for a few days. After we were nearly run down by a truck that led to Lindsay flipping off the driver, the truck came back at us and an old guy jumped out with a gun. The worst day with the best line ever – here's a guy with a gun who yells at Lindsay, "Girl, you made the biggest mistake of your life" to which Lindsay replies, "What are you gonna do, f**king shoot us?" Uh, Lindsay, he might! Luckily for us, the guy didn't want any part of her so he jumped back in his truck and took off. Lindsay says to me, "I am so sorry! Where I come from, I flip you off, you flip me off, we go get a beer! That's why they call us Massholes." Late, late that night, at 5:00 am, the tornado sirens sounded in town and she and I were down in a shelter with a family that was letting us crash at their place. In one 24-hour window we went face to face with a crazy guy with a gun and a tornado.

My journey was a vast collection of moments impossible to sort into bests and worsts. I get asked a lot what my favorite/least favorite moment/state/city/day, etc. and it's impossible to answer. There were just too many awesome moments and a whole lot of crappy ones. To pinpoint best and worst can't be done. I loved Alabama and did NOT love Texas. That said, I met so many cool people in Texas! I loved Alabama even though that's where the guy followed me and I almost pulled my weapons out to defend myself. But Alabama was absolutely beautiful and the roads were awesome and the people were great. I hated Texas not because of anything Texas did to me, it was just flat and super hot and I didn't have Wink anymore because he had to go home due to the heat. I loved the people in Oklahoma a TON except for the guy with the gun but I hated Oklahoma because it took me six weeks to walk what should have taken me four because there were dozens of tornadoes and the thunderstorms were crazy. Oh, and I got a tattoo in OKC after Wink went home and I love my tattoo so I have that connection to Oklahoma. I loved Oregon. Period. Loved it.

I will add an entire paragraph to the most surprising thing about my walk. My home state, where I was born and raised and still lived within, was the WORST state to walk and I would NEVER walk down it again. Now, let me add that I met some of the most awesome people in California. A few of them saved my butt for days on end. But California felt different. In general, the people were just not as nice, not as caring, far more judgmental and it was the first time in months where a human actually refused to help me when I was in absolute dire need of help and all they would have had to do was let me fill my water bottle with their hose. It was the worst moment of my walk and it shattered my feelings of good humanity for a few days. Long story short, it was about 104 degrees and I was on a dirt road eight miles from town with nothing around me. I had gotten lost earlier in the day and, due to the increase in mileage to get back on course, I ran out of water. I found a house where two young men were outside and I asked if I could fill up from their hose which was hanging on the wall ten feet away. They told me to get off their property. I was stunned and, needless to say, very worried. There wasn't another building for miles and I was OUT of water in those temperatures. As I sat under a tree on the edge of a never traveled dirt road contemplating how miserable and agonizingly slow death would be, a little car appeared and he just so happened to have a cooler full of water bottles. He may have saved my life.

Two days later, compassionate humanity was restored. I had been letting the water incident bother me quite a bit which I shouldn't have done. I should have just let it go. On another long dirt road in the crazy heat, I saw a guy on a bike coming towards me. As he got closer I saw that he had a big heavy bag hanging around his neck. At about ten feet out he reached down into the bag as my hands went down to my weapons. I'm always vigilant. The man pulled out a peach and, without ever stopping or making eye contact, he held it out and I snatched it out of his hand as he rode by. We never spoke and never looked at each other but that single moment with that one man made everything better. I no longer cared about the water incident. It didn't matter anymore.

My point is this: looking at our world from way up high it's easy to see how messed up and divided we are as a country. But down on the road, face to face, we are all good people with a just a few bad seeds mixed in. My journey changed the way I feel and how I act and how I respond to people who don't think like me. I'm a slightly moderate liberal from California who walked through the bible belt with a cart and a dog and found love, compassion, kindness, and care amongst people that the media would leave me to normally believe were against me. My ideologies couldn't have mattered less. I found true hope out on those highways and rural roads, in the big cities and one light towns. Red, blue, God, no God, black, white, Hispanic, Asian and every other nationality – we're all down here together just trying to carve out a meaningful life. Whether we hang out together or not, we all have a common goal and maybe, just maybe, the path to get there doesn't have to be so treacherous and rocky.

I met my son about a mile from my finish line at one of my favorite local restaurants. We had a big breakfast and enjoyed a moment alone. I was in a state of mind that I can't quite explain. My journey was almost over. Only one mile to go. I wanted that water so badly but I was terrified of the end. When I made it to the pier and saw crowds of friends and family cheering me on, it became overwhelming. I made it to the sand, ditched my cart and ran to the water where I dove in, made my way back to the sand, plopped down on my knees and cried. I had done it. I had walked across America. And my first thought was, "Now what? It's really over?"

I've been home for about two months and I miss the road every moment of every day. Getting back to real life has been hard. I knew it would be. I was warned. I wonder what it is about my journey that continually calls me to go back out and keep walking. Is it the freedom? The challenge? The beauty of so much country I've yet to see? I think it's all of those but, mostly, I just want to experience more great people and share some food and drink and good stories. I miss that. I miss every person I met. I love being near my friends again and my bed is so, so comfy. But I feel different. I kinda feel like a tourist in my own town. My friend summed it up best when she said, "You were a piece in a large puzzle. Then you left that puzzle for awhile and, when you returned, your piece had grown and it no longer fit in the space it used to." I choke up a bit every time I say those words. They are so spot on.

I didn't mention any names in this chapter except former crossers who helped me out. I did that because there were just too many and, although some may have helped more than others, it was every single one of them that made my entire journey the most incredible experience of my life. I couldn't possibly single out just a few without listing them all and I don't have that much space in this chapter. If you helped me in any way, shape or form for one minute or eight days or donated a dollar to my cause or a couple thousand, you know who you are and this chapter of this incredible book is for you.

I will finish on this note. If you ever want to do anything in your life that you think you're not capable of, you are wrong! Don't wait till it's too late. Try it, do it. Don't let anybody tell you that you can't or shouldn't. There's the old saying, "You only live once." Well, that's a load of crap. You live every day, you only die once. So, go live!

Chapter 27

Patrick Binienda
June 7, 2019 to October 23, 2019
Rehoboth Beach, Delaware to Florence, Oregon
Atlantic Ocean to Pacific Ocean

"Only those who will risk going too far can possibly find out how far one can go." T.S. Eliot

Includes excerpts from Patandterrysexcellentadventue.com – The Blog – printed in *italics*

More than 20 years ago, running across America was in my 5-year plan, and then life happened. Years passed with multiple ultras and year-after-year completion of my favorite races, but the run across America was put on the back burner because of the commitment it required. In the fall of 2017, my wife, Terry said to me "What ever happened to that idea about running across America?" We found ourselves at a place in life where we had a house that was too big, jobs winding down or needing change, and family commitments declining. The doors opened for us to run across America.
From the Blog:

The question most asked by those we meet on the road: "Why"? Pat doesn't have a clear answer for this but said "It's not a vacation, it's not a trip, it is our life right now. It has to come from the heart or it can't happen. You can't just say here are the pros and cons of running across the country or achieving some feat so this is why I am doing it. It has to be in your heart. I knew it was in your heart and mine to do this, so…

In 2017 I was managing a vacation property we owned after leaving my "real" job in 2016. We decided to start seriously planning for the run that fall. I had a lot of flexibility with my schedule so I was able to fully dedicate myself to training. I started out going for long runs focusing on length of time on the road. I had a lot of experience running ultras, and a few events behind me with journey runs that lasted up to a week. I knew that stacking up 3 or 4 days in a row with 8 – 10 hours out on the road was where I needed to focus. I would typically cover 25 miles or so each day, and while this was not enough mileage to get me across the U.S. I imagined that the mileage and physical requirements of the run would take shape as I muscled through the mental training needed for long hours, day after day.

I began to think of my training as a routine - just part of my day – going out for a long run and pacing my speed in order to stay out on the road for at least 8 hours. I've always been plagued with hydration issues and maintaining energy in ultra-events - either too much hydration or dehydration, and nausea from anything and everything I ate. As part of my training, I made a point of eating before setting out for the day, stopping for lunch and snacks during the day, and hydrating with only water and Gatorade. No fancy endurance drinks or potions with the exception of Succeed Tablets, occasionally, to get through the extreme Atlanta heat and humidity. After every run, I supplemented with Endurox R4 Muscle Recovery drink which has been a staple in my running routine for many years. I used this training routine throughout the actual run.

Another important part of my training was learning to rest for recovery. Most runners have experienced the adrenalin filled nights before a big event – lack of sleep from the excitement is typical. The day after a big race or ultra-event is usually filled with a physical sense of needing rest, but at least for me, it is not always easy to settle down and get the needed rest. Training to rest required discipline and the development of a routine. Immediately after my recovery drink, I put my focus on the basics – showering and food and then rest. I tried to avoid stressful situations requiring big decisions until fully rested and didn't go out much to social events, etc. Meals were not specifically designed using a runner's diet but I tried to eat healthy proteins and a balanced amount of carbs. I rested though - knowing that I needed to be ready for more of the same the next day. Getting to a position where I could make my training my first priority was 20 years in the making. While many of my other events took rigorous training, everything I had done up to this point had a distinct start and finish and I understood the limits of the event, and also what would be needed from me. This run, however, was something of a different animal. I didn't know, fully, how I would piece it all together and, more importantly, what it would take to get to the finish.

Training went well during the summer of '18 and into the Fall – reaching an average of 120 miles per week – multi-day runs lasting 8 hours and covering 25 miles or so, just as planned. However, in December '18, my mother was diagnosed with cancer and was almost immediately admitted into Hospice. From December '18 to February '19, when she passed away, Mom was my first priority and my training took a backseat. In addition, in early April we put our home up for sale and with all the organizing, packing, and moving that comes with that, my training came to a halt. For the six months leading up to our departure on June 3rd, my training was in minimal maintenance mode. I had to trust that the training I had already put in would get me through to the finish.

Planning for the Event – Logistics

We had to be "all in". For me, this meant clearing up commitments. Sell the house, put a pause on our careers and "jobs", pare down other obligations, and set expectations with family and friends before leaving. I felt if there was a possibility I could fall back on the safety-net of a comfortable home, or contrive a burning need to get back to our jobs, the opportunity existed for me to quit when the going got tough. Terry, on the other hand, wanted to eliminate distractions so she was all in on the house sale and leaving her job, however, she says she never had any doubt that we would finish. Quitting wasn't an option. I am grateful to have had the opportunity to start the run from this position of commitment and privilege.

My crew would consist of Terry, my wife, and Ginny, our little dog, a very important companion and cheerleader. To prepare for the trip beyond training, we read articles written by other cross-country runners to glean advice. One recommendation that stuck with us on the crew vehicle was "take the biggest vehicle you can manage." Terry has crewed on a lot of ultras and she thought the most important things for the vehicle was that it had to be ready to go into godforsaken places, in all kinds of weather and terrain, and it must have room for all of the gear, all the time. It is important not to leave anything behind that you have to backtrack to pick up. With this in mind, we settled on a 27' RV Motorhome built on a van chassis. With a motor home, we would never be leaving a trailer behind, and the narrow profile of the van would maneuver in and out of tight spaces easily. The vehicle performed well for us going across the mountains, and with the diesel engine, we could keep the engine running for a/c and heat whenever it wasn't convenient to plug into power or start up the generator. The RV had an onboard kitchen, bathroom and easy to manage sleeping spaces. While we had an extra slide out to expand the space inside by 30 sq. ft., we more often made-do without the extra space. If we got too comfortable, using the queen-sized bed, etc., our intensity diminished, and we lost our focus and flow. The one drawback on the RV was it did not have 4x4 capability. There were a lot of times it would have come in handy but we figured out by trial, error, and more than a few stressful moments, where the machine would take us and where it would not.

In addition to acquiring the best RV for the trip, we also focused our preparation on what we thought would be our necessities:

- **Running clothes** – X-bionic brand was used exclusively for shirts and tights. This gear, scientifically designed and tested to keep body temperatures below 99 degrees, was the key to managing my issues with the heat and dehydration. SPF hats, jackets or vests, compression knee socks, and arm sleeves were all high visibility. Ten- pair of the lightest weight shoes available from New Balance, and gel inserts pretty much completed the wardrobe. At approximately 800 miles, I had to go from my usual 10.5 D shoe to 10.5 EE and stayed in the EE to the end. Many days, I dressed for the next day's run the night before. I rarely dressed in street clothes the entire 5 months we were on the road.

- **Technology and Applications** – having several Garmin devices was helpful so when the power cords or wrist bands failed, we had backups. Multiple power cells for recharging mobile devices while on the road, and cell phones kept us connected and going in the right direction. All Stays App for the mobile phone was a necessity for finding overnight RV parking and LP gas. Also, Life 360 App was literally a life-saver – this GPS personal locator also provides directions to find each other, and messaging. Life 360 does not work, however, without cell service so there may be something better out there, but this was my primary way for Terry and myself to keep track of each other.

- **Creature comforts for the RV** – we initially packed way too much stuff into the RV, mainly kitchen items, food and clothing. After 6 weeks or so, Terry started sending things back to Atlanta via UPS. It was interesting to learn how few "necessities" we really needed. One of the best buys the entire trip was a $5 gadget to hold the mobile phone/GPS unit on the windshield of the car. A 7-Day Cooler (Cabela's version is $100 < Yeti) - keeps ice for up to 7 full days, and 2- Pendleton wool blankets top off the list of most used creature comforts. We had heat in the RV but the woolies made it much easier to boondock on BLM land and various parking lots when needed.

- **Maps** – Starting out, we didn't leave home with too many maps. As we gained experience, we added some great map books and folding paper maps from AAA. In the planning stages, we pasted a 6' x 9' map of the US on the wall in our home office. We used that map to directionally map out the route and to inspire us every day about the run. When we left home, however, there were only two certainties about the course. We would start at Rehoboth Beach, DE, and finish on the Oregon Coast. We started out with Data Books for the American Discovery Trail, as we initially planned the ADT would be the course to take us from Indiana through Nebraska. We had on-line access to Rail Trail Maps, and AAA Triptik planner, a great tool for getting the big-picture image of the course. We started off using Google Maps, Waze, and Apple Maps and had little experience with any of them. We finally decided to use Google Maps day to day, and we printed detailed directions on a portable, rechargeable printer. Having detailed directions for turns made navigating easy even in the midst of the brain fog that plagued me often. Benchmark Maps Road and Recreation Atlas (by State) came into our lives for Wyoming, Idaho, and Oregon and saved the day. There are so few roads across these states that we needed the details this map line gives you to get across. Also, these maps show elevations, county roads, dirt roads, and other undeveloped access, all very much needed details for backroad travel. We were, by design, taking the roads less traveled.

The Run –
From The Blog on 7/21/19:

We've gotten several comments on the name of our Blog – Patandterrysexcellentadventure – mainly that the first thing many see in the address is "sex". While out on the trail, Pat figured out that if we left off "excellent" in order to edit out the word "sex", our Blog address would be Patandterrysadventure. A "sad venture" is hardly better than sex. tb/ 7/21/19

At the onset, the course mapped in AAA Triptik was 3071 miles from Rehoboth Beach, Delaware to Newport, Oregon. However, this didn't accurately measure distance using the trails in the early segments: Maryland Rail Trail; C&O Canal Trail; Great Allegheny Passage Trail (GAP Trail); the USBRS Ohio 50 Trail. It was my plan to "enjoy myself" running on as many trails as I could and just enjoy the journey. At the end of the USBRS Ohio 50 Trail just outside Richmond, IN, I had covered 800 miles linking the trails but discovered I could have come to the same point on the roads with only 600 miles. We were also fighting against our late start the first week in June and we had to get over the Sierras and Rockies before snowfall. At this point, I decided to get off the trails and find the shortest, most practical route to the Oregon Coast. This major change in course and philosophy about the run tested our commitment. Terry was especially against leaving the defined trails and moving to county roads and US/State highways. She didn't want me running with traffic, but mostly, she had very little experience navigating with maps. Not using the ADT Data Books, and other trails as planned, meant we would have to navigate the entire distance from Richmond, Indiana to the Oregon coast ourselves. At this point in the run, Terry was still spinning the maps around in circles trying to find her way East to West and North to South. At the time, I was afraid this change would push her to call it quits – it was a real blow-up - she tells me today that quitting never entered her mind.

We took a day off and went to a local library with all our maps, markers, Google, and AAA programs and mapped out the new course. The roads across Indiana, Illinois, Iowa, and Nebraska were straight forward, primarily using state highways and farm roads directly E to W, however, there would be more changes as we moved across Wyoming, Idaho, and Oregon, testing once again, our ability to flex and evolve with the Run.

- Indiana – From Richmond followed backroads N to Gaston; W on county roads along IN 28; N in Attica to IN border at Ambia using IN 26.
- Illinois – IL 9 W to Pekin; W on county roads to Ft. Madison, IA.
- Iowa – IA 2 W to Nebraska City, NE.
- Nebraska – NE 6 and county roads W to Kearney; US 30 W to Pine Bluffs.

From the Blog - Terry's early description of the Run:

... it is the sheer magnitude of it all. Kind of like slamming the car door on a finger... it isn't usually a serious injury but the pain is stunning, unexpected, and you are overwhelmed by the stupidity of it – the magnitude of it all brings you to tears. Tb 7/21/19

I ran through 13 states – approximate mileage by state is shown below – totaling 3470 miles run, and 11,050 miles driven by the RV. It may be a surprise that the RV traveled 3 x the running miles – at least we were surprised. We planned for something closer to 2 x but spent a lot of miles backtracking early on looking for places to park overnight, and then scouting out the route sometimes 20 miles in advance. We were tracking 4 x running miles at one point but made a "rule" for no backtracking to sleep or shop, and tried to keep the scouting miles to about 10, and only when necessary.

My route is obviously not the shortest route across the US. I had the extra 200 miles for DE to OH due mostly to using the trails, and starting at Rehoboth Beach, DE required running directly N nearly 80 miles to get to where I could cross into Maryland. Mileage logged included all miles run each day. This includes detours and backtracking for road closures, unpassable bridges, flooded roads through corn fields, wrong turns ... you get the idea.

From the Blog – approximately one week following the IN re-route:

This past week – ending 7/28 – was our best week yet for mileage with 186 miles forward (and with a day off for the toe) – for a total of 1130 miles after 7 weeks. Pat is physically strong, emotionally balanced (for Pat) and ready to go every day. He is cheerful in the morning and goes out to bring coffee back to the RV anytime there is a vendor nearby. The navigation is going pretty well for both of us. Pat has slowed down to give more attention to the directions. We review the maps every morning and plot out the turns, meeting places, and end points for the day. Most days, he listens but I make copious notes and addendums to the printouts just in case :). I am trying to text less because he says he doesn't have time to search for shade every time I send him a message. The days are long for me and quiet. If I can find someone to talk to during the day, I likely will just talk and talk too much. I talk to Ginny. She listens! She looks at my face for expression and then reacts accordingly – generally I think she is looking for a smile. tb/7/30

Everywhere I ran, people were so nice to me. There was not a day that went by without at least one person slowing to ask me if I needed something. There were many cars that stopped to give me cold water on the hottest days. People in Illinois were probably the most attentive – not sure if it was due to the 95+ temps or if these mid-westerners are just the nicest folks in America. Whatever the reason, I sure did appreciate the breaks in the monotony of mile after mile and the water always seemed to come when I needed it the most. We had friends and family host us in their homes along the way, calling us on the phone for weekly check-ins, and also coming out to run and ride along in the RV. I would be remiss to not mention how much it meant also, to have followers on social media - the Blog and Instagram - all along the way. These daily messages cheered us on and kept us connected to the real world when going across some of the most isolated sections of the run.

My goal was to run 30 miles per day and finish in approximately 102 running days. I knew that 30 miles per day would work for me over the long-run as it had during training, although, it would be important to pace myself to meet the 30-mile goal, day after day. I tried a few times to push beyond the 30 miles but when I exceeded more than about 32-34 miles, my running the next day was compromised. I finished the run after 123 total running days with an overall average of 30 miles per day. We were on the road a total of 139 days.

From the Blog:

My pace remains slow and steady. I'm holding up well though I have small aches and pains in my feet. Perhaps my biggest asset or liability is persistence. I propel myself with persistence. Not sure where it comes from, just that each day I wake up and go forward with the thought that I'm going for the finish wherever that is. I use it like a cup of coffee whenever I'm failing a bit I just reach for and sip some persistence to keep moving. Fortunately, my cup has been full each time I've sipped. Don't know what I'd do without it. pb/ 9/2/19

I focused on running vs. walking – no matter how slow the running. As long as I was running, meaning that during my stride I had both feet off the ground at the same time, I could maintain a pace that would get me through. This was, after all, a run across America. I did, however, have periods of determined walking breaks when the energy just wasn't available. For an energy boost, I opted for a cup of coffee or iced tea in hot weather. There were a couple of days when I had plenty of daylight, I climbed into the RV for a midday nap when I felt I just couldn't go any further.

My speed depended largely on road conditions – traffic, width of shoulders (if any), quality of the directions and signage, and the number of historical markers present on the route. I could not stop myself from pausing to read every historical marker I passed. I also took a lot of photos along the way. I worked on a "trip project", photographing unique signage that included names of friends and family members to be framed later as souvenir gifts from the Run.

Injuries were few and far between. Early on in the trip, I fell while climbing over a fence on a "shortcut" and sprained my big toe. For fear it was broken, Terry urged me to the ER for an x-ray but found it as only a painful sprain. The biggest injury was when I almost stepped on a rattlesnake in Wyoming and fell backward. I injured my hip and knocked a tooth loose. Somewhere in Idaho, the pain in my feet that started much earlier, increased. By then, the pain was excruciating every night when I took my shoes off – so much so that it was painful to have the sheets or blankets laying on them. Epsom Salt soaks, Lidocaine, and Tylenol got me through the final weeks. Overall though, I was amazed at how well my body stood up, after all, I celebrated receiving my Medicare Card while out on the run.

I took scheduled breaks every 8 days or so from the running, and we also had forced days off for RV maintenance. I found if I maintained a steady rhythm, with steady mileage each day, my endurance held up. The breaks were not so much for physical rest, but the rest was welcomed. The breaks were more for mental rest. We didn't want to break on weekends because traffic was lighter on weekends, for faster and easier running. We also tried to measure the distance between breaks so the stopping point would be a meaningful milestone, for example state lines, and larger cities. The intensity of the quest to finish built up over the days between breaks to a point where Terry and I both just felt crazy, in a literal way heading into a break.

From the Blog regarding breaks:
The trek to get to IA border was intense with 9 days in a row of 30+ miles. We've had a couple of other long stretches without breaks and it seems that 7-8 days is really the max for us. When we get into a "push" toward a milestone, our intensity and drive for the finish builds and builds. It is a manic experience that takes us into another realm of being; one where conscious decisions are made with unconscious, possibly negative, impacts to self-preservation and well-being. It is only when we hit the destination, step back and take a breath, that we realize how tightly we have wound the ropes. I looked back during the IA break and realized how much we need the milestone breaks to maintain any kind of balance in this great adventure. We'll just have to see how crazy we seem once we get to NE on Wednesday. Tb

Terry drove the RV to meet me at regular intervals every day providing food, water, Gatorade and moral support. Each day, we logged the starting point and ending point and mileage covered, and also a brief note of where we slept or parked the RV just to jog our memories of the individual sections for storytelling and future analysis. Terry was responsible for locating suitable overnight parking, maintaining supplies, logistics, mapping, and pretty much everything but my running and human bodily functions. My daily routine was fairly predictable – Eat, Sleep, Walk Dog,

Run, Eat, Run, Eat, Sleep, Repeat. It was easy to get mixed up about the days of the week and dates as the days were indistinguishable from each other.

From the Blog:
Friday Sept 13 – Is it really Friday? I woke up this morning and went thru my morning ritual of "where am I?", "what day is it?", "what are we doing today?" and announced "Today is Thursday. It is almost Friday again." Even though Friday is no longer the day we look forward to for intro to the weekend, we still seem to recognize Friday as different. A life-long practice is hard to break. Pat was confused by my announcement that today is Thursday – questioned it – and then accepted it. Today is in fact Friday. Pat's blind trust in me is surprising.
Tb/9/13/19

I was so happy to finish 500 miles across NE and enter WY but my attitude about WY changed pretty quickly. Getting to Cheyenne on US 30 was easy but then 30 merged with I-80 and the struggle to find alternates began. We used the Benchmark Maps for WY, (and also ID and OR) and found small roads to get us across but met with the challenge of private land ownership and gated barriers not included on the maps. Just outside Laramie we dug in for another major re-routing, primarily to get across WY but this led to changes for ID and OR as well. This rerouting put me out on some pretty narrow, winding, highways with narrow or no shoulders, and more traffic than what I had seen previously.

- Wyoming – I-80 Service Road W to Cheyenne; county roads to WY 230 & 70; CO 4 to WY 430 N to Rock Springs. US 30 W/NW to Montpellier.
- Idaho – US 30 N/NW to Pocatello; county roads W to ID 24; US 26 W; ID 78 to US 95 at Nyssa, OR.
- Oregon – US 26 W to OR 126 to Sisters; US 20 to OR 126 W over Santiam Pass; OR 126 S & W to Florence, OR.

From the Blog – Highways vs. Byways:
Saturday 9/21/19 – Since leaving Rock Springs on Tuesday we have had winds of 35 mph or more, three out of five days. In addition, the route we have planned has Pat running on US 30, a busy truck route, for 125 miles. We have wrestled with trying some of the off-road routes, leaving US 30, but Pat is fine with running with the trucks – like running with the bulls but he is going in the opposite direction. It is dangerous. Pat says that when he is off in the brush alone (and frequently without cell service), it is worse than navigating traffic on the highway. We visited the BLM office in Kemmerer to check out a number of dirt roads. The rangers and others in the office were fascinated by Pat's story-telling, very knowledgeable about the back roads, elevations, and road conditions. They advised against the dirt roads for the RV. We decided to continue on US 30 after a heart-to-heart, head-to-head battle ensued.

I dropped Pat at Nugget Canyon in Kemmerer this morning. US 30 is winding and steep here with a reduced shoulder. I sat at the entrance of the canyon yesterday and the traffic headed down seemed to be taking on air as they were going so fast. When I dropped him off, I promised to take a leap of faith that he would pay attention, be smart, and play it safe. Pat agreed and off he went. His drive to get in the miles and my fears for his safety separated today for at least 4 hours.

Ending the run in Florence, OR, was the perfect decision. The sand dunes at the Oregon coast provided a dramatic finish – I ran down US HWY 101 to South Jetty Road to enter the dunes area; I ran my fastest mile of the trip – a 7:57 – climbed over a tremendous sized dune with Terry, and our adventure dog Ginny. At the summit of the dune, the Pacific Ocean opened its arms for me. It was a spellbinding moment, taking my breath away. At 6:15 p.m. on October 23, 2019, at sunset, my journey was complete. There will be many stories written as we are able to gain the clarity of mind to reminisce and document the full journey. So many lessons learned about what to do, how to do it, and what not to do. It almost makes it seem we should do it again just to put all the lessons learned into action. Almost.

It is an honor to be invited to write my story here along with other successful USA Crossers.

Top Left Clockwise: Abandoned Welcome Station in Montpelier ID, Rural Mailbox in IN, Roadside Banners Near Centerville, IA, Maryland Rail Trail.

Patrick, Terry, and Ginny, RV, Trusted Directions

States	3470
DE	100
MD	183
PA	188
WV	42
OH	337
IL	219
IN	184
IA	267
NE	496
CO	66
WY	455
ID	467
OR	467

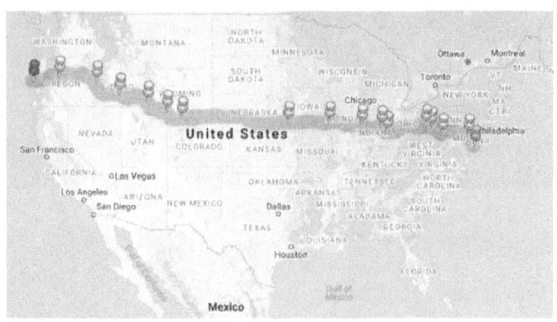

Run Across America Route-Patrick Binienda – Rehoboth Beach, DE, to Florence, OR 6/7/19 – 10/23/19

About the Authors

Alan Tardy — Born 1954. Have lived in Massachusetts all my life. House painter by trade. Ran San Francisco, CA. to Northampton, MA. in 1978. Carried a knapsack. Raised funds and awareness for a birth defect (Spina Bifida) and our efforts have been credited, by many, to have helped change medical history.

Frank Giannino — Frank Giannino (b1952), from the Hudson area of New York, ran across the USA twice. Run #1 from Los Angeles to NYC in 60d6h (3/1/79-4/30/79)(50 mpd). Run #2 from SF to NYC in 46d8h36m (9/1/80-10/17/80)(67 mpd). Held the Guinness Book Record for 36 years.

Jay Birmingham — Born in 1945. Lived in Ohio, Colorado, Nebraska, Florida. Profession: college and high school science teacher and coach. 72 marathons, 35+ ultramarathons. Ran from Los Angeles to New York City in 1980, unsupported with a backpack. Ran from Ft. Kent, Maine to Key West, Florida in 1982.

LouisMichael Figueroa — LouisMichael Figueroa is best known for inspiring the famous words of Forrest Gump during his 1982 run across the US to fulfill a promise to a dying friend. "When I got tired, I slept. When I got hungry, I ate. And when I had to go, you know, I went."

Jim Starkovich	After retiring from IBM and one of the older transcon runners, at age 56, Jim ran 2381 miles from Fernandina Beach, FL to La Jolla, CA in 77 days. He was supported by a van with driver wife Jo. Jim has run 14 marathons and has run in all US states and provinces and territories of Canada plus 60 different countries.
Brian Stark	Running solo and with only a 10-pound hip pack, Brian, 26, was the first to run nearly 5,000 miles across the US from Delaware to California on a collection of trails called the American Discovery Trail.
Jim McCord	Ran supported with RV and driver in 2002 from San Diego to Wash DC. Purpose was to raise public awareness (through radio, tv and newspapers) to the underfunding of Diabetes research through NIH. Had only run one marathon previously. Life-changing experience. Born 1957, four children, five grandchildren.
John Wallace III	Starting on his dad's birthday and ending on his mom's, John covered over 3800 miles and 12 states during his 2004-2005 solo crossing. Using James E. Shapiro's initial crossing list as a guide, John created usacrossers.com to promote and archive transcontinental USA crossings as well as provide a resource for former, current, and future crossers.
Helene Neville	Helene, a cancer survivor, became the first woman to run across every state in

About the Authors

	the United States - 13,850 miles/nine years to Rethink Impossible. Helene has authored five books, is a nurse, a health care advocate, and an Inspirational speaker.
Jeff Grabosky	Jeff ran solo and unsupported for more than 3,700 miles over the course of exactly four months from California to New York in 2011. He gathered prayer intentions from thousands of people all over the world and prayed a decade of the Rosary for each of those requests as he ran.
Milton Miller	After a long career in Information Technology, Milton Miller chose to become a professional vagabond, adventurer, ultra-runner, motorcycle enthusiast, sailor, entrepreneur, and writer. Since 2009 he has been traveling the world nearly full time, not worrying very much about being an adult.
Chris Finill & Steve Pope	Chris was born in the street where Roger Bannister lived so he had no choice but to run. He has represented Great Britain at both 100k and 24 hours and has completed every edition of the London Marathon since its inception in 1981. Steve is a free spirit and author having written several books covering education and great British inventions. He plans to retire soon so that he can spend more time with his debts.
Doug Masiuk	Doug Masiuk is the first person with Type 1 Diabetes to run across the US. His mission was to share with a world

	that if he could run across the continent that anything is possible with Diabetes. Along the way he met and spoke with over 100,000 people to share this message. Doug was diagnosed in 1977.
Rosalynn Frederick	Traveler who loves exploring the physical world, as well as the spiritual world. Jogged ⅔ of the way across the country in Vibram Five Fingers (walked the rest in regular running shoes). Wore the same shirt every single day on the road for her 5-month journey.
Benjamin Lee	At 24 years old, Ben had hoped to become the youngest Australian to cross America on foot. From San Francisco to Delaware Bay, his adventure of a lifetime took 6.5 months to complete while raising money for Oxfam. During his solo walk, he spent three weeks crossing the Rocky Mountains with Joe Bell (as portrayed in the film *Good Joe Bell*).
Newton Baker	B1942, January 16, 2015 start on my birthday, finished Race Across USA 140 days later, 2nd oldest (73) to finish a Transcon. 25 consecutive USA National 24-Hour races with 14 Age Group 1sts, 7 AG 2nds, 2 AG 3rds. Finished 8th Overall in Canadian Open section of 2007 World 24 Hour Championship.
Pete Kostelnick	In 2016, broke Frank Giannino's long standing record for fastest run across America, averaging 72 miles per day over 42 days/6 hours/30 minutes. In 2018, ran self-supported with a stroller from Kenai, Alaska to Key West, Florida in

About the Authors

	just under 100 days, averaging 55 miles per day.
Henrik Aarup Svendsen	First Dane to run across USA. Born in Aalborg in 1966, 49 years when running. Profession: Entrepreneur and owner of valve company; Mars Valve Europe A/S. My crossing was Inspired by Andrew Payne, the winner of the first foot race across the USA in 1928. Running for a good cause: Youth For Understanding. (YFU).
Jan Walker	A native of Knoxville, TN, Jan had always been active outdoors. But by her 50's, she found herself severely overweight. Beginning with a simple "get off the couch and walk out the door", she soon began completing long distance runs, and even completed an Ironman! At 57, solo and unsupported, she ran 3,154 miles across the U.S. from Oceanside, CA to Ocean City, MD in 7 months.
Lindsay Monroe	In November of 2017, left her jobs as a photographer and bartender to walk across America. Walked from South Carolina to Oregon in 9 months and 2 days, in Arkansas a stray dog started following her and never left.
Noah & Robert Barnes	At 16 months of age, Noah was diagnosed with Type 1 diabetes. When he was 10, he convinced his father, Robert, to March across the America with him to find a cure. He is the youngest person on record to have walked across the United States. Robert is the only person on record to walk across America, then ride a bicycle back.

Nicholas Ashill — Born in 1964. Started his run at the end of Santa Monica Pier, Los Angeles on 14 May 2017. Following historical Route 66. Ran 4000km but was hit by a pickup truck in Ohio on 2 August 2017. The driver did not stop. Spent 4 months in hospital. Returning to Ohio in May 2020 to finish his run. Running to raise awareness of Pulmonary Fibrosis, a disease of the lungs.

Amanda Standley — Walked from Cape Henlopen, Delaware to Bodega Bay, California in 2017 (3,300 miles and 8 ½ months) at the age of 22. Woke up from a dream with the idea, convinced to do it by a student, and raised money for underprivileged children along the way. The greatest gift from my walk was learning about human connection.

Sandra Villines — In 2017, Sandra, a wife, mom, grandma, and ultra-unner coach, set a new women's transcontinental speed record of 54 days, 16 hours, 23 minutes. She broke the longstanding record from 1979 by more than 15 days. Currently living in San Jose, California, Sandra is the General Manager at a flagship store for Skechers.

lazarus lake — began running in 1966,
and have competed at events ranging from 440 yards to 6 days,
on roads, tracks, and trails.
began journey running in 1980,
the 2018 transcon was the realization of a lifelong dream....

About the Authors

but, the itch has not been cured.

Thomas Curran Ditched a 30-year career as a chef and restaurant owner to walk 3,235 miles across America in 2019 and re-discover life. During my walk, I raised $21,220 for the Pediatric Cancer Research Foundation. I started my walk on February 2, 2019 at Holden Beach, NC and finished 231 days later at Newport Beach, CA at the pier I hung out at growing up. My dog, Wink, made it 1300 miles to Oklahoma City before being sent home due to excessive heat and a minor shoulder strain. During my walk, I wrote a murder mystery using my journey as the backdrop which will be published early 2020.

Patrick Binienda In 1976 after watching the Olympic marathon Patrick said to his roommates "I can do that." In 1978 Patrick ran his first marathon and in 1984 took it a step further by becoming an ultramarathoner. Forty+ years of running and twenty years of planning Patrick and his wife Terry cast everything aside to take on the adventure of their lives.

Thanks for reading. If you enjoyed this book, please consider leaving an honest review on Amazon.com or at your favorite bookstore.

Printed in Great Britain
by Amazon